# Claus Mayrhofer Barabbas

## Gegenwelten eines Grenzgängers
## The Transcultural Worlds of an Out-There Artist

HerausgeberInnen für die Kulturabteilung der Stadt Wien (MA 7)
Gunda Achleitner, Berthold Ecker, Elisabeth Voggeneder

MUSA AMBRA | V

Die im Katalog abgebildeten Werke befinden sich in folgenden Sammlungen
The works shown in the catalogue are part of the following collections:
Artothek des Bundes: Abb. | fig. 41, 42
Galerie Gans, Wien | Gallery Gans, Vienna: Abb. | fig. 66, 67
Privatsammlungen, Wien | Private collections, Vienna: Abb. | fig. 1, 2, 3, 4, 5, 6, 9, 11, 15, 19, 20, 21, 22, 23, 24, 25, 26, 27, 29, 30, 31, 32, 33, 34, 35, 36, 37, 38, 39, 40, 43, 44, 45, 46, 51, 52, 53, 54, 55, 56, 57, 58, 59, 60, 61, 63, 64, 65, 69, 71, 72, 74, 75, 76, 77, 78, 79, 80, 81, 82, 83, 84, 85, 86, 87, 88, 89, 90, 91, 92, 93, 94, 95, 96, 97, 98, 99, 101, 103, 104, 105, 106, 107, 108, 109, 110, 111, 112, 114, 115, 116, 117
Sammlung der Kulturabteilung der Stadt Wien – MUSA
Collection of the Department for Cultural Affairs of the City of Vienna – MUSA:
Abb. | fig. 8, 12, 13, 14, 16, 17, 28, 47, 48, 49, 50, 62, 68, 70, 73, 100, 102, 113
Wien Museum: Abb. | fig. 7

# Inhalt
# Content

# On Tiptoes?

*Berthold Ecker*

Barabbas has struck me as one of the most paradigmatic painters of 1960s and 1970s Austria ever since I first saw some of his work in the MUSA collection more than twenty-five years ago. And he seemed to come by his achievements so effortlessly, so buoyantly, as though he were gamboling through the Viennese arts scene on tiptoe. His vigorously colorful creations between biomorphic abstraction and figurative narration, I believe, are emblematic of a time shaped by modernization, the rise of technology, and a spirit of anything goes as much as by the incipient struggles over ever scarcer resources (remember the oil price shock) and the confrontation between industry and environmentalists. The peculiar aesthetic of hippie culture, too, finds itself reflected in these works, though in a highly individual adaptation that integrates aspects of contemporary artistic developments in Vienna. Traces of Fantastic Realism – especially of the variety spearheaded by Friedensreich Hundertwasser – are unmistakable, but other influences were of at least equal significance. Padhi Frieberger, whose name stands for one of the most important and earliest avant-garde positions in post-World War II Vienna, introduced Barabbas to the artists around Galerie nächst St. Stephan and was presumably also influential in steering him toward his musical career.

With the "Masters of Unorthodox Jazz," Barabbas played a part in Vienna's musical history that is no less significant than his essential contributions to our city's art history, which we are slowly coming to recognize, and so our Barabbas project devotes particular attention to the musical side of his creative output, drawing on the expertise of Andreas Felber.

Curated by Elisabeth Voggeneder, the exhibition at MUSA is the first to survey the entire oeuvre of this exceptional artist. As it turns out, I should qualify my initial impression of lightness and carefree playfulness. The show unfolds the panorama of a forceful and deliberate oeuvre developed with great assiduity in which the interplay between the artist's playful ease and the elemental forces of nature generated stunning artistic energies.

The Collection of the Department for Cultural Affairs of the City of Vienna – MUSA was able to acquire several important works during the artist's lifetime. A legendary monumental painting (entitled "Big Bang" or "Genesis") Barabbas had

# On Tiptoes?

*Berthold Ecker*

Barabbas gilt mir, seit ich vor mehr als 25 Jahren einige seiner Werke in der Sammlung des MUSA gesehen habe, als einer der paradigmatischsten Maler der 1960er und 1970er Jahre in Österreich. Und das schien ihm auf eine wunderbar leichte, beschwingte Weise zu gelingen, so als würde da einer auf Zehenspitzen durch die Wiener Kunstlandschaft tänzeln. Seine farbstarken phantastischen Gebilde zwischen biomorpher Abstraktion und figurativer Narration erscheinen mir als Inbegriff einer Zeit, die von Modernisierung, Technisierung und einem Anything-goes-Denken genauso geprägt war wie vom beginnenden Kampf um knapper werdende Ressourcen (Ölschock) und der Konfrontation zwischen Industrie und Umweltschutz. Die spezielle Ästhetik der Hippiekultur spiegelt sich in diesen Werken gleichfalls wider, wenn auch in einer sehr individuellen Anverwandlung, die auch Elemente aus dem Wiener Kunstschaffen verarbeitet. Spuren des Phantastischen Realismus – besonders in seiner Ausprägung durch Friedensreich Hundertwasser – sind klar erkennbar, doch andere Einflüsse waren zumindest von gleichem Gewicht. Padhi Frieberger, der für eine der wichtigsten und frühesten avantgardistischen Positionen in Wien nach dem Zweiten Weltkrieg steht, machte Barabbas mit den Künstlern der Galerie nächst St. Stephan bekannt und war wohl auch für dessen musikalische Karriere ein wichtiger Impuls.

Da Barabbas mit den „Masters of Unorthodox Jazz" für die Wiener Musikgeschichte ebenso bedeutend ist, wie seine bildnerischen Hervorbringungen einen festen Platz in der Kunstgeschichte unserer Stadt einzunehmen beginnen, wird im Rahmen unseres Barabbas-Projektes dem musikalischen Aspekt seines Schaffens – betreut durch Andreas Felber – besondere Aufmerksamkeit geschenkt.

Die Ausstellung im MUSA, kuratiert von Elisabeth Voggeneder, ermöglicht erstmals eine Übersicht über das gesamte Schaffen dieses Ausnahmekünstlers. Dabei relativiert sich der erste Eindruck von Leichtigkeit und spielerischer Unbekümmertheit. In seiner Gesamtheit offenbart sich ein kraftvolles, bedachtes und sehr konsequent entwickeltes Werk, in dem spielerische Leichtigkeit und die Urgewalt der Naturkräfte in einem spannungsreichen Austausch stehen.

Die Sammlung der Kulturabteilung der Stadt Wien – MUSA konnte zu Lebzeiten des Künstlers einige wichtige Werke erwerben. Ein sagenumwobenes Monumentalgemälde („Big Bang" bzw. „Genesis"), das Barabbas 1975 für seine große

created in 1975 for his grand show at the Künstlerhaus here in Vienna has long haunted me and aroused my collector's passion early on. My desire to see "Big Bang" in the permanent and expert care of MUSA's conservators was stoked further when the artist himself called from Australia and offered to sell the work to the City of Vienna. Unfortunately, we were unable to accept his offer at the time. After Barabbas had died in 2009, the estate passed to a community of heirs. With the assistance of the artist's first wife and the mother of three of his children, Rosemarie Sebek, we launched our search for the monumental picture, which was believed to have been lost; our quest finally led us to the Künstlerhaus's sub-basement. One sunny day, we brought the painting into the light of day and unrolled it on the adjacent square in front of the Wiener Musikverein. A few minor injuries aside, the "Big Bang" had lost none of its overwhelming power. To my mind, that first hour with "Big Bang" was a truly unforgettable experience and a real visual sensation. Thanks to a generous donation, the exceptional painting has now entered MUSA's municipal collection. It made obvious sense to present the work in the very place where it was created, the Sculptors' Hall of the Künstlerhaus, before moving it to MUSA, where it is on display as part of the retrospective.

The present volume is published on occasion of this first comprehensive retrospective of an oeuvre that has not received the attention it merits. The book features a representative selection of Barabbas's works.

I am especially grateful to the artist's family, and foremost to Rosemarie Sebek, as well as to all lenders who have made this project possible. The curator of the exhibition, Elisabeth Voggeneder, explored the visual-arts side of the oeuvre, while Andreas Felber studied Barabbas's music; I would like to thank both for their outstanding work and the amicable collaboration. Heimo Watzlik and Michael Wolschlager worked with great dedication to set up the exhibition and all technical equipment; they also took all photographs and edited the images. The overall project management was in the hands of Gunda Achleitner, who calmly guided everyone involved to ensure the success of the endeavor. I am grateful, finally, to the entire team at MUSA for their commitment to the project.

Ausstellung im Wiener Künstlerhaus geschaffen hatte, weckte schon früh meine Sammlerleidenschaft und spukte mir beständig im Hirn herum. Mein Wunsch nach einer dauerhaften und fachgerechten Aufbewahrung des „Big Bang" in der Sammlung des MUSA wurde noch angefacht, als der Künstler selbst aus Australien anrief und das Werk der Stadt Wien zum Kauf anbot. Damals konnten wir leider nicht darauf eingehen. Nach Barabbas' Tod im Jahr 2009 wurde der Nachlass von einer Erbengemeinschaft übernommen. Auf Vermittlung der ersten Frau des Künstlers und Mutter dreier gemeinsamer Kinder, Rosemarie Sebek, begann unsere gemeinsame Suche nach dem verschollen geglaubten Monumentalbild, die letztlich im zweiten Keller des Künstlerhauses von Erfolg gekrönt war. An einem sonnigen Tag holten wir das Gemälde ans Tageslicht und entrollten es auf dem benachbarten Platz vor dem Wiener Musikverein. Abgesehen von kleineren Blessuren hatte der „Big Bang" nichts von seiner gewaltigen Wirkkraft verloren. Diese erste Stunde mit dem „Big Bang" war für mich ein wahrhaft unvergessliches Ereignis und eine echte optische Sensation. Im Rahmen einer Schenkung wurde diese exzeptionelle Malerei der Stadt Wien – MUSA übertragen. Es lag nahe, das Werk zunächst an genau dem Ort, an dem es geschaffen worden war, im Plastikersaal des Künstlerhauses, zu zeigen, bevor es als Teil der Retrospektive auch im MUSA zu sehen ist.

Die vorliegende Publikation erscheint anlässlich dieser ersten Gesamtschau und bietet einen repräsentativen Querschnitt durch Barabbas' bisher viel zu wenig beachtetes Werk.

Mein Dank gilt ganz besonders der Familie des Künstlers, allen voran Rosemarie Sebek, sowie allen Leihgebern, die dieses Projekt ermöglicht haben. Die Kuratorin der Ausstellung Elisabeth Voggeneder hat den bildnerischen Aspekt des Werkes bearbeitet, während Andreas Felber dessen musikalischen Teil übernommen hat. Beiden danke ich für ihre hervorragende Leistung und die freundschaftliche Zusammenarbeit. Heimo Watzlik und Michael Wolschlager haben mit großem Engagement für den Aufbau und die gesamte technische Betreuung gesorgt. Auch alle fotografischen Arbeiten sowie die Bildbearbeitung stammen von den Letztgenannten. Die Leitung des Gesamtprojektes lag in den Händen von Gunda Achleitner, die alle Kräfte souverän zu einem guten Gelingen gebündelt hat. Zuletzt gilt mein Dank dem gesamten Team des MUSA für seinen hoch motivierten Einsatz.

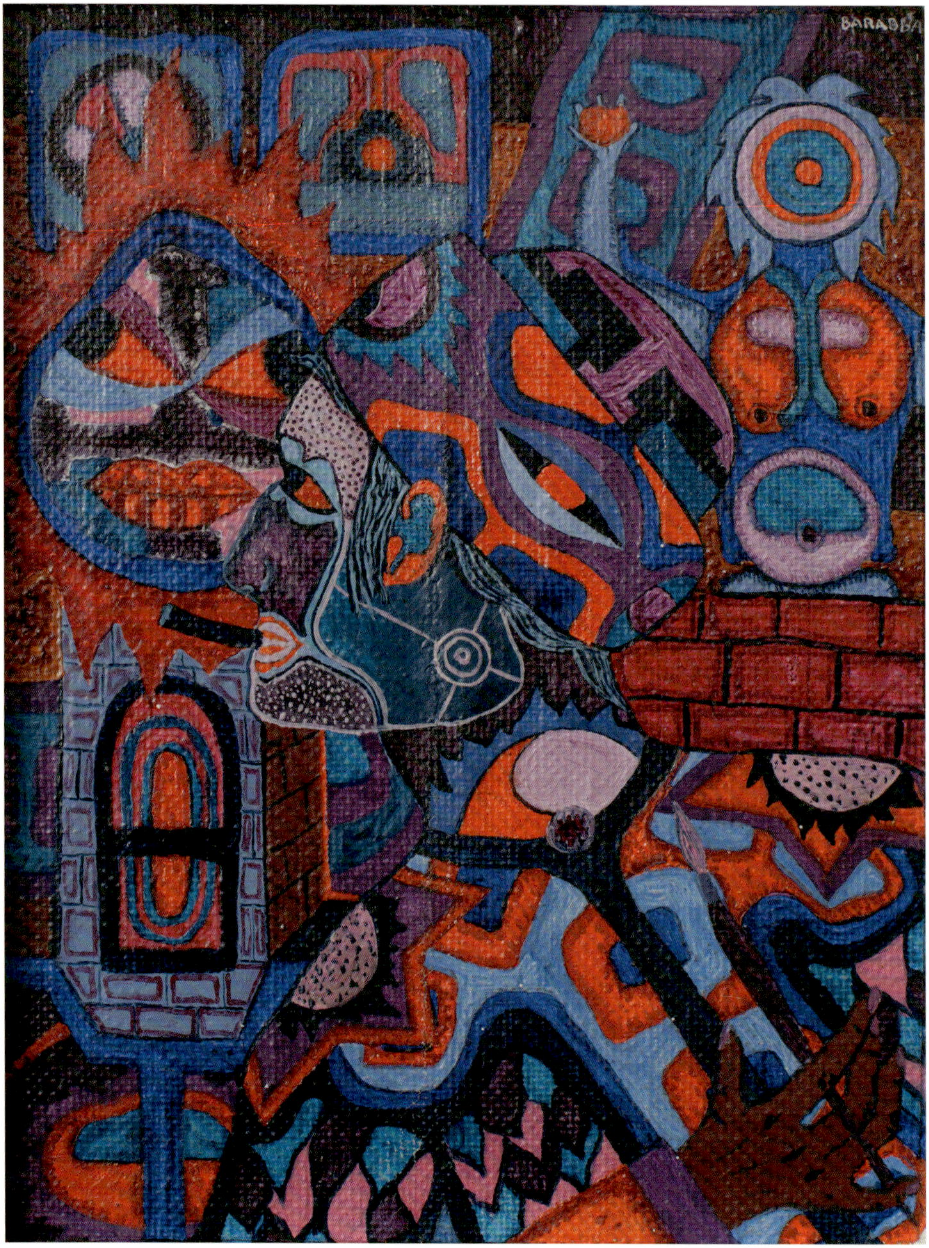


1
Selbstporträt, 1962
Öl auf Leinwand (auf Holz aufgezogen), 18 x 14 cm
Self-Portrait, 1962
oil on canvas (stretched on wood), 18 x 14 cm

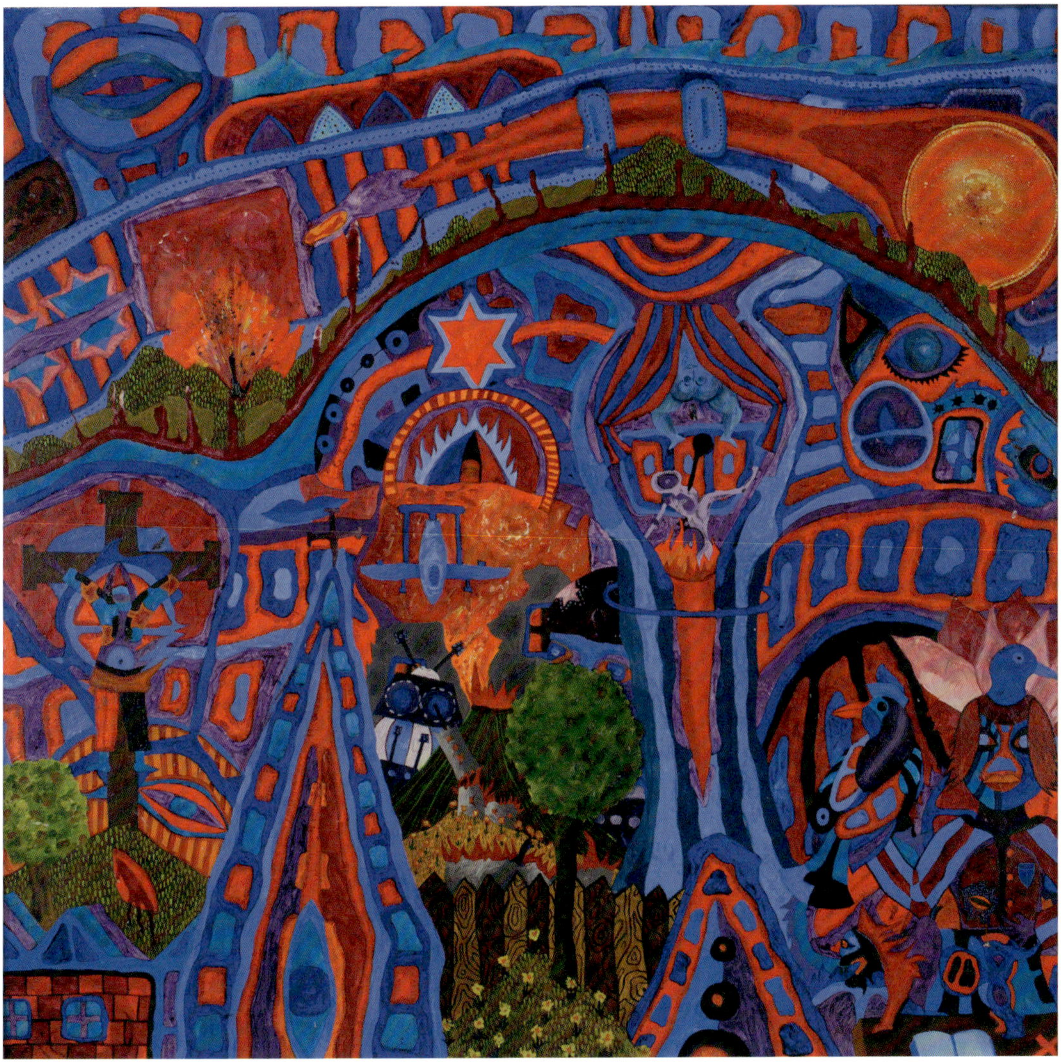

2
Der Untergang des Christentums/Atompilz, August 1962
Öl auf Holz, 71 x 75,5 cm
The Demise of Christianity/Atomic Cloud, August 1962
oil on wood, 71 x 75,5 cm

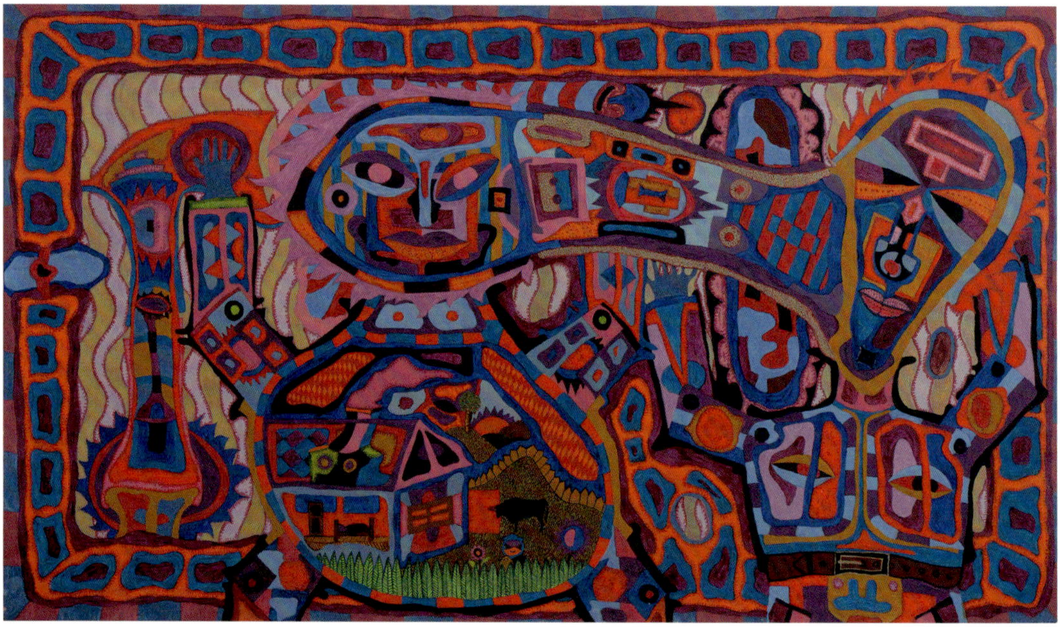

3
Ich und meine Frau, 1966
Öl auf Pressspan, 79 x 140 cm
I and My Wife, 1966
oil on particleboard, 79 x 140 cm

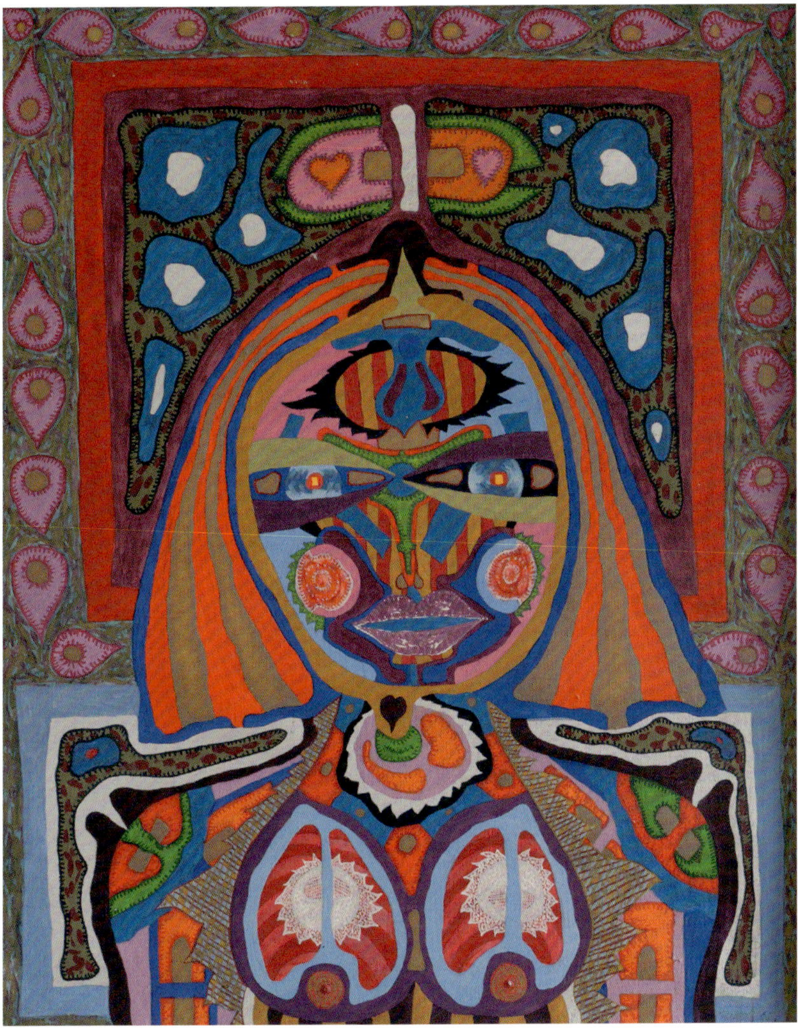

4
Wardi, 1965
Öl auf Leinwand, 70 x 60 cm
Wardi, 1965
oil on canvas, 70 x 60 cm

# Claus Mayrhofer Barabbas

## The Transcultural Worlds of an Out-There Artist

*Elisabeth Voggeneder*

Claus Mayrhofer Barabbas was out there.

When he was fifteen, he refused to go to school and graduate, having resolved to be an artist. He styled himself Barabbas, choosing the name of the insurrectionist who, according to the biblical tradition, rebelled against Roman rule and was sentenced to death; Pontius Pilate pardoned him instead of Jesus of Nazareth.

Barabbas identified with the idea of rebellion, and that stuck; in every respect. With a flowing beard, shoulder-length hair, and a jackdaw as his constant companion, he set out to reject the tradition and look for alternatives: in art, in faith, and in life. He made friends with Padhi Frieberger, the *enfant terrible* of Vienna's arts community, and together they explored the scene. He visited Friedensreich Hundertwasser in Paris, created abstract-gestural paintings, then ornamental and garishly colorful picturesques, and founded a jazz ensemble that caused a stir. He married and became father to three daughters, converted to the Baha'i faith, stumbled, wrestled with life. After a separation, he was remarried, and a son was born. He moved to New York; having returned to Vienna, he painted only in black. At some point, he had to flee the stuffy atmosphere of his hometown for Bali, where he created lushly colorful pictures. But his roving spirit soon urged him onward, to the last station of his quest, Australia: the happiness of a new love, paintings of vast expanses and the cosmic fantastic. *"There's something to be said for living in a country where there aren't borders everywhere to impose boundaries on you,"*[1] he wrote in 1989, the first year he spent in Australia; he would stay – until his death in 2009.

In his life's journey as much as his creative output, Barabbas embodies a distinctive personality; more than virtually anyone else, he lived the idea of the artist, between romanticism and avant-garde. To do something that was unheard of: that impulse is regarded as the paradigm that drove the visual arts forward in the twentieth century.[2] From Paul Gauguin to Vincent van Gogh, from Marcel Duchamp to Gelatin, the avant-garde saw and still sees itself as an anti-bourgeois counter-movement, promising progress in the arts through innovation and rebellion. The goal is to burst through barriers and find new ideas and techniques.

# Claus Mayrhofer Barabbas

## Gegenwelten eines Grenzgängers

*Elisabeth Voggeneder*

Claus Mayrhofer Barabbas war ein Grenzgänger.

Mit fünfzehn Jahren verweigerte er den Besuch und Abschluss der Schule, um Künstler zu sein. Er gab sich den Namen Barabbas, jenes biblischen Aufrührers, von dem überliefert wird, er habe sich gegen die Herrschaft der Römer aufgelehnt und sei, zum Tode verurteilt, von Pontius Pilatus anstelle von Jesus von Nazareth begnadigt worden.

Barabbas identifizierte sich mit der Idee der Rebellion, und das blieb so; in jeder Hinsicht. Mit wallendem Bart, schulterlangem Haar und einer Dohle als ständiger Begleiterin machte er sich auf, um Hergebrachtes zu verweigern und nach Alternativen zu suchen: in der Kunst, im Glauben und im Leben. Er freundete sich mit Padhi Frieberger an und durchstreifte mit ihm, dem Enfant terrible der Wiener Künstlerschaft, die Szene. Er besuchte Friedensreich Hundertwasser in Paris, malte abstrakt-gestisch, dann ornamentale, schreiend bunte Pittoresken und gründete eine Aufsehen erregende Jazzband. Er heiratete und wurde Vater von drei Töchtern, wechselte zur Bahá'i-Religion, stolperte, haderte. Trennung, neuerliche Heirat und die Geburt eines Sohnes folgten. Er ging nach New York und malte – zurück in Wien – nur noch in Schwarz. Es kam zur Flucht vor der Enge der Heimatstadt nach Bali. Blumig bunte Bilder entstanden. Doch auch hier hielt es ihn nicht lange. Letzte Station seiner Suche wurde Australien: neues Liebesglück, Bilder von Weite und Kosmisch-Phantastisches. *„Es hat schon etwas für sich, in einem Land zu leben, wo einem nicht an allen Ecken Grenzen durch Grenzen gesetzt werden",*[1] schrieb er in seinem ersten Jahr in Australien 1989 und blieb – bis zu seinem Tod 2009.

Mit seinem Lebensweg wie mit seinem Schaffen verkörpert Barabbas eine Persönlichkeit, die, wie kaum eine andere, der Idee des Künstlers – zwischen Romantik und Avantgarde – lebte. Etwas Unerhörtes zu tun: Dieser Impuls gilt als Paradigma, das die bildende Kunst im 20. Jahrhundert beherrschte.[2] Von Paul Gauguin über Vincent van Gogh bis zu Marcel Duchamp und Gelatin, Avantgarde verstand und versteht sich als antibürgerliche Gegenbewegung und verspricht das Fortschreiten der Kunst durch Erneuerung und Aufbegehren. Es gilt, Grenzen zu sprengen und neue Ideen und Verfahrensweisen zu finden.

But hasn't the vision of the artist as such – the emblem of the artistic life – always been the acrobat, which is to say, someone who tests limits? The "acrobat" – from the Greek ἀκροβάτης, which combines ἄκρος, "high," and βαίνειν, "to walk" – is one who walks on tiptoe; in a pars pro toto figure, the Greeks used the term to characterize artistic feats. More figuratively, walking on the peaks also meant going to extremes. Yet even as "one who goes to extremes," the artist remains an actor in a social system: the system of art. That was not least among the reasons why the idea of the avant-gardes foundered.

An uncompromising fighter for individualistic ideas, a maverick, an artist who was out there, Claus Mayrhofer Barabbas stood no chance in the art system; even a brief sketch of his life indicates as much. His painterly oeuvre, which was sustained by great determination and continuity, drew little attention from the outset; once he had left Vienna, his art was virtually forgotten in his native country.

How should we assess his oeuvre, which developed along biographical disruptions rather than according to some evolutionary logic, in a contemporary perspective? Which influences can we discern in it? And which ideas, innovations, and peculiarities does it manifest? These are the questions the following pages will seek to shed some light on for the first time.

## Between tachism and ornament
### *The 1960s and early 1970s*

In a self-portrait (fig. 1) created in 1962, Claus Mayrhofer Barabbas is virtually invisible; his likeness is embedded in an ornamental pattern of surfaces and contours. The small painting is paradigmatic of the artist's early pictures. Background and foreground are interfused. The motif is part of an ornament that covers everything. Slowly, gradually, figurative elements emerge from it. Barabbas appears in profile. He is wearing a cap, holds a cigarette between his lips, and gazes into the distance as he paints.

At the time this picture was created, Barabbas was a member of the group "Zum roten Apfel." The loosely organized association, which included Erich Brauner Thage, Karl Anton Fleck, Martha Jungwirth, Jürgen Leskowa, Walter Malli, Lia Pechoc, Richard Pechoc, Drago Prelog, and Wilfried Zimmermann, was among the protagonists of the gallery of the same name, which had been set up in 1959 in an apartment at Landstraßer Hauptstraße 74. With Galerie St. Stephan, founded in 1954, Galerie Würthle, and Galerie im Griechenbeisl, which opened in 1960, the "romantic rear courtyard-facing cabinet" was one of the earliest innovative

Doch ist der Entwurf des Künstlers per se – das Sinnbild des Künstlertums – nicht seit alters her der Akrobat, also jemand, der Grenzen auslotet? Der „Akrobat" – von griechisch ἀκροβάτης, aus ἄκρος „hoch" und βαίνειν „gehen" – ist der auf den Zehenspitzen Gehende und wird im Griechischen in einer Pars-pro-toto-Übertragung zur Charakterisierung des Artistischen herangezogen. Im übertragenen Sinne bedeutet das Auf-den-Spitzen-Gehen auch ein Ans-Äußerste-Gehen. Doch auch als „Ans-Äußerste-Gehender" bleibt der Künstler Akteur eines gesellschaftlichen Systems: der Kunst. Nicht zuletzt daran scheiterte die Idee der Avantgarden.

Dass es Claus Mayrhofer Barabbas, einem kompromisslosen Kämpfer für individualistische Ideen, einem Einzel- und Grenzgänger, nicht möglich war, im System Kunst zu bestehen, wundert angesichts seines Lebensabrisses nicht weiter. Sein malerisches Schaffen, das von großer Konsequenz und Kontinuität getragen ist, wurde von Beginn an nur wenig wahrgenommen und geriet mit seiner Flucht von Wien hierzulande nahezu in Vergessenheit.

Wie ist sein Œuvre, das sich abseits einer Entwicklungslogik entlang biografischer Bruchstellen entfaltete, aus heutiger Sicht einzuschätzen, welche Einflüsse sind spürbar und wo liegen seine Ideen, Innovationen und Besonderheiten – auf diese Fragen soll hier erstmals ein Streiflicht gerichtet werden.

## Zwischen Tachismus und Ornamentik

*Die sechziger und frühen siebziger Jahre*

Kaum sichtbar, in ein Musterwerk aus Flächen und Kontur eingeschrieben, stellte sich Claus Mayrhofer Barabbas 1962 in einem Selbstporträt (Abb. 1) dar. Das kleine Gemälde ist paradigmatisch für die frühen Bilder des Malers. Hintergrund und Vordergrund verschmelzen zu einer Einheit. Das Motiv ist Teil einer alles bedeckenden Ornamentik. Aus dieser löst sich allmählich Figürliches. Barabbas zeigt sich im Profil. Er trägt eine Kappe, hat eine Zigarette im Mund und blickt in die Ferne, malend.

Das Bild entstand während der Zeit, als Barabbas Mitglied der Gruppe „Zum roten Apfel" war. Die lose Gruppe, bestehend aus Erich Brauner Thage, Karl Anton Fleck, Martha Jungwirth, Jürgen Leskowa, Walter Malli, Lia Pechoc, Richard Pechoc, Drago Prelog sowie Wilfried Zimmermann, gehörte zu den Protagonisten der gleichnamigen Galerie, die seit 1959 in einer Wohnung des Hauses Landstraßer Hauptstraße 74 bestand. Neben der 1954 gegründeten Galerie St. Stephan, der Galerie Würthle sowie der 1960 eröffneten Galerie im Griechenbeisl zählte das „romantische Zimmer im Hinterhof" zu den ersten innovativen Plattformen

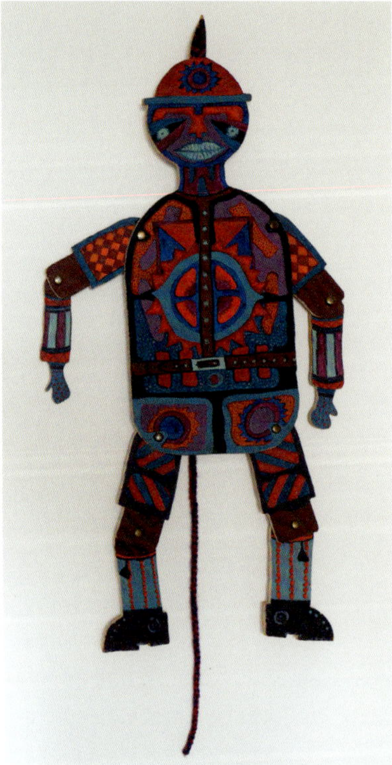

5
Ba'bas-Männchen, 1965
Öl auf Sperrholz, Höhe 43 cm
Ba'bas Manikin, 1965
oil on plywood, height 43 cm

platforms in Vienna's culturally conservative atmosphere; the city otherwise blinked drowsily at new ideas. "A new generation is revving it up here, and right away things are getting interesting,"[3] the art historian and journalist Alfred Schmeller, who would later direct the Museum des 20. Jahrhunderts ("20er Haus"), remarked about the gallery's activities in the *Kurier*.

Operating in Vienna's 3rd district, Zum roten Apfel sought to distinguish itself from the two major downtown galleries. "The establishment of Galerie zum roten Apfel [...] serves the purpose of an informal and cheerful exhibition activity. We have no intention of competing with larger (which is to say: real) galleries (nor could we if we wanted to) or trying to emulate them." The goal, instead, was to "present very young artists [...] who dislike the neutered, aesthetic, affected, and impersonal exhibitions at galleries,"[4] Walter Malli, one of the gallery's founding fathers, harangued.

The program was limited to presentations of work by a small number of artists; with its emphasis on tachism, it initially engaged the debate over informel painting. Abstract expressionism – in its American variety – was regarded as the tendency associated with liberation; its Austrian interpretation had dominated the small Viennese scene since the 1950s. Monsignore Otto Mauer, the cathedral preacher at St. Stephen's and founder of Galerie nächst St. Stephan, who construed informel painting as an expression of religious-spiritual ideas, was especially instrumental in paving the way for this avant-garde movement. "The St. Stephan boys" – Arnulf Rainer, Josef Mikl, Markus Prachensky, Wolfgang Hollegha – are now considered the chief representatives of Austrian informel; their shows at the gallery behind the cathedral made art history.

Pechoc and Malli, who had been Carl Unger's students at the Academy of Fine Arts Vienna and cofounded Galerie zum roten Apfel, likewise experimented with abstraction around 1960, while also trying to distance themselves from the informel of the St. Stephan group and the gallery's affiliations with party politics and the Church. Almost as though to defy Monsignore Mauer's Catholic mindset,

im kulturkonservativen Nachkriegswien, das neuen Ideen ansonsten verschlafen entgegenblinzelte. „Hier geht eine neue junge Generation auf Hochtouren und hier wird's sofort interessant",[3] kommentierte Alfred Schmeller, Kunsthistoriker, Journalist und später Direktor des Museums des 20. Jahrhunderts („20er Haus"), die Aktivitäten der Galerie zum roten Apfel im „Kurier".

Man versuchte sich im dritten Bezirk von den beiden großen Innenstadtgalerien zu unterscheiden. „Die errichtung der galerie zum roten apfel [...] dient der ungezwungenen, heiteren ausstellungstätigkeit. Wir wollen nicht mit grösseren (sprich: richtigen) galerien konkurrieren (wir können es auch gar nicht) oder ihnen nacheifern." Vielmehr wollte man „ganz junge künstler zeigen [...], denen die kastrierten, ästhetischen, gekünstelten und unpersönlichen ausstellungen in galerien unsympatisch sind",[4] ereiferte sich Walter Malli, Gründungsvater der Galerie.

Das Programm beschränkte sich darauf, Arbeiten weniger Künstler zu zeigen, und gliederte sich zunächst mit dem Schwerpunkt Tachismus in die Debatte um die informelle Malerei ein. Der abstrakte Expressionismus – amerikanischer Prägung – galt als die Kunstströmung der Befreiung und dominierte in österreichischer Interpretation die kleine Wiener Szene seit den fünfziger Jahren. Besonders der Domprediger und Gründer der Galerie nächst St. Stephan Monsignore Otto Mauer wurde mit der Interpretation der informellen Malerei als Ausdruck religiös-spiritueller Inhalte zum Wegbereiter der Avantgardebewegung. „Die St. Stephan Buam" – Arnulf Rainer, Josef Mikl, Markus Prachensky, Wolfgang Hollegha – gelten heute als Hauptvertreter des Informel in Österreich und schrieben in der Galerie hinter dem Stephansdom Kunstgeschichte.

Auch Pechoc und Malli, ehemals Schüler von Carl Unger an der Akademie der bildenden Künste Wien und Mitbegründer der Galerie zum roten Apfel, experimentierten um 1960 mit der Abstraktion, versuchten sich aber gleichzeitig vom Informel der St.-Stephan-Gruppe und dem parteipolitischen und kirchlichen Hintergrund der Galerie zu distanzieren. Pechoc und Malli definierten ihre Malerei – fast möchte man meinen, der katholischen Geistesauffassung Monsignore Mauers trotzend – als Ausdruck ihrer „Islamischen Haltung". Pechoc dazu: „Dieser Haltung sind sämtliche Ergebnisse und Stimmungen untergeordnet. Das Malen ist eine rituell-pulsive Handlung [...]."[5]

Als Barabbas die Kunstszene betrat, landete er mitten in diesem Diskurs. In der Galerie nächst St. Stephan hatte Barabbas seine ersten Kontakte mit aktueller Kunst geknüpft, als er sich als 15-Jähriger mit Padhi Frieberger anfreundete und mit ihm die Szene durchstreifte; dort hatte er Arnulf Rainer kennengelernt, mit

Pechoc and Malli defined their painting as an expression of their "Islamic stance." As Pechoc noted, "all results and moods are subordinate to this stance. Painting is a ritualized-pulsive action."[5]

When Barabbas entered the arts scene, that was the discourse he got involved in. At Galerie nächst St. Stephan, Barabbas had first become acquainted with contemporary art, making friends, at the age of fifteen, with Padhi Frieberger and roaming the scene in his company; it was there that he had met Arnulf Rainer, with whom he briefly maintained a friendship; and it was from the gallery that everyone left for the Theater am Fleischmarkt, where, in 1959, Georges Mathieu held his legendary painting action.

The French painter's action would turn out to be an initiation experience for Barabbas. Mathieu, the protagonist of *art informel*, performed in front of a giant canvas he spattered with paint straight from the tube in a gesture that anticipated Viennese Actionism. "The French star's public painting action – at the time, he was at the height of his renown – lasted just under fifty minutes. The atmosphere in the auditorium was explosive, not least because pastose oil paints, binders and solvents, and vapors released for the eight-by-twenty-foot canvas created a latent fire hazard."[6] The master then bequeathed leftovers of these same paints to the enthusiastic young painter, and Rainer gave him painted canvases on the condition that he must use them by overpainting them.[7] Now seventeen years old, Barabbas painted his first tachist pictures, trying out working blindfolded and experimenting.

Few of these works are extant today, but they exemplify the characteristics of the early oeuvre. Georges Mathieu's influence is palpable (fig. 6). Like the French artist, Barabbas puts a palette of yellows and reds on the canvas in wild and unbridled gestures; the expansive application in linear brushstrokes and the paths of the paint tube are clearly recognizable.

At his friend Walter Malli's suggestion, Barabbas exhibited these tachist works at Galerie zum roten Apfel in 1960. The show, his first, marked his entrée to the Vienna scene: "ring the bell, wait, open, narrow iron stairway, a warm welcome in a living room, that's Galerie zum roten Apfel [...] where a very young painter who calls himself Barabbas is putting his fantasies on display [...] Bright controlled splotches spread out over a serenely colorful ground; above them, the precious paint is applied directly from the tube, in thin and thicker filaments or blobs, in straight or curved lines. The Romans prophesied from the entrails of animals, and if I may offer a smiling augury from these intestine-shaped visions, the young man has a sense of color; the cosmic evolutions out of midnight blue, for example, are captivating,"[8] a critic in a daily summed up the show with mild amusement.

dem er für kurze Zeit freundschaftlich verbunden war; und von dort war man auch zum Theater am Fleischmarkt aufgebrochen, als Georges Mathieu 1959 seine legendäre Malaktion durchführte.

Die Aktion des Franzosen sollte für Barabbas ein Initiationserlebnis werden. Der Protagonist der Art Informel agierte vor einer riesigen Leinwand, die er mit Farbe aus der Tube, aktionistischem Gestus gleich, bespritzte. „Die öffentliche Malaktion des französischen Stars, der zu dieser Zeit am Zenit seiner Anerkennung war, dauerte knapp 50 Minuten. Die Atmosphäre im Saal war nicht zuletzt auch deshalb explosiv, weil pastose aus der Tube gepresste Ölfarben, Malmittel und Dämpfe, die für die 2,5 x 6 Meter messende Leinwand freigesetzt wurden, eine latente Feuergefahr bildeten."[6] Reste eben dieser Farben schenkte der Meister dem begeisterten jungen Maler, und von Rainer bekam er bereits bemalte Leinwände mit der Auflage, er dürfe sie nur für seine eigenen Übermalungen verwenden.[7] Und der 17-jährige Barabbas malte seine ersten tachistischen Bilder, versuchte sich mit verbundenen Augen und experimentierte.

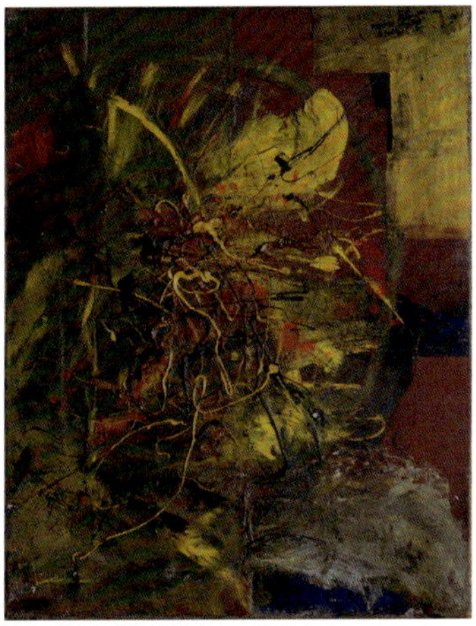

6
O.T., 1960
Mischtechnik auf Leinwand, 118 x 92 cm
Untitled, 1960
mixed technique on canvas, 118 x 92 cm

Heute sind von diesen Werken nur wenige erhalten, doch charakterisieren diese das Frühwerk beispielhaft. Der Einfluss Georges Mathieus ist deutlich spürbar (Abb. 6). Ebenso wie der Franzose setzt Barabbas wild und ungebändigt eine Palette aus gelben und roten Tönen auf die Fläche, in großräumigem Auftrag und linearer Spur bleiben Malauftrag und Führung der Farbtube sichtbar.

Auf Anregung seines Freundes Walter Malli stellte Barabbas die tachistischen Werke 1960 in der Galerie zum roten Apfel aus. Mit dieser, seiner ersten Ausstellung betrat er die Wiener Szene: „läuten, warten, öffnen, schmale Eisenstiege, herzliches Willkommen in einem Wohnraum, das ist die Galerie zum roten Apfel [...]. Dort zeigt ein ganz junger Maler, der sich Barabbas nennt, [...] seine Phantasien. Auf ruhig farbigem Grund breiten sich helle gelenkte Kleckse aus, darüber wird kostbare Farbe direkt aus der Tube, also in dünnen und dickeren Fäden oder Würstchen gerade oder in Kurven geführt. Die Römer prophezeiten aus dem Gekröse der Tiere, wenn ich von diesen Visionen in Darmform als Augur lächeln darf, dann hat der Jüngling Farbsinn, die kosmischen Evolutionen aus dem Nachtblau etwa fesseln",[8] resümierte man in der Tagespresse dazu ein wenig mit einem Lächeln.

In Austria, tachism, like Mathieu's performance, was a hotly debated phenomenon, while the rest of Europe and America had long accepted it. That was why the activities at the Roter Apfel, as a phenomenon on the periphery of Vienna's informel scene, could cause a stir. Labeled "Islamic tachists" – Malli and Pechoc professed the Muslim faith, inspiring Barabbas to convert in 1960 – the team became part of the history of Galerie zum roten Apfel.[9]

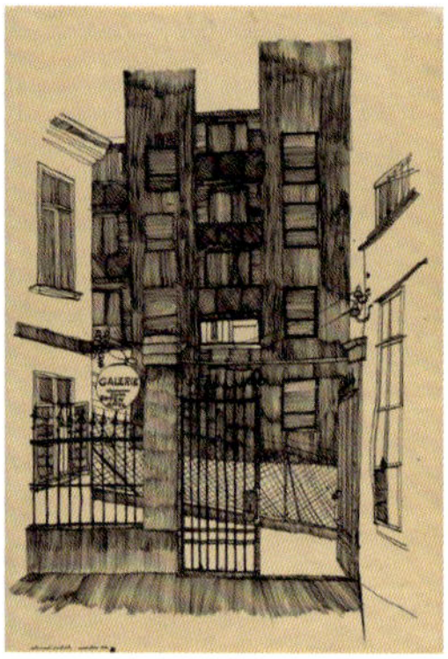

7
Richard Ahmad Pechoc
Galerie zum roten Apfel, 1964
Tusche auf Papier, 63 x 45 cm
Richard Ahmad Pechoc
Galerie zum roten Apfel, 1964
drawing ink on paper, 63 x 45 cm

During this period, Malli's and Pechoc's paintings tended toward an abstract approach realized chiefly in the graphical register. Delicate webs of lines forming dense gestural conglomerations are the signature feature of their intuitive technique (fig. 7). Meanwhile, the work of Carl Anton Fleck – another close friend of Barabbas's from the Roter Apfel clique – evinces distinctly greater realism, with figurative formations (fig. 8).

Yet Pechoc and Malli, too, changed course in 1960. They once again turned to naturalism, drawing on the skills in *en plein air* painting they had acquired as Carl Unger's students to produce sensitively composed cityscapes. Barabbas similarly soon lost interest in tachist performance.

His break with tachism came shortly after the first show at the Roter Apfel; he also explicitly addressed this step in his art itself, in a picture entitled "Barabbas Ploughs through Tachism" (fig. 9).[10] Barabbas visited Friedensreich Hundertwasser in Bellême, France, and left abstract-gestural painting behind for good. From this moment on, a technique of composing surfaces out of minute fields that translates what the painter has seen into pattern-like structures predominates in his oeuvre. In terms of themes, religious issues are a central concern.

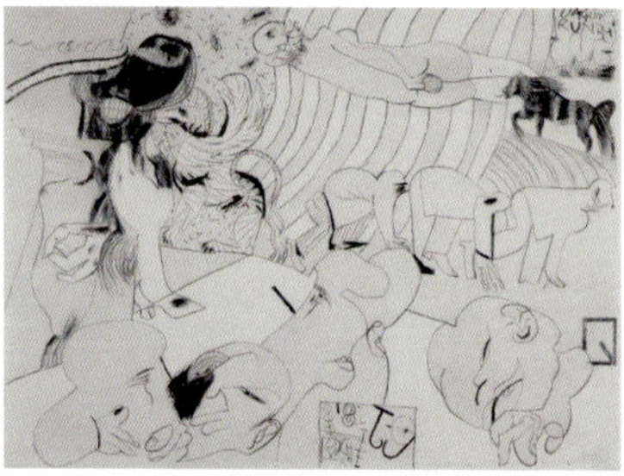

8
Karl Anton Fleck, Umgliederung, 1969
Bleistift auf Papier, 60 x 79,7 cm
Karl Anton Fleck, Restructuring, 1969
pencil on paper, 60 x 79,7 cm

"The Demise of Christianity/Atomic Cloud" (fig. 2) was the title Barabbas gave to a 1962 work in oil on fiberboard that is reminiscent of a naïve narrative style. A cross and church spires rise shakily right next to a gigantic atomic cloud that bursts the format's constraints, bearing witness to the menace to humankind. Barabbas builds the composition in rigorously contoured fields and segments, producing a dense fabric of abstract structures and simplified representational elements. What is striking is the painting's palette. Barabbas limits himself to a triad of blues, reds,

In Österreich war der Tachismus, wie auch der Auftritt Mathieus, ein heiß diskutiertes Ereignis, während diese Strömung in Europa und Amerika längst anerkannt war. So konnten die Aktivitäten im Roten Apfel als Randerscheinung der informellen Szene Wiens aufhorchen lassen. Unter der Bezeichnung „Islamische Tachisten" ging das Gespann – Malli und Pechoc waren bekennende Muslims, und auch Barabbas war, von den beiden angeregt, 1960 zum Islam übergetreten – in die Geschichte der Galerie zum roten Apfel ein.[9]

Die Malerei von Malli und Pechoc tendierte in diesem Zeitraum zu einer abstrahierten Auffassung, die sich vornehmlich im Grafischen realisierte. Feine Liniengespinste, die sich zu gestisch dichten Formationen ballen, kennzeichnen ihre intuitive Malweise (Abb. 7). Im Unterschied dazu zeigte sich die Arbeit Carl Anton Flecks – ebenfalls enger Freund Barabbas' aus der Clique im Roten Apfel – mit seinen figurativen Formationen (Abb. 8) deutlich realistischer.

1960 kam es jedoch auch bei Pechoc und Malli zu einer Umkehr. Sie wandten sich neuerlich dem Naturalismus zu und knüpften an ihre bei Carl Unger erlernte Arbeit nach der freien Natur an: Sensibel gezeichnete Stadtansichten entstanden. Das tachistische Agieren blieb auch für Barabbas nur kurzfristig interessant.

Bald nach der ersten Schau im Roten Apfel kam es zu einem Bruch mit dem Tachismus, der sich auch in einer selbstreflexiven Arbeit mit dem Titel „Barabbas durchpflügt den Tachismus" (Abb. 9) niederschlägt.[10] Barabbas besuchte Friedensreich Hundertwasser in Bellême in Frankreich und wandte sich gänzlich von der abstrakt-gestischen Malerei ab. Von diesem Moment an überwiegt eine kleinteilige flächenhafte Malerei im Œuvre des Malers, die Gesehenes ins Musterhafte übersetzt. Thematisch bilden religiöse Fragestellungen ein zentrales Anliegen.

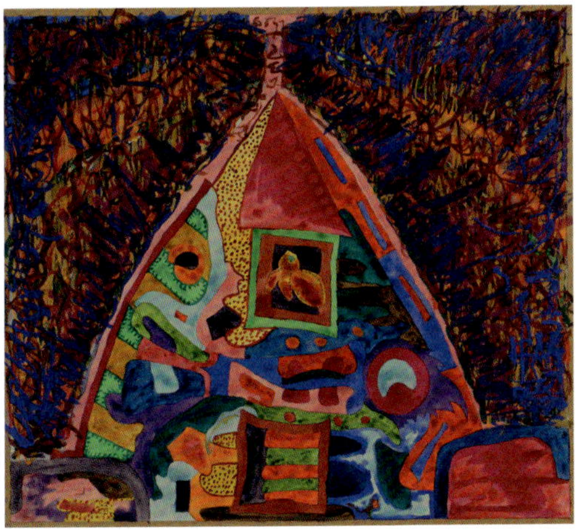

9
Barabbas durchpflügt den Tachismus, 1965
Mischtechnik auf Papier, 39,5 x 44 cm
Barabbas Ploughs through Tachism, 1965
mixed technique on paper, 39,5 x 44 cm

„Der Untergang des Christentums/Atompilz" (Abb. 2) nannte Barabbas eine 1962 entstandene Arbeit in Öl auf Faserplatte, die an naiven Erzählstil mahnt. Kreuz und Kirchtürme erheben sich schwankend unmittelbar neben einem riesenhaft anwachsenden, das Format sprengenden Atompilz und verkünden die Bedrohung der Menschheit. In streng konturierten

and blacks, creating an emphatic contrast; this color scheme prevails in his art between 1961 and 1963.

In these works, Friedensreich Hundertwasser's influence is most prominent in the compositional structure: the picture is clearly laid out and emphasizes flatness. Yet his artistic position evinces parallels with Hundertwasser's as well; the older artist "came to public notice as an early activist championing an extreme environmentalist worldview."[11] Barabbas's graphic works from the early 1960s such as "Prophet Jeremiah" (fig. 25) and "Annunciation to the Blessed Virgin Mary" (fig. 23), in particular, are remarkable illustrations of the painter's gift. Most striking about them is the crystalline structure subdividing the surface into innumerable segments in which different patterns emerge; the motif, equally broken up into fragments, is inscribed in these segments so as to be virtually imperceptible. With what would seem almost obsessive attention to detail, Barabbas produces a minimized translation of the figuration into a band of black-and-white, into a progression leading from contour to form, from the large to the small, and from the exterior ever deeper into the interior.

The beholder feels reminded of the sprawling series of minute pattern units and ribbons of Adolf Wölfli, who filled countless books with figured pictures. The art of the mentally ill, which is today described as rooted in their psychological states – it is also publicized under the art brut or "outsider art" labels – drew a great deal of interest in the 1960s and was regarded as a point of reference for painting, as were the naïve, children's drawings, and exotica. It is possible that Barabbas received impulses from these directions. What we know is that he was fascinated by the paintings of Paul Klee, whose highly detailed and imaginative imagery is akin to his own scenarios and dream worlds. Time and again, magical narratives appear in his art. "Early Christian Squid in the Neighbor's Garden" (fig. 24) and "Three Space Probes Fly Through Mars Full of Holes" (fig. 34) speak to the painter's playful and wide-ranging imagination.

In ornamentation, Barabbas had discovered a register that counterbalanced his abstract-gestural roots. After his return to Vienna from France, he next appeared on the scene in 1963 with an exhibition entitled "Innen- und Außenschau der Welt" ("Inside and Outside View of the World") at Galerie zum roten Apfel. Alfred Schmeller wrote a wonderful review that reads in part: "When we were boys, one game we would play was ringing all bells of the various tenants at the same time, using all fingers or an arm. We loved it when, all at once, furious faces emerged from all windows and doors. The painter Barabbas plays the same game in his pictures. Take a closer look, and you'll find heads and faces looking out everywhere. The colors are pealing at full throttle. Between his low blue and his high

Flächen und Segmenten baut Barabbas die Komposition auf, es ergibt sich ein dichtes Gefüge aus abstrakten Strukturen und vereinfachten Darstellungen. Auffallend ist die Farbigkeit des Bildes. Barabbas beschränkt sich auf einen Dreiklang aus Blau-, Rot- und Schwarztönen und erzeugt damit einen betonten Kontrast, eine Farbgebung, die in den Jahren 1961 bis 1963 vorherrscht.

Der Einfluss Friedensreich Hundertwassers wird bei diesen Werken vor allem im Bildaufbau deutlich: Das Bild ist klar gegliedert und an der Fläche orientiert. Aber auch hinsichtlich der künstlerischen Position tun sich Parallelen zu Hundertwasser auf, der „als früher Aktivist einer extrem ökologisch-grünbewegten Weltsicht an die Öffentlichkeit trat".[11] Besonders Barabbas' grafische Arbeiten aus den frühen sechziger Jahren wie „Prophet Jeremia" (Abb. 25) und „Mariä Verkündigung" (Abb. 23) erscheinen bemerkenswert und zeigen die Begabung des Malers. Erstaunlich ist vor allem die kristallin angelegte Flächenteilung in zahllose sich eröffnende Segmente unterschiedlicher Musterung, in die das Motiv, ebenso gegliedert, nahezu nicht wahrnehmbar eingeschrieben wird. Fast manisch wirkt die minimierte Übersetzung des Figürlichen in ein Band von Schwarz-Weiß, in einen Ablauf, der von der Kontur zur Form, vom Großen ins Kleine, vom Außen immer mehr ins Innere führt.

Man fühlt sich an die kleinteiligen Serien mit Rapporten und Bändern von Adolf Wölfli erinnert, der unzählige Bücher mit musterhaften Bildern füllte. Die heute als zustandsgebundene Kunst bezeichnete Arbeit von psychisch Kranken – auch unter dem Begriff Art Brut rezipiert – wurde in den sechziger Jahren viel diskutiert und galt als Orientierungspunkt für die Malerei, ebenso wie das Naive, die Kinderzeichnung und das Exotische. Möglich, dass Barabbas diese Impulse aufnahm. Sicher aber war er von der Malerei Paul Klees fasziniert, deren kleinteilige, imaginative Bilderwelt seinen Szenarien und Traumwelten verwandt ist. Märchenhafte Narrationen treten in seinem Schaffen immer wieder auf. „Urchristlicher Tintenfisch in des Nachbars Garten" (Abb. 24) und „Drei Raumsonden durchfliegen den löchrigen Mars" (Abb. 34) erzählen von der spielerischen Gedankenwelt des Malers.

Mit dem Ornament hatte Barabbas einen Gegenpol zu seinen abstrakt-gestischen Anfängen entdeckt. Aus Frankreich zurück in Wien, trat er 1963 mit der Ausstellung „Innen- und Außenschau der Welt" in der Galerie zum roten Apfel auf. Wunderbar liest sich die Kritik, die Alfred Schmeller dazu verfasste: „Als Buben spielten wir mit allen Fingern oder mit dem Arm gleichzeitig auf alle Glocken der Hausparteien drücken. Es war so schön, wenn mit einem Schlag aus allen Fenstern, aus allen Türen erboste Gesichter herausschauten. Dasselbe Spiel spielt der Maler Barabbas auf seinen Bildern. Überall schauen bei näherem Zusehen Köpfe

red, turquoise rings shrilly, orange clatters. And yet harmony results. The small pictures roar like a large organ."[12]

It is not by accident that Schmeller's metaphorical language refers to acoustic phenomena. Around 1963, Barabbas started to make music with Malli, Fleck, and Pechoc. From the outset, the gallery, which had always been conceived as an open meeting-point, also hosted public concerts and music events. Pechoc, Malli, and Fleck had performed together on several occasions and aroused attention with appearances at Forum Stadtpark in Graz. Now Barabbas, who had played the piano to pay his way during his tour of France, joined them. Since the ensemble already had a pianist in Pechoc, Barabbas had to choose another instrument, and his choice was the saxophone.

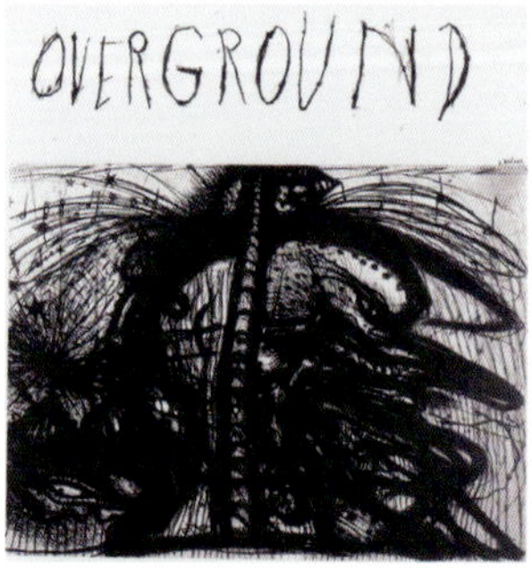


10
1969 produzierte Barabbas mit den „Masters of Unorthodox Jazz" die erste österreichische Free-Jazz-Platte OVERGROUND. Für das Cover stellte Arnulf Rainer eine teilübermalte Grafik zur Verfügung.
In 1969, Barabbas and the "Masters of Unorthodox Jazz" produced OVERGROUND, Austria's first-ever free jazz record. Arnulf Rainer provided a partially overpainted piece of graphic art for the cover.

His gift and his enthusiasm for improvisation led to a major decision: the musicians founded the "Masters of Unorthodox Jazz." They performed at various venues, including the Museum des 20. Jahrhunderts, which had been founded in 1962, and in 1969, they successfully recorded a first LP entitled "Overground."

"Overground," a term coined by Barabbas, designates an idea he wanted to see realized in his visual oeuvre as well as in music; the goal is a "timeless recording of what cannot be measured."[13] The extent to which structural affinities exist between his music and his visual art beyond this general idea has been documented only for his early works.[14] The overall significance of the interplay between visual art and music, however, is illustrated not only by the venues where the band performed, but also by the LP cover, which features a picture by Arnulf Rainer, copy by the painter and art theorist Claus Pack, and photographs by Gerhard Trumler.[15]

Direct references to music are rare in Barabbas's painting. One example is the painting "Sonny Rollins" (fig. 42) created in 1969, which he dedicated to the noted American saxophonist, one of his heroes.

The "Overground" concept, which the press also read in ironic contrast with "underground,"[16] is the key to an attitude of mind rooted mainly in the spirit of the era – the love and peace movement of the 1960s. The author of one opening invitation card quoted: "Overground means a lifestyle to which relaxing is fundamental, the effort to achieve unity through love, subtle spirituality. Overground is unity in art and the endeavor to integrate that art into all domains of life."[17]

und Gesichter heraus. Die Farben läuten auf Hochtouren. Zwischen tiefem Blau und hohem Rot schrillt Türkis, scheppert Orange. Trotzdem ergibt sich eine Harmonie. Die kleinen Bilder dröhnen wie eine große Orgel."[12]

Die metaphorische Sprache Schmellers bezieht sich nicht von ungefähr auf Akustisches. Um 1963 begann Barabbas mit Malli, Fleck und Pechoc zu musizieren. Die Galerie, stets als offener Treffpunkt angelegt, war von Beginn an auch mit Konzerten und Musikveranstaltungen an die Öffentlichkeit getreten. Pechoc, Malli und Fleck hatten bereits mehrfach gemeinsam musiziert und mit Auftritten in Graz im Forum Stadtpark Aufmerksamkeit erregt. Nun gesellte sich auch Barabbas hinzu, der sich während seiner Frankreich-Reise als Pianist durchgeschlagen hatte. Da Pechoc am Piano saß, blieb ihm nur die Wahl eines anderen Instrumentes, und er wählte das Saxofon.

Seine Begabung und seine Improvisationsfreude führten zu einer Weichenstellung. Man gründete die „Masters of Unorthodox Jazz", trat an verschiedenen Orten auf, etwa auch im 1962 gegründeten Museum des 20. Jahrhunderts, und es gelang 1969, eine erste Schallplatte mit dem Titel „Overground" zu produzieren.

„Overground", dieser von Barabbas geprägte Ausdruck, verweist auf eine Vorstellung, die er in seiner bildnerischen Arbeit wie auch in der Musik verwirklicht wissen wollte und bei der es um „das zeitlose Erfassen von nicht Messbarem"[13] ging. Inwieweit über diese allgemeine Idee hinaus strukturelle Beziehungen zwischen seinem musikalischen und seinem bildnerischen Schaffen bestanden, ist nur für seine Frühwerke belegt.[14] Dass die Verschränkung von bildender Kunst und Musik jedoch generell von Bedeutung war, wird nicht nur an den Spielorten der Band, sondern schon am Cover der LP sichtbar, das mit einem Bild von Arnulf Rainer und einem Text des Malers und Kunsttheoretikers Claus Pack sowie Fotos von Gerhard Trumler versehen ist.[15]

Nur selten bezieht sich Barabbas in seiner Malerei direkt auf Musikalisches. Beispiel dafür ist das Gemälde „Sonny Rollins" (Abb. 42) aus dem Jahr 1969, das er dem bekannten amerikanischen Saxofonisten, einem seiner Vorbilder, widmete.

Mit den Begriff „Overground", der von der Presse auch ironisch als Antonym zu Underground gesetzt wurde,[16] erschließt sich eine Geisteshaltung, die vor allem im Zeitgeist – der Love-and-Peace-Bewegung der sechziger Jahre – verwurzelt ist. Bei einer Vernissage zitierte man dazu: „Overground bedeutet eine Lebenshaltung aus dem Relaxing, das Streben nach Einheit durch Liebe, subtile Geistigkeit. Overground ist Einheit in der Kunst und das Bestreben, diese Kunst in alle Lebensbereiche zu integrieren."[17]

At the time, the American hippie and flower power movement reached Europe's shores. This revolt expressed through lifestyle choices, music, and dress drew the vociferous disapproval of ordinary citizens. Experimentation with drugs and rambunctious scenes were part of the young generation's self-image. As a "rebel," Barabbas welcomed this movement, which brought a surge of like-minded people, and its influence is palpable in his music as well as his paintings.

Around the mid-1960s, Barabbas's creative output suggests a fresh start. He gradually approaches larger formats, producing a series of monumental works in oil and casein on canvas. Although he was an autodidact, he had studied painterly techniques early on. His old friend Heinz Stangl – the two had attended the same high school – supported this exploration. Barabbas taught himself many different techniques, and he kept a detailed diary of his work in which he explained various procedures: *"In the oil painting [...] I used alkyd resin as a binder. In order to make it evenly matte, for example, I use a bit of beeswax. Oil paints also dry more rapidly and, what is more important, more uniformly when this resin is added. For egg tempera, I use damar or mastic gum or linseed oil ..."*[18] Barabbas filled page after page with observations like these, evidence of his close study of the technical aspects of his craft, in which he first achieved a degree of maturity in the 1960s.

"Malli's Island" (fig. 29), a painting from the middle of that decade, is a key work of the period. Barabbas augments the ornamental compositional structure by broadening his palette and adding nuance. As in the earlier graphic works, the surface is now broken up in many places and resolved into minute formations. Differently patterned zones blend and slide into one another, although they remain clearly circumscribed. The painting faintly suggests musical improvisation. Each planar structure responds to its counterpart, complementing or enhancing it or setting it off.

What seems crucial is that Barabbas disassociates his art from representational points of reference and probes the picture's abstract dimensions. That also holds for associations on the levels of content and theme, which he now visualizes in the iconic and universal, rather than the figural and allegorical, register. An exemplary illustration of this development is the "Prayer Rug" (fig. 30) from the mid-1960s, whose religious connotation is unfolded entirely by means of abstraction.

The title "Malli's Island" refers to the history of the picture's genesis. The anecdote is this: Barabbas, seated next to his friend Malli at Café Krugerhof, told him about the concept for a painting. The art critic Kristian Sotriffer sat nearby. Malli was somehow uncomfortable with the critic's presence. Barabbas explained: *"Basically, the concept for this picture was about a theory Othmar Zechyr and I had de-*

Die Hippie- und Flower-Power-Bewegung schwappte zu diesem Zeitpunkt von Amerika auf Europa über. Das Aufbegehren mittels Lebensstil, Musik und Kleidung rief bei den BürgerInnen laut geäußertes Missfallen hervor. Experimente mit Drogen und wilde Auftritte gehörten zum Selbstverständnis der jungen Generation. Für Barabbas den „Rebellen" bildete die Bewegung eine willkommene Strömung Gleichgesinnter, deren Einfluss in seiner Musik ebenso wie in seiner Malerei spürbar ist.

Mitte der sechziger Jahre zeichnet sich in Barabbas' Schaffen ein Aufbruch ab. Er nähert sich dem großen Format, und es entstand eine Serie monumentaler Werke in Öl-Kasein-Technik auf Leinwand. Obwohl Barabbas Autodidakt war, hatte er sich schon früh mit malerischen Techniken beschäftigt. Sein Schulkollege Heinz Stangl, mit dem er das Gymnasium besucht hatte, wirkte hier unterstützend. Viele technische Spielarten brachte sich Barabbas selbst bei, und er führte ein ausführliches Werktagebuch, in dem er diverse Techniken erklärte: *„Beim Ölbild [...] habe ich Alkydharz als Malmittel verwendet. Um es z. B. matt zu machen verwende ich ein wenig Bienenwachs. Ölfarben trocknen auch schneller und vor allem zeitlich gleichmäßig durch die Verwendung dieses Harzes. Für Ei Tempera verwende ich Damar, Mastix oder Leinöl ..."*[18] So oder ähnlich schrieb Barabbas Seite um Seite und verdeutlicht damit seine intensive Beschäftigung mit den handwerklich-technischen Aspekten der Malerei, die er in den sechziger Jahren zu einer ersten Reife führte.

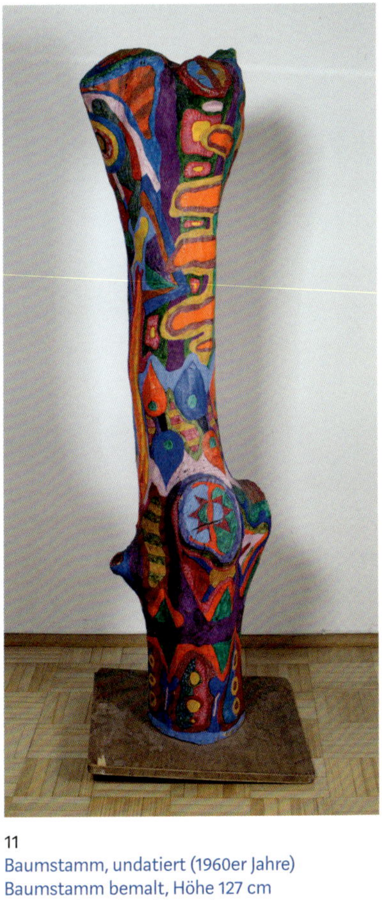

11
Baumstamm, undatiert (1960er Jahre)
Baumstamm bemalt, Höhe 127 cm
Tree Trunk, undated (1960s)
tree trunk, painted, height 127 cm

„Mallis Insel" (Abb. 29) aus der Mitte des Jahrzehnts bildet ein Schlüsselwerk dieser Phase. Barabbas erweitert den ornamentalen Bildaufbau hinsichtlich Farbigkeit und Differenziertheit. Wie schon bei den Grafiken ist die Fläche nun vielfach durchbrochen und in kleinteilige Formationen aufgelöst. Verschieden gemusterte Zonen schwimmen und gleiten ineinander, sind aber dennoch klar abgegrenzt. Bei diesem Gemälde fühlt man sich ein wenig an die musikalische Methode der Improvisation erinnert. Jede Flächenstruktur antwortet auf ihr Gegenüber, ergänzt es, kontrastiert es oder steigert es.

*veloped of leaving the idea behind a painting in the painting, rather than visualizing a detail from an overall action. So, for example, of taking an island in the sea as an identity in its own right; depicting a tower, a rock formation, a haystack, a skeleton, or a microscopic detail as singular."* [19]

"Malli's Island" symbolizes this anecdote as well as the figure of the friend – his world – as such. Barabbas's explanation is interesting also with regard to a group of works created between 1966 and 1969 for which he used maps (fig. 35-37) and pattern sheets (fig. 38-40) of various sizes as support media, adding colorful accents and ornaments that highlight their various specific features. Southeast Asia, Japan, Asia are thus identified by the emphasis on their shapes.

This group of works evinces parallels with the art of Christian Boltanski, who archived his own life. Invited to contribute to documenta 5 in 1972, he exhibited woven maps – visualizations of stages in his life's journey – in which, as in Barabbas's maps, the shapes of the continents were covered with patterns. In actions and documentary works, Boltanski's oeuvre reflects on the relation between art and the real in the widest sense of the term. Barabbas, by contrast, seeks out the imagination as a place of sojourn that develops out of the real.

Between 1964 and 1969, Barabbas's life entered a phase of new beginnings in terms of his art as well as private life. In 1964, he married Rosemarie Sebek – he called her Wardi, Arabic for Rose, and liked to paint her portrait (fig. 4). They had three children together. The family lived in the upscale summer resort town of Reichenau, in an apartment in his parents' villa. The village at the foot of the Rax mountain range inspired the idea in Barabbas of founding an artists' colony, though his romantic vision of such a life mostly remained just that. Still, the house was always open to his colleagues and friends, who came to discuss, work, and collaborate, and were invited to stay at the villa as needed. Othmar Zechyr, who was among Barabbas's closest friends, spent months in Reichenau. Richard Pechoc, Walter Malli, and Heinz Stangl visited the family on a regular basis; Erwin Ringel, Robert Zeppel-Sperl, and Peter Pongratz came, and Ernst Fuchs and Arnulf Rainer supported their friend by buying his work.[20]

The paintings the members of the circle produced during this period show growing similarities in some respects. They preferred graphic techniques such as quill and ink drawing or etching. Malli's and Pechoc's drawings (fig. 12+13), like Othmar Zechyr's (fig. 14), present highly subtle shadings and hatchings condensed and concentrated to produce lively formations. The cityscape becomes the central motif, transformed into a dynamic architectural and landscape space. With a view to the detailed ornamentation in Barabbas's graphic art, we might speak of

Wesentlich erscheint, dass Barabbas sich von gegenständlichen Bezugspunkten löst und das Bild ins Abstrakte auslotet. Dies gilt auch für inhaltliche und thematische Assoziationen, die nun nicht mehr ins Figürlich-Allegorische, sondern ins Ikonisch-Universelle übersetzt werden. Beispielhaft für diese Entwicklung ist der „Gebetsteppich" (Abb. 30) aus der Mitte der sechziger Jahre, dessen religiöse Konnotation gänzlich abstrahiert entwickelt wird.

Bei „Mallis Insel" verweist der Titel auf die Entstehungsgeschichte des Bildes. Dazu ist überliefert: Im Café Krugerhof sitzend, erzählte Barabbas seinem Freund Malli vom Konzept eines Gemäldes. Der Kunstkritiker Kristian Sotriffer saß neben den beiden. Malli schien es irgendwie unangenehm, den Kritiker neben sich zu wissen. Barabbas erklärte: *„Grundsätzlich ging es bei diesem Bildkonzept um eine von Othmar Zechyr und mir entwickelte Theorie, die Bildidee im Bild zu belassen und nicht einen Ausschnitt eines Gesamtgeschehens darzustellen. Also z. B. eine Insel im Meer als eigene Identität zu nehmen, einen Turm, eine Felsenformation, einen Heuhaufen, ein Skelett, oder einen mikroskopischen Ausschnitt singular darzustellen."*[19]

„Mallis Insel" steht sinnbildhaft für diese Begebenheit, aber ebenso für die Figur des Freundes – seine Welt – als solche. Interessant ist die Erklärung Barabbas' auch im Hinblick auf eine Werkgruppe, die zwischen 1966 und 1969 entstand. Dabei verwendete Barabbas Landkarten (Abb. 35-37) und Schnittbögen (Abb. 38-40) diverser Größe als Bildträger und versah diese mit farblichen Akzenten und Musterungen, die deren jeweilige Spezifik unterstreichen. Südostasien, Japan, Asien werden damit durch ihre betonte Form erkennbar.

Bei dieser Werkgruppe lassen sich Ähnlichkeiten zu Christian Boltanski feststellen, der 1972 bei der documenta 5 vertreten war und sein eigenes Leben archivierte. Er stellte dort gewebte Landkarten – als Bezugsmomente seines Lebensweges – aus, die, den Karten Barabbas' gleich, die Form der Kontinente mit einer Musterung überzogen. Boltanskis Werk reflektiert mit Aktionen und Dokumentationen die Beziehung von Kunst und Realem im weitesten Sinn. Barabbas hingegen sucht das Imaginative als Ort des Verweilens, der sich aus dem Realen heraus entwickelt.

Zwischen 1964 und 1969 durchlebte Barabbas eine Phase des Aufbruchs in künstlerischer, aber auch in privater Hinsicht. Er heiratete 1964 Rosemarie Sebek, die er Wardi (arabisch für Rose) nannte und gerne in Porträts darstellte (Abb. 4). Gemeinsam hatten sie drei Kinder. Die Familie lebte in der noblen Sommerfrische Reichenau, in einer Wohnung der elterlichen Villa. Der Ort am Fuß der Rax inspirierte Barabbas zur Idee, eine Künstlerkolonie zu gründen, was allerdings

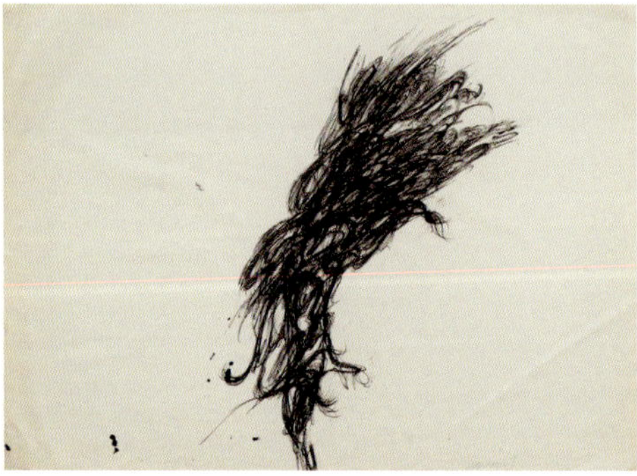

12
Walter Muhammad Malli, Ohne Titel, 1958/59
Tusche auf Papier, 50 x 70 cm
Walter Muhammad Malli, untitled, 1958/59
drawing ink on paper, 50 x 70 cm

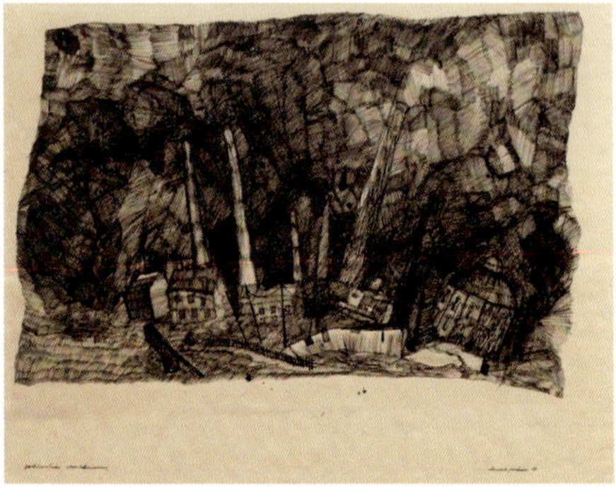

13
Richard Ahmad Pechoc
Fortschreitende Verschlammung, 1967
Tusche auf Papier, 53,5 x 70 cm
Richard Ahmad Pechoc, Progressive Siltation, 1967
drawing ink on paper, 53,5 x 70 cm

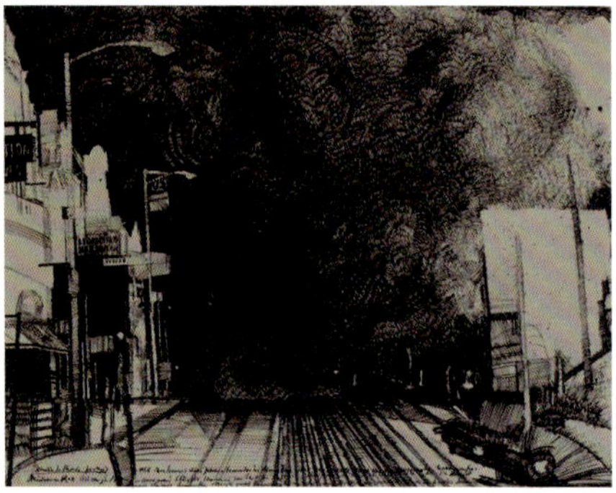

14
Othmar Zechyr, Chicago, Black Power, 1967
Tusche auf Papier, 46,2 x 61,5 cm
Othmar Zechyr, Chicago, Black Power, 1967
drawing ink on paper, 46,2 x 61,5 cm

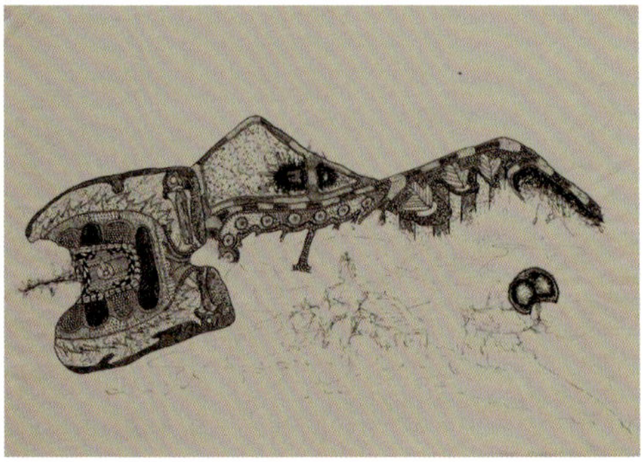

15
Landschaft, 1966
Tusche auf Transparentpapier, 31 x 45 cm
Landscape, 1966
drawing ink on tracing paper, 31 x 45 cm

an extension of microstructure into the perspectival register. The motif seems to come to life.

Zeppel-Sperl and Stangl likewise pursued a translation of form into pattern-like designs. Unlike Malli and Pechoc, they primarily engaged with the figure, which they kaleidoscopically dissolved into esoteric spaces. Barabbas, on the other hand, turned more and more resolutely to subjects pertinent to his frame of mind and ideals. One example is the work "Black Power No. II" (fig. 41), which examines the American Civil Rights Movement around Martin Luther King – a struggle for recognition and against the establishment – and of course also contains references to the Nation of Islam and Malcolm X.

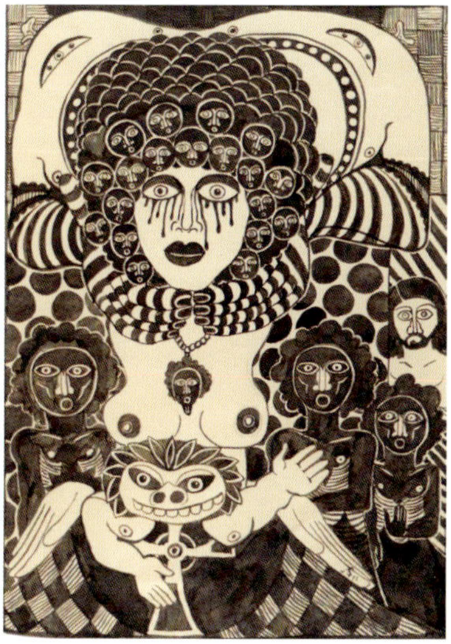

16
Robert Zeppel-Sperl, Afrikanerin, 1971
Tusche auf Papier, 61,2 x 45,6 cm
Robert Zeppel-Sperl, African Woman, 1971
drawing ink on paper, 61,2 x 45,6 cm

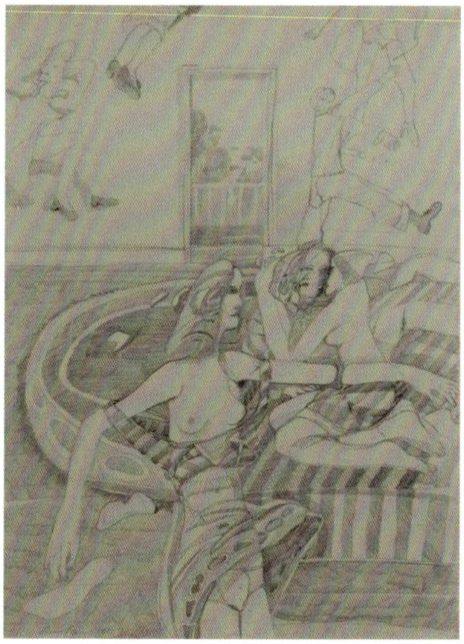

17
Heinz Stangl, Zerrinnender Nachmittag, 1972
Bleistift auf Papier, 64 x 48 cm
Heinz Stangl, Afternoon Melting Away, 1972
pencil on paper, 64 x 48 cm

mehr romantische Vorstellung als gelebte Vision blieb. Das offene Haus bot jedoch für Kollegen und Freunde einen Ort der Diskussion, der gemeinsamen Arbeit, und bei Bedarf war es auch möglich, in der Villa zu wohnen. Othmar Zechyr, der zu den engsten Freunden Barabbas' zählte, blieb für Monate in Reichenau. Richard Pechoc, Walter Malli und Heinz Stangl besuchten die Familie regelmäßig, Erwin Ringel, Robert Zeppel-Sperl und Peter Pongratz waren da, und Ernst Fuchs sowie Arnulf Rainer förderten den Freund durch Ankäufe.[20]

Die Malerei dieses Freundeskreises näherte sich in dieser Zeit punktuell an. Man bevorzugte grafische Techniken wie das Zeichnen mit Tusche und Feder oder die Radierung. Mallis und Pechocs Zeichnungen (Abb. 12+13) zeigten sich ebenso wie jene Othmar Zechyrs (Abb. 14) in feinsten Schraffuren und Parallelen verdichtet und zu bewegten Formationen konzentriert. Die Stadtansicht wird zum zentralen Motiv und in einen dynamischen Architektur- und Landschaftsraum transformiert. Mit Blick auf die kleinteilige Ornamentik von Barabbas' Grafiken könnte man von einer Erweiterung der Mikrostruktur ins Perspektivische sprechen. Das Motiv erscheint belebt.

Zeppel-Sperl wie Stangl verfolgten ebenfalls eine Übersetzung der Form ins Musterhafte. Anders als Malli und Pechoc setzten sich die beiden vorwiegend mit der Figur auseinander, die in esoterische Räume kaleidoskopisch aufgelöst wird. Barabbas wandte sich hingegen immer deutlicher Inhalten zu, die seiner Geisteshaltung und seinen Idealen entsprachen. Beispiel dafür ist die Arbeit „Black Power Nr. II" (Abb. 41), die sich auf die Bürgerrechtsbewegung in Amerika rund um Martin Luther King – einen Kampf um Anerkennung und gegen das Establishment – bezieht und damit natürlich auch Bezüge zur Nation of Islam und Malcolm X aufweist.

Das Religiöse war für Barabbas eine wichtige Inspirationsquelle und Lebenshaltung. In der Reichenauer Zeit wandte er sich der Bahá'i-Religion zu, einer 5 bis 8

Religion was an important source of inspiration for Barabbas and shaped his attitude toward life. During his time in Reichenau, he converted to the Baha'i Faith, a universal religion with between five and eight million followers, most of them in India, Africa, and South America. The mystical belief in man's union with God is central to the religion's emphasis on social and humanitarian values. In the West, it was primarily perceived as a peace movement.[21]

In the late 1960s, Barabbas's new religious persuasion begins to show in his visual art; see, for example, the work "Baha" (fig. 49), which is based on the calligraphic ring symbol for *Baha* (magnificence, grace, splendor, and beauty). The ideogram consists of three wavy horizontal lines crossed by a vertical and ending in small circular shapes. The horizontals symbolize three planes: the plane of God, the plane of the messengers, and the plane of humanity; they are interconnected by revelation. Barabbas translates the Arabic calligram into an abstract "Western" interpretation. At the center of a wide landscape format, he places an organic-looking rounded shape produced by connecting the outermost points of the Arabic letters. He then adds a contour to lend it graphical unity, before inserting abstract patterns. The ground is patterned as well and encircled by an animated ribbon that matches the contour of the formation at the center.

Barabbas developed an ever more complex individual mythology out of religious symbols, abstract shapes, simplified depictions of animals and humans, and emblematic signs he embedded in a lively panorama. Besides the subjects directly related to religious iconography, his art tends toward spiritual and cosmic themes of a universal nature. The paintings "Astral Travelin" (fig. 48) and "Milky Way with White Hole" (fig. 45) are characteristic examples from this period of his oeuvre. They reflect the brightly cheerful world of 1960s and early-1970s pop culture, echoing the psychedelic vibes of the decade as it draws to a close. Gaily colorful and flowing, the abstract shapes have shed all traces of small-scale and rigorous ornamentation. The generously laid-out pictorial structure unfolds in billowing arches, rhythmic modulations, and picturesque curves. And all these shapes radiate an incredible wealth of color. "The transition from the figurative magical pictures to an abstract pictorial structure, though still interspersed with the former, was a fluid one, because an almost messianic spiritual attitude is at the heart of this fabulist's invention in radiant colors, psychographic linear ornaments, and planar shapes that proliferate like sprawling vegetation,"[22] Maria Buchsbaum aptly describes the evolution of Barabbas's art.

This luminous and exuberant "fabulist's" painting reached a climax when Barabbas decided to paint a room in his apartment on Payergasse in Vienna's 16th district (fig. 18). Having broken up with his first wife and left Reichenau, he briefly lived there

Millionen Gläubige umfassenden Universalreligion, die ihre Anhänger vorwiegend in Indien, Afrika und Südamerika hat. Der mystische Glaube an die Einheit des Menschen mit Gott steht im Zentrum dieser sozio-humanitär orientierten Haltung. Im Westen wurde die Religion vor allem als Friedensbewegung wahrgenommen.[21]

In den späten sechziger Jahren findet Barabbas' neue Glaubensrichtung Einzug in sein bildnerisches Schaffen, etwa bei der Arbeit „Baha" (Abb. 49), die sich auf das kalligrafische Ringsymbol für „Baha" (Herrlichkeit, Anmut, Glanz und Schönheit) bezieht. Das Zeichen besteht aus drei geschwungenen Horizontallinien, die, von einer Senkrechten geteilt, durch kleine Kreisformen abgeschlossen werden. Die Horizontalen symbolisieren drei Ebenen: die Ebene Gottes, die Ebene der Stifter und die Ebene der Menschheit, die durch die Offenbarung verbunden werden. Barabbas übersetzt das arabische Schriftsymbol in eine abstrakte „westliche" Interpretation. In einem breiten Querformat platziert er eine zentrale, organisch wirkende Rundform. Diese entsteht aus einer Verbindung der äußeren Punkte des arabischen Zeichens. Barabbas versieht diese mit einer Kontur, sodass sich eine flächige Einheit bildet. In diese Form fügt er abstrakte Musterungen ein. Der Grund ist ebenfalls gemustert und von einem bewegten Band eingekreist, das sich der Kontur der zentralen Formation angleicht.

Barabbas entwickelte eine immer komplexere individuelle Mythologie aus religiösen Symbolen, abstrakten Formationen, vereinfachten Darstellungen von Tieren und Menschen sowie sinnbildhafter Zeichen, die er in ein bewegtes Panorama einbettete. Neben unmittelbar auf religiöse Ikonografie bezogene Bildthemen tendiert sein Werk zu spirituell-kosmischen Fragestellungen universeller Natur. Die in der ersten Hälfte der siebziger Jahre entstandenen Gemälde „Astral Travelin" (Abb. 48) und „Milchstraße mit weißem Loch" (Abb. 45) sind charakteristisch für diese Werkphase. Die Gemälde reflektieren die poppige Welt der sechziger und frühen siebziger Jahre; die psychedelische Schwingung des ausklingenden Jahrzehnts findet einen Widerhall. Buntfarbig und fließend haben die abstrakten Formen nun jede kleinteilig starre Ornamentik verloren. Großflächig entfaltet sich die Bildstruktur in wogenden Bögen, rhythmischen Modulationen und pittoresken Schwüngen. Und über all den Formen erstrahlt eine unglaubliche Farbigkeit. „Der Übergang von figurativen Märchenbildern zu einer von diesen immer noch durchsetzten abstrakten Bildstruktur war ein fließender, weil diesem Fabulieren in leuchtenden Farben und vegetabilisch wuchernden, psychografischen Linienornamenten und Flächenformen eine nahezu messianische Geisteshaltung zu Grunde liegt",[22] beschreibt Maria Buchsbaum die Entwicklung des Künstlers treffend.

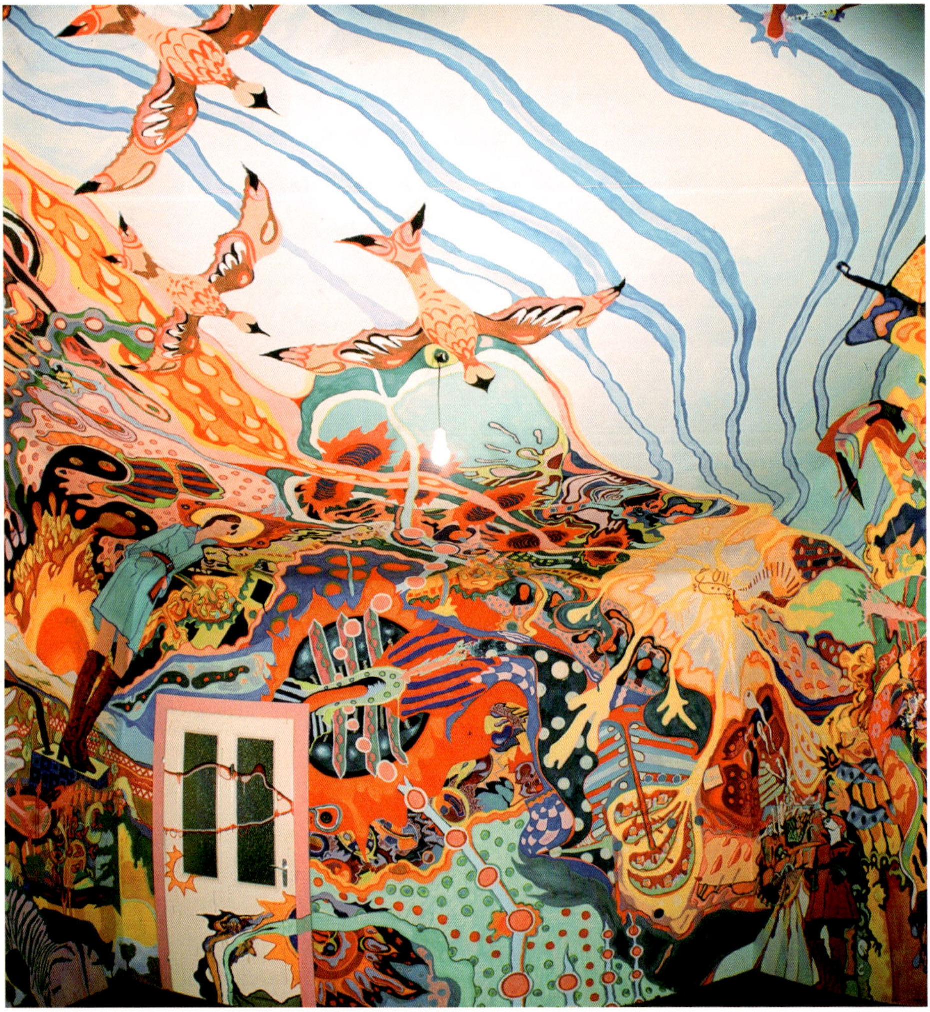

18
Anfang der 70er Jahre wohnte Barabbas kurze Zeit in der Payergasse 7/2/29 im 16. Bezirk, wo er ein Zimmer bemalte. Nachdem er ausgezogen war, wohnte dort noch etwa zwei Monate lang der Dichter Hermann Schürrer, mit dem Barabbas befreundet war. Die Malerei dieses Zimmers existiert leider nicht mehr. (Foto: Gerhard Trumler)
In the early 1970s, Barabbas briefly lived at Payergasse 7/2/29 in the 16th district, where he painted on the walls of a room. After he moved out, the poet Hermann Schürrer, a friend of Barabbas's, lived there for around two months. Unfortunately, the paintings on the walls have been lost. (Photograph: Gerhard Trumler)

before moving into an apartment on Fenzlgasse. The wall painting survives only in documentary photographs, which nonetheless indicate its size and style. Like a cosmos unto itself, painted patterns extended toward forever new points of reference, growing across corners and around doors and windows into a picturesque universe exploding in blazing colors.

Zu einem Höhepunkt dieser „fabulierenden", leuchtenden, vegetabilisch wuchernden Malerei kam es, als Barabbas beschloss, ein Zimmer seiner Wohnung in der Payergasse in Wien 16 zu bemalen (Abb. 18). Dort lebte er, nachdem er von Reichenau ausgezogen und sich von seiner ersten Frau getrennt hatte, für kurze Zeit, bevor er eine Wohnung in der Fenzlgasse bezog. Zwar ist die Wandbemalung nur in dokumentarischen Fotografien erhalten, diese geben aber dennoch Aufschluss über die Ausdehnung und Machart der Arbeit. Wie ein Kosmos dehnte sich die Malerei in Musterungen zu immer neuen Bezugspunkten aus, wächst über Ecken, Türen und Fenster zu einem pittoresken Universum, das in leuchtenden Farben explodiert.

Barabbas eröffnete mit der Wandbemalung eine neue Dimension seines Schaffens: das Monumentalbild. War er in seinen Anfängen eher dem kleinen Format zugetan, so steigerte er die Größe seiner Malgründe in den sechziger und siebziger Jahren allmählich. Sein Spektrum an Formaten reicht von miniaturhaften Größen – 18 x 14 cm maß das „Selbstporträt" aus dem Jahr 1962 – bis zu Großformaten von 200 x 200 cm bei „Mallis Insel". Das Wandgemälde stellte im Œuvre des Malers jedoch das bis dahin monumentalste Format dar.

Auch im Amerika der sechziger Jahre war das Großformat en vogue. Im Kontext der Farbfeldmalerei erreichten die Leinwände Raumdimension, um die kontemplative Wirkung der Arbeiten in Bezug auf den/die Betrachter/in zu steigern. Meditative Versenkung im Raumgefühl war das Ziel. Bei Barabbas war die spirituelle Erlebbarkeit seiner Kosmologien wohl ebenfalls ein Impuls, zum Monumentalformat zu gehen.

1975 erarbeitete er einen ca. 3, 50 Meter hohen und 50 Meter langen Fries, „The Big Bang" oder „Genesis" (s. Leporello), der im Künstlerhaus in Wien im August 1975 ausgestellt wurde. „Das Riesenbild von Wien!", hieß es in den Presserezensionen dazu. „Mehr als 200 Quadratmeter bemalte Leinwand, über 50 Meter lang, fast vier Meter hoch: das ist das größte Bild, das seit Hans Makarts Riesenschinken je in Österreich gemalt wurde."[23]

Das in Acryl auf Leinwand gefertigte Gemälde entstand in drei Monaten kontinuierlicher Arbeit und wurde vor Ort gemalt. Bei den Rezensionen wurde primär die Farbigkeit des Bildes wahrgenommen. „Les- und deutbar ist das farbenfrohe Credo ähnlich orientalischer Schrift, von rechts nach links: Abstraktes mit barockem Zug gepaart mit viel Mystik und einem Schuss lebensfroher Heiterkeit",[24] stellte Erwin Melchart in der „Kronen Zeitung" fest.

Doch das Gemälde ist nicht nur monumental, sondern auch inhaltlich vielschichtig. Es zeigt eine Interpretation der Schöpfungsmythologie, die von multikulturel-

This wall painting inaugurates a new dimension in Barabbas's oeuvre: the monumental picture. In his early years, his preference had been for small formats, but over the course of the 1960s and 1970s, he gradually chose larger and larger support media. His formats range from miniature-like sizes – the 1962 "Self-Portrait" measures 7 by 5.5 inches – to pictures as large as 80 by 80 inches in the case of "Malli's Island." Still, the wall painting was the most monumental format to date in the painter's oeuvre.

Large formats were fashionable in 1960s America as well. In the orbit of Color Field painting, the canvases grew to the dimensions of entire rooms; the idea was to heighten the sense of contemplation the works would instill in the beholder. Meditative immersion in the atmosphere of a space was the goal. In Barabbas, facilitating the beholder's spiritual experience of his cosmologies was presumably also one purpose driving the move toward monumental formats.

In 1975, he created a frieze entitled "The Big Bang" or "Genesis" (fanfold); almost twelve feet tall and 165 feet wide, it went on display at the Künstlerhaus, Vienna, in August 1975. "The Giant Picture of Vienna!" one press review read. "More than 2150 square feet of painted canvas, more than 165 feet wide, thirteen feet tall: it's the biggest picture ever to be painted in Austria since Hans Makart's giant extravaganzas."[23]

Executed in acrylic on canvas, the painting was painted on site in three months of continuous work. The reviews primarily noted the picture's colors. "The colorful credo can be read and interpreted not unlike Oriental writing, from right to left: abstract elements with a baroque streak in combination with a lot of mysticism and a dash of cheerful joie de vivre,"[24] Erwin Melchart remarked in the *Kronen Zeitung*.

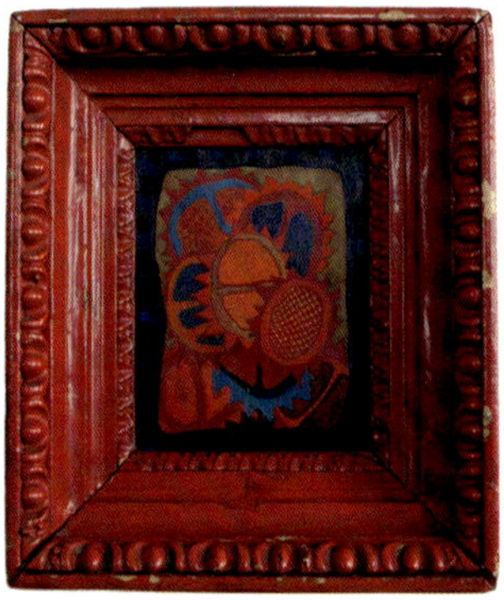

19
Sonnenblumen in rotem Rahmen, undatiert (1960er Jahre)
Mischtechnik auf Holz, 19 x 17 cm
Sunflowers in a Red Frame, undated (1960s)
mixed technique on wood, 19 x 17 cm

Yet the picture is not just monumental; it is also the visualization of a complex set of ideas. It presents an interpreta-tion of the mythology of creation based on multicultural influences and the artist's personal reflections on the cosmos and being. Barabbas's first wife, with whom he exchanged letters about his work for many years after they separated, offers this reading: "On the far right: the first scream – man, the artist, all in all. The path leads across the mountain through the gate. We plunge into the inconceivable. The tabernacle (the yellow center) holds for all eternity that which defies all signification, the everlasting being, the origin and end of things. From that point, everything begins afresh, everything is in flux. The future leads back to a new beginning, a new world comes into being."[25]

len Einflüssen und individuellen Überlegungen zum Kosmos und zum Sein ausgeht. Barabbas' erste Ehefrau, mit der er nach der Trennung lange Jahre über sein Werk korrespondierte, deutet: „Ganz rechts: der erste Schrei – der Mensch, der Künstler, Alles in Allem. Der Weg führt über den Berg durch das Tor. Man taucht in das Unfassbare ein. Im Tabernakel (gelbes Zentrum) ist das über jede Bezeichnung Erhabene verewigt, das immerwährend Seiende, der Ursprung und das Ziel der Dinge. Von dort aus beginnt alles von Neuem, alles ist im Fließen. Die Zukunft führt wieder zu einem neuen Anfang, eine neue Welt entsteht."[25]

Barabbas selbst hat die Idee zum Bild ebenfalls erläutert: *„Eigentlich tropft und rinnt das ganze Bild aus meinem sehnsüchtigen Herzen. Es ist der Einheit der Menschheit gewidmet. Das Bild ist so gedacht, dass die beiden Enden nahe beieinander sein sollten. [...] Die beiden Enden wären dann das Tor, durch das man eintritt. Der Sinn ist, dass Anfang und Ende eins sind. Von allen Seiten steuert die Schöpfung zum Tabernakel, von wo aus alles Sein erleuchtet wird. Wir alle kommen von dort und kehren wieder dorthin zurück. Das Bild hat aber noch viele andere Inhalte."*[26]

Barabbas ist mit dieser Arbeit am Höhepunkt einer mystisch geprägten individuellen Symbolik angelangt, deren Interpretation – abseits persönlicher Aussagen des Künstlers – für den/die Betrachter/in schwer nachzuvollziehen ist und offen bleibt. Interessant erscheint, dass einzelne Bildelemente immer wieder auftauchen, also durchaus im Sinne einer persönlichen Zeichensprache zu verstehen sind. Ein solches Motiv ist die Sonnenblume, die Barabbas in typisch ornamentaler Gliederung mehrfach verwendet.

Erstmals erscheint die Sonnenblume Anfang der sechziger Jahre, etwa bei einem Paravent, den Barabbas in Reichenau malerisch gestaltete (Abb. 19), und findet sich in zahlreichen Gemälden aus allen Perioden wieder. *„Man könnte sagen, dass es mein Markenzeichen ist. Auch verwende ich dieses Symbol einfach als dekoratives Element",*[27] berichtet der Künstler. Die Sonnenblume als Sinnbild für Wärme, Ruhe und Kraft, auch von der Hippiebewegung gerne zitiert, verortet Barabbas noch einmal in den psychedelisch-esoterischen Strömungen der sechziger und frühen siebziger Jahre, die maßgeblich den soziokulturellen Kontext der ersten Schaffensphase bilden.

Doch geht seine Intention weit über eine Mode hinaus. Fragen des Seins und der Existenz des Menschen bestimmen seine geistige Welt in einer komplexen Reflexion, die in vielen Briefen und Korrespondenzen erhalten ist und in seiner Malerei mündet.

Formal scheinen divergente Einflussfaktoren greifbar. Einerseits steht er in Bezug zur zeitgenössischen österreichischen Malerei – das wird besonders deutlich bei

Barabbas himself also elucidated the idea behind the painting: *"Ultimately, the entire picture drips and trickles from my yearning heart. It is dedicated to the unity of humankind. The painting is conceived such that the two ends ought to be close to each other [...] The two ends would then be the gate through which one enters. The point is that beginning and end are one. From all sides, creation strives toward the tabernacle, from which light issues to illuminate all that is. It is where we all come from and where we return. But there is a great deal more content to the picture as well."*[26]

With this work, Barabbas's art has reached the climax of a mystically inspired individual symbolism; such personal statements by the artist aside, its intended meaning is difficult to reconstruct, leaving it open to interpretation by the beholder. What seems interesting is that there are pictorial elements that recur frequently and must accordingly be read as constituting a personal ideogrammatic language. One such motif is the sunflower, which Barabbas uses several times, visualizing it as a characteristically ornamental structure.

The sunflower first appears in the early 1960s, as on a folding screen Barabbas painted in Reichenau (fig. 19); it can also be found in numerous paintings from all periods of his oeuvre. *"One might say that it's my trademark. I also use this symbol simply as a decorative element,"*[27] the artist notes. As an emblem of warmth, calm, and strength also widely quoted by the hippie movement, the sunflower is another indication of Barabbas's association with the psychedelic-esoteric tendencies of the 1960s and early 1970s, which constitute the defining sociocultural context of the first phase of his oeuvre.

Yet his intention goes far beyond a passing fashion. Questions about being and man's existence shape his spiritual world in a complex reflection that is documented in many extant letters and correspondences and ultimately finds expression in his painting.

In formal terms, we may discern divergent influences. On the one hand, Barabbas is in dialogue with contemporary Austrian painting, as is especially evident in works such as the Portrait of a Woman (fig. 55), whose theme and compositional structure distinctly recall Kiki Kogelnik's figurations from the 1970s, or the "Archangel" series (fig. 53+54), which exhibits affinities with Robert Zeppel-Sperl's portraits. Still, Barabbas transforms such references, fusing them with his personal visual language and his preference for the ornamental.

The significance of ornament in Barabbas is comparable to the employment of abstract geometrical patterning in Islamic art, where the prohibition of images recommends it as a representation of the infinite cosmos and the will of God. Barabbas's own intention in using it is quite comparable to this spiritual dimen-

der Darstellung einer Frau (Abb. 55) aus der Mitte der siebziger Jahre, die thematisch und vom Bildaufbau her deutlich an Kiki Kogelniks Figurationen der siebziger Jahre erinnert, oder der Serie „Archangel" (Abb. 53+54), die Verwandtschaft mit Robert Zeppel-Sperls Porträts aufweist. Doch transformiert Barabbas diese Bezüge und vereinigt sie mit einer persönlichen Zeichensprache und einer Vorliebe für das Ornament.

Die Bedeutung des Ornaments bei Barabbas lässt sich mit dem Gebrauch des abstrakt-geometrischen Musters im Islam vergleichen. Ausgelöst durch das Bilderverbot fungiert es dort als Repräsentation des unendlichen Kosmos und des Willens Gottes. Barabbas' Intention kann durchaus mit dieser spirituellen Dimension islamischer Musterung verglichen werden. Hinzu kommt eine Auseinandersetzung mit dem künstlerischen Ausdruck verschiedener Kulturen, wie den Indianern oder den Aborigines, die das Geometrische gleichfalls als magisch aufgeladene Zeichensprache benützen.

Die Arbeit „Big Bang" spannt demnach einen formalen Bogen zwischen poppig buntem Farbenrausch, kaleidoskopischer Musterung, narrativer Monumentalität und spiritueller Ornamentik und verbindet eine westliche mit einer östlichen Sichtweise, die in ihrer Gesamtaussage ins Mystische tendiert. Das Werk bedeutet einen Höhepunkt im Weg des Malers. Gleichzeitig markiert es aber auch einen Wendepunkt.

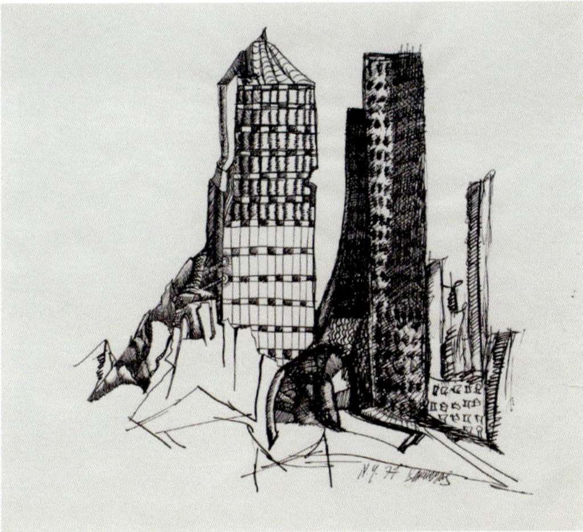

20
O.T., 1977
Tusche auf Papier, 41 x 34 cm
Untitled, 1977
drawing ink on paper, 41 x 34 cm

## Von der Monochromie zum Valeur
### *Die späten siebziger und achtziger Jahre*

Schwarze, braunschwarze und grauschwarze Flächen, matt und glänzend, fügen sich zu einem Gebilde von bizarrer Form. Auf weißem Grund scheint die Formation die Fläche zu zerschneiden und wird ihrerseits auseinanderklaffend durchbrochen (Abb. 59). Die unbetitelte Arbeit aus dem Jahr 1979 ist exemplarisch für Barabbas' Malerei in der zweiten Hälfte der siebziger Jahre.

Unmittelbar nach der Ausstellung der Arbeit „Big Bang" im Künstlerhaus – einer der wichtigsten Erfolge von Claus Mayrhofer Barabbas – fand eine dra-

sion of Islamic patterns. Another factor was his engagement with the artistic expressions of different cultures, such as those of the Native Americans or Australia's Aborigines, which likewise use geometric figures as a visual language charged with magic.

"Big Bang," that is to say, forges a formal bridge between the wealth of bright colors of pop culture, kaleidoscopic patterning, narrative monumentality, and spiritual ornament, blending a Western with an Eastern way of seeing to frame a statement inflected by an encompassing mysticism. The work constitutes an apex on the painter's path. But it would also prove a turning point.

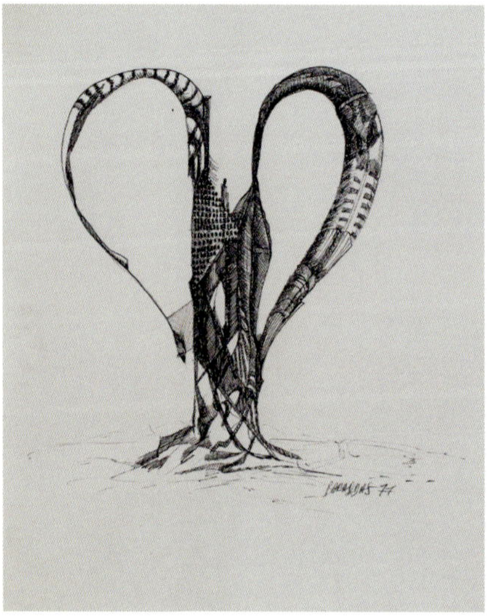

21
O.T., 1977, Tusche auf Papier, 41 x 34 cm
Untitled, 1977, drawing ink on paper, 41 x 34 cm

## From the monochrome to chromatic nuance
### *The late 1970s and 1980s*

Black, brownish-black, and grayish-black surfaces, some matte, some glossy, coalesce into a construct of bizarre formation. Set before a white ground, this entity seems to cut through the surface while for its part breaking up to reveal gaping chasms (fig. 59). The untitled work from 1979 is exemplary of the paintings Barabbas creates during the second half of the 1970s.

Immediately after the exhibition of "Big Bang" at the Künstlerhaus – one of the moments of greatest success in Claus Mayrhofer Barabbas's life – a dramatic disruption changed his art profoundly. Barabbas left Vienna for New York, where he increasingly came to call his work in painting in question. A few works of graphic art survive from his time in New York that illustrate the crisis Barabbas experienced with regard to his themes (fig. 21). He turned to an entirely new motif: architectural drawing. The drawings, mostly small formats, translate New York's imposing buildings into subtle and delicate systems of lines articulated in a wealth of detail. The metropolis's skyscrapers appear as fragmentary and deformed colossuses and seem brittle and menacing at once.

Back in Vienna, Barabbas took up painting again, but he abandoned color altogether and painted exclusively in black. The decision to do so was motivated by his artistic aspirations, as many statements by the artist show. He wrote, for example, that *"in order to prevent my painting from becoming repetitive and trivial, I*

matische Zäsur in seinem Werk statt. Barabbas reiste nach New York und stellte seine eigene Malerei immer mehr in Frage. Aus der New Yorker Zeit sind einige Grafiken erhalten, die Barabbas' Krise im Thematischen verdeutlichen (Abb. 21). Er wandte sich einem gänzlich neuen Motiv zu: der Architekturzeichnung. Die beeindruckenden Bauwerke New Yorks zeigen sich bei den meist kleinformatigen Blättern in eine subtile und feine Lineamentik übersetzt, die sich detailreich ausformuliert. Die Hochhäuser der Metropole erscheinen als fragmentarisch verformte Kolosse und wirken in ihrer Brüchigkeit bedrohlich.

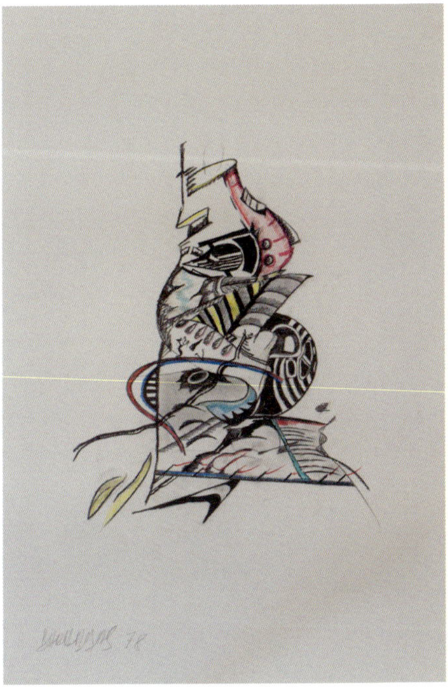

22
Das Suggestive im Gebilde einer Flasche, 1977
Bleistift auf Karton, 60 x 40 cm
The Suggestive Aspect of the Figure of a Bottle, 1977
pencil on cardboard, 60 x 40 cm

In Wien zurück nahm Barabbas die Malerei wieder auf, wandte sich aber gänzlich von der Farbe ab und malte ausschließlich in Schwarz. Die Entscheidung dazu wurde aus einem künstlerischen Anspruch heraus getroffen, wie zahlreiche Aussagen des Künstlers belegen. Etwa: *„Um nicht in repetitive Malerei zu verflachen, nahm ich mir vor, sieben Jahre dunkle Bilder zu malen."*[28] Oder: *„Ich riss mich zusammen und disziplinierte mich. Denn Schwarz als Farbe ist eine harte Disziplin."*[29]

Zwischen 1977 und 1984 verfolgte Barabbas sein Ziel der Disziplinierung. Doch realisierte sich dieses nicht nur in einer Reduktion der Farbe, sondern auch in einer Straffung der Komposition und Konzentration der Formen. Das Bild scheint nicht mehr aus einer Farbenwelt voller sprühender Assoziationen und erzählerischer Figurationen entwickelt, bei der Fläche in Fläche fließt, es ist vielmehr eine Konstruktion der Kontemplation. Fast hermetisch schließen sich die dargestellten Gebilde.

Die Arbeiten legen die Frage nach der persönlichen Befindlichkeit des Künstlers nahe, und es bestätigt sich mit Blick auf seine Vita, dass Barabbas eine schwierige Zeit durchlebte. Finanzielle und persönliche Probleme beherrschten die „schwarze Periode". Barabbas kämpfte um sein Überleben und kam immer mehr in Schwierigkeiten. Dieser persönliche Hintergrund veranlasste Maria Buchsbaum zu einer psychologischen Interpretation der Werkperiode. „Im folgenden Jahrzehnt schloss sich der frühere Farbdynamiker, von Mystik erfüllt, in eine schwarze Phase ein [...]".[30]

*made a plan of painting dark pictures for seven years";*[28] and that *"I bucked up and imposed discipline on myself. Because black as a color means hard discipline."*[29]

From 1977 to 1984, Barabbas pursued this form of self-discipline, which eventually extended beyond the reduction of color to more streamlined compositions and greater focus in his forms. The picture no longer seems to elaborate a colorful world full of spirited associations and narrative figurations in which color flows into the surface; instead, it is now a construction, the result of painting as an act of contemplation. The structures Barabbas visualizes are self-contained, almost hermetically sealed.

The works invite the question as to the artist's state of mind at the time, and a look at his biography confirms that Barabbas was going through a rough patch. Financial and personal problems abounded during the "black period." Barabbas struggled to stay afloat and found himself in ever-mounting difficulties. This personal background led Maria Buchsbaum to offer a psychological interpretation of this period in his oeuvre. "Over the decade that followed, the erstwhile dynamist of color, his mind full of mystical ideas, locked himself into a black phase."[30]

Yet the artist's own statements contradict this view, and a comparison between these pictures and his earlier suggests otherwise as well. Barabbas had experimented with painting in a single color as early as the 1960s, during his Reichenau days, when he produced monochrome pictures in red, blue and yellow. See, for example, the painting "Aztec Sun" (fig. 57), created in 1967: although a geometrically resolved pattern governing the sequencing of a single hue once again defines the surface, we may discern crucial differences between the Reichenau monochromes and those of the black period. What is essential here is the relation between foreground and background. In the 1960s, Barabbas had always striven to cover the entire surface with an all-over structure, but now he clearly distinguishes figure from ground. The effect is one of focusing the picture on the subject; the artist has renounced the holistic integration of the surface. The sense of elements flowing into each other is lost.

One exception with respect to this technique is the large-format painting "Psychopathic Petrol" (fig. 58). Created in 1969, it operates by contrasting motif and background, showing a central figure modeled in black-and-gray set off against a yellow ground. It may be seen as anticipating the monochrome works of the late 1970s and early 1980s.

In the late 1970s, Barabbas slowly returned to visualizing corresponding forms that suggest dynamic tension and movement in space. In fact, he explicitly entitled one of these canvases "Space Shuttle" (fig. 60). The critical study of spatial

Doch dieser Ansicht widersprechen nicht nur die Aussagen des Künstlers, sondern auch ein Vergleich mit seinem früheren Schaffen. Bereits in den sechziger Jahren in Reichenau hatte Barabbas den Versuch begonnen, ausschließlich mit einer Farbe zu malen. Monochrome Bildwerke in Rot, Blau und Gelb waren entstanden. Beispielhaft dafür ist das Gemälde „Aztekensonne" (Abb. 57) aus dem Jahr 1967. Obwohl auch hier eine geometrisch aufgelöste Musterung in der Abfolge eines Farbtones die Fläche bestimmt, lassen sich wesentliche Unterschiede zwischen den monochromen Werken der Reichenauer Zeit und jenen der schwarzen Periode feststellen. Zentral dabei ist die Relation von Vordergrund und Hintergrund. War Barabbas in den sechziger Jahren stets bestrebt, die gesamte Fläche mit einer All-over-Struktur zu bedecken, so unterscheidet er nun klar zwischen Motiv und Grund. Das Bild erscheint dadurch auf das Sujet fokussiert, die ganzheitliche Integration der Fläche ist aufgegeben. Das Gefühl des Ineinanderfließens ist verloren.

Eine Ausnahme im Hinblick auf dieses Verfahren bildet das 1969 entstandene großformatige Gemälde „Psychopathic Petrol" (Abb. 58), das mit dem Kontrast zwischen Motiv und Hintergrund arbeitet. Das Gemälde zeigt eine schwarzgrau modellierte zentrale Figur, die sich von einem gelben Hintergrund abhebt, und kann als Vorläufer der monochromen Werke der späten siebziger und frühen achtziger Jahre gelten.

In den späten siebziger Jahren begann Barabbas erst allmählich wieder korrespondierende Formen darzustellen, die dynamische Spannung und die Bewegung im Raum suggerieren. Tatsächlich nannte Barabbas eine dieser Leinwände auch „Space Shuttle" (Abb. 60). Die Auseinandersetzung mit der räumlichen Struktur und die Klärung der Formen bilden die wichtigsten Errungenschaften der schwarzen Periode. Diese Errungenschaften machte sich Barabbas in den folgenden Jahren künstlerisch zunutze.

1986 verließ er Wien. Die finanziellen und persönlichen Schwierigkeiten erschienen unlösbar. Barabbas ging mit einer neuen Liebe nach Bali, der „Insel der Tausend Tempel". Der nun folgende Bruch in der malerischen Auffassung könnte nicht größer sein. Wie in einem Farbenrausch erblühen zart duftige Bildwelten. „Eine psychophysische Wende spiegeln dann die in Bali [...] gemalten Bilder. In ihren beschwingten Formen und durchlichteten Farben wird eine ganz neue Gelöstheit spürbar. Biomorphe Gestaltfindungen bringen den zyklischen Ablauf des Lebens, dessen Auferstehung aus Abgestorbenem zum Ausdruck. Sie lassen in flammenden Feuerzungen die Dynamik des Seins erkennen. Das aus den früheren Werkphasen weiterwirkende ornamentale Element, dessen geistiger Inhalt über alle dekorative Notwendigkeit obsiegt, verbindet sich mit einem dy-

structure and the clarification of forms are the most significant accomplishments of the black period, which Barabbas would rely on in his art in the years that followed.

In 1986, he left Vienna. His financial and personal difficulties seemed insurmountable. With a new lover, Barabbas left for Bali, the "Island of a Thousand Temples." The resulting discontinuity in his approach to painting could not have been any greater. As though the painter were intoxicated with color, visual worlds full of delicate fragrant hazes blossom before his eyes. "The pictures created in Bali then reflect a psycho-physical watershed moment [...] Their buoyant shapes and transparently luminous colors convey an utterly new sense of serenity. Biomorphic figurative inventions articulate the cyclical course of life, its resurrection from what has died away. In the licking flames of fire, they reveal the animating force of being. The ornament, a residue from the earlier phases of his oeuvre, continues to be operative, its spiritual substance vanquishing any decorative necessity; it is now fused with a breath of intellectual energy that, with explosive force, engenders a materialization of the spiritual as such,"[31] Maria Buchsbaum writes.

"The Dawn-Breakers" (fig. 82), a canvas created in 1988, is a key work, exemplifying the period in the artist's oeuvre delimited by his sojourn in Bali between 1986 and 1989, which marks the transition to his late work. Painted in vigorous yellows interspersed by delicate blue and pink – almost invisible, like a puff of air – the pictorial plane opens toward a billowing space of virtuosic density. A jet of spheres, like light, punctuate a central moving figuration, a hazily iridescent cloudlike shape. The evocation of depth in the painting, in particular, is unprecedented in the artist's oeuvre. The planarity that had been the defining trait of the ornamental work of the 1960s and 1970s has evolved in the direction of three dimensions.

The picture's theme pays homage to Barabbas's faith. "The Dawn-Breakers" is one of the central historic texts of the Baha'i and Babi Faiths. The Baha'i explain the title as referring to "the messengers proclaiming the dawn of a new day (age)." In this work, the painter's spiritual worldview has found a new expression.

Again and again, Barabbas's art revolved around the question of the genesis of being. Besides allegorical works, he also created a number of personifications related to this theme. One central motif in this context is the figure of Mama Ocollo (fig. 63), which he adopted from the mythological history of the Inca. The daughter of the sun-god Inti, she founded the Inca empire with her brother and was worshipped as a fertility goddess. Barabbas uses this motif with some regularity, especially in his graphic art. The theme suggests his interest in genesis mythologies as well as his affinity for other cultures.

namisch-geistigen Zug und führt explosionsartig zur Materialisierung des Spirituellen an sich",[31] schreibt Maria Buchsbaum.

„The Dawn-Breakers" (Abb. 82), eine 1988 entstandene Leinwand, bildet ein Schlüsselwerk und steht exemplarisch für die Werkperiode des Künstlers, die mit dem Aufenthalt in Bali von 1986 bis 1989 einzugrenzen ist und in die letzte Werkphase überleitet. In kräftigen Gelbtönen, durchbrochen von zartem Blau und Rosa – kaum sichtbar wie ein Hauch –, öffnet sich die Bildebene in einen wogenden Raum von virtuoser Dichte. Eine zentrale bewegte Figuration in nebelig-schillernder Wolkigkeit wird von einem Strahl von Kugeln lichtgleich durchbrochen. Besonders die Plastizität der Malerei ist ein Novum im Schaffen des Künstlers. Die Flächigkeit, die für die Ornamentik in den sechziger und siebziger Jahren charakteristisch gewesen war, ist zugunsten einer Dreidimensionalität weiter entwickelt.

Das Thema des Bildes zollt dem Glauben Barabbas' Tribut. „The Dawn-Breakers" ist eine der zentralen historischen Schriften der Bahá'í- und Babi-Religion. Der Titel wird von den Bahá'ís übersetzt mit: „Die Boten, die den Anbruch eines neuen Zeitalters ankündigen". Die spirituelle Weltsicht des Malers hat mit dieser Arbeit einen neuen Ausdruck gefunden.

Immer wieder kreiste Barabbas in seiner Arbeit um die Frage der Entstehung des Seins. Neben allegorischen Werken findet sich auch eine Reihe von Personifizierungen zu dieser Thematik. Ein zentrales Motiv dabei ist die Figur der Mama Ocollo (Abb. 63), die aus der mythologischen Geschichte der Inkas entnommen ist. Als Tochter des Sonnengottes Inti begründete sie gemeinsam mit ihrem Bruder das Inkareich und wurde als Fruchtbarkeitsgöttin verehrt. Das Motiv wird von Barabbas vor allem im Grafischen immer wieder aufgegriffen. Die Thematik verweist auf sein Interesse für Entstehungsmythologien ebenso wie auf seine Affinität zu anderen Kulturen.

Barabbas' ständige Beschäftigung mit existentiellen Menschheitsfragen und religiösen Werten fand in der Tradition der Balinesen – mit ihrer deutlichen Neigung zu einer spirituellen Grundhaltung – einen fruchtbaren Boden. Mit über 20.000 Tempeln und unzähligen Prozessionen ist das Religiöse Teil des Alltags der Insel. Dies und die wunderbare Landschaft und sonnige Atmosphäre führten bei Barabbas zu einer Grundstimmung, die sich auch in der Weichheit und Subtilität der Malerei zeigt.

Einen Höhepunkt der balinesischen Bilder findet man mit einer unbetitelten Arbeit aus dem Jahr 1988 (Abb. 83). Das hochformatige Gemälde eröffnet eine ineinanderfließende Woge von Bändern, Blüten und knospenartigen Formen, die sich in einer ungekannten Räumlichkeit in die Tiefe entfalten. Die Farbigkeit ist in

Barabbas's ongoing study of humankind's existential questions and religious values found fertile ground in the traditions of the Balinese, who show a clear tendency to integrate spirituality into their basic attitudes. With more than twenty thousand temples and innumerable processions, Bali is a place where religion is part of everyday life. This environment, the wonderful landscape, and the sunny atmosphere lifted Barabbas's spirits, a shift reflected in the softness and subtlety of his painting.

One highlight among his Balinese pictures is an untitled work created in 1988 (fig. 83). The portrait-format painting reveals a surge of ribbons, blossoms, and bud-like shapes flowing into each other and unfolding into a space whose depth is without precedent in his oeuvre. The colors, gentle pastels, are modulated in subtle nuances, forming a harmoniously attuned ensemble captured in a quasi-natural movement of blossoming.

To the beholder aware of the artist's roots, the paintings from his time in Bali may seem distant echoes the flower paintings of, say, Wolfgang Hutter or the subtle chromatic worlds of Ernst Fuchs. Yet it seems clear that these formal characteristics in Barabbas's art are inspired by the encounter with the light, colors, and exuberant flora of the tropical island. The ornamental register has developed into a vivid structure of formations blending into one another.

## Of the real, surreal, fantastic, and cosmic
### *The 1990s and 2000s*

In 1989, Barabbas left the Island of a Thousand Temples and moved to Australia, where he settled in Bendigo in the southeastern state of Victoria. His sister had been living there for twenty years and invited Barabbas to come. The artist, who would enter a third and a fourth marriage in Australia and live in a vacant house owned by his sister, was deeply impressed by the country's landscapes.

He produced numerous landscape paintings; a three-part series created in 1990, comprising the paintings "Warrumbungles," "View," and "The Spirit of Coonawarra" (fig. 86-88), is among the most compelling works of the early 1990s. Barabbas retained the use of patterning in space he had developed in Bali, but shifted to a different palette. Earth tones such as ochre, brown, and sienna predominate, in combination with hues of blue used for shadowing. As a result, the works hew more closely to reality while appearing abstract in their composition.

There is one work from this period of his oeuvre that Barabbas himself was especially fond of: the painting "Transfiction" (fig. 90).[32] Created in 1990, it likewise renders a view of a landscape. It represents a high point in terms of chromatic

zarten pastelligen Tönen in feinen Valeurs moduliert und in einer harmonischen Tonlage zu einem Ensemble naturhafter Bewegung des Erblühens vereinigt.

Im Blick auf die Wurzeln des Malers erinnern die Gemälde der Bali-Zeit ein wenig an die Blumenbilder eines Wolfgang Hutter und die subtilen Farbwelten eines Ernst Fuchs. Doch scheint diese formale Ausprägung bei Barabbas deutlich aus der Begegnung mit der Licht-, Farb- und Blumenwelt der tropischen Insel angeregt. Die Ornamentik hat sich nun in eine plastische Struktur ineinanderlaufender Formationen entwickelt.

## Vom Realen, Surrealen, Phantastischen und Kosmischen

### *Die neunziger und zweitausender Jahre*

1989 verließ Barabbas die Insel der tausend Tempel und ging nach Australien, nach Bendigo im südöstlichen Bundesstaat Victoria. Seine Schwester Ilse lebte bereits seit zwanzig Jahren dort und hatte Barabbas zu der Reise angeregt. Barabbas, der dort ein drittes und viertes Mal heiratete und in einem leer stehenden Haus seiner Schwester wohnte, war von der Landschaft Australiens beeindruckt.

Es entstanden zahlreiche Landschaftsbilder, wobei die dreiteilige Serie aus dem Jahr 1990, bestehend aus den Gemälden „Warrumbungles", „View" und „The Spirit of Coonawarra" (Abb. 86-88), zu den gelungensten Werken der frühen neunziger Jahre zählt. Barabbas behielt die in Bali entwickelte räumliche Musterhaftigkeit bei, veränderte aber die koloristische Tonlage. Erdtöne wie Ocker, Braun, Siena überwiegen und werden mit einer Abschattierung von Blauwerten kombiniert. Die Arbeiten bleiben damit deutlicher am Realen, wirken in ihrer Komposition aber abstrakt.

Aus dieser Werkperiode gibt es eine Arbeit, die Barabbas selbst besonders schätzte: das Gemälde „Transfiction" (Abb. 90).[32] Es wurde 1990 gemalt und gibt ebenfalls eine Landschaftsansicht wieder. Die Reduktion der Farbe erreicht hier einen Höhepunkt, beschränkt sich Barabbas doch auf einen betonten Kontrast von Blau und Braun, der die Komposition hervortreten lässt. Die Kraft der eruptiven Formationen macht die Intensität der Landschaftserfahrung deutlich. Die Landschaft selbst bleibt aber offen: Ist im Hintergrund eine Bergkette zu sehen? Ein Wirbelwind im Vordergrund? Oder ist es eine abstrakte Umsetzung für ein Ereignis?

Die weiten Landschaften des südlichen Australiens mit den plötzlich auftauchenden Bergformationen und Hügelketten, wie sie für den Kontinent charakteristisch sind, bilden jedenfalls den Ausgangspunkt für diese Landschaftsbilder, gleichzeitig führt das Motiv aber auch zurück zu den großen Themen des Künst-

reduction; Barabbas confines himself to an emphatic contrast between blue and brown that throws the composition into sharp relief. The force of the eruptive formations conveys the intensity of his experience of the landscape. But the exact nature of the setting remains indeterminate: Is what we see in the backdrop a mountain range? Is that a tornado in the foreground? Or does the picture translate an incident into an abstract visualization?

Be that as it may, the vast sceneries of southern Australia with the continent's characteristic mountain chains and hill ranges suddenly coming into view form the point of departure for these landscapes, while the motif also leads the artist back to his great themes; time seems to have a different presence in this setting than in his native country. *"Gondwanaland – the most ancient continent – I feel like everything has existed from time immemorial, and yet it also seems that it came into existence just now – timelessness,"*[33] Barabbas writes.

"Time Cycle" (fig. 89) is the title of a work, also created in 1990, that Barabbas devotes to the life and death of his father. As in the landscapes, the artist hews to reality in the basic composition, but then transforms its rendition into a surreal defamiliarized landscape he interprets as a holistic view of the course of a life. In these works, Barabbas has found a form of expression that operates amid the tensions between abstraction, the depiction of nature, and spirituality. Nature is reinterpreted and transformed into a metaphor for existential questions.

The culmination of this tendency appears in the works "Milky Head" and "Travel through the 4$^{th}$ Dimension" (fig. 91+92). Painted in 1991, they show an exploding tangle of loops, surges, waves, lines, and shapes amid a bizarre cosmic thunderstorm: eruptive, dynamic, and disorganized. The formal structure of these paintings reflects the impenetrable nature of cosmic space.

The origin of the world, the big bang, Genesis: in the vast expanses of Australia's landscapes, Barabbas found a new foothold for his exploration of questions that had occupied him since the 1960s. That is also the context in which to see the work "$E = mc^2$" (fig. 95), which he created in 1996. In a letter, Barabbas gave a complex analysis of this painting, which is worth quoting in full:

*"As you can see at first glance, I've reused a detail in the picture 'Genesis' (Big Bang) in order to 'rework an old idea,' as it were. Of course, the special and then the general theory of relativity pose virtually insurmountable obstacles to 'thematic' depiction, but that's not what I was/am interested in. What's important is that I pondered the matter and studied it with great focus as I was painting. (I don't claim that I've understood everything completely, especially when it comes to the general theory of relativity.)*

lers, scheint die Zeit in dieser Umgebung in anderer Form präsent als in der Heimat. *„Gondwanaland – der älteste Kontinent – Ich habe das Gefühl, dass alles uralt ist und gleichzeitig als wäre es in diesem Moment entstanden – Zeitlosigkeit",*[33] schreibt Barabbas.

„Time Cycle" (Abb. 89) ist der Titel einer im selben Jahr entstandenen Arbeit, die Barabbas dem Leben und Tod seines Vaters widmet. Wie schon bei den Landschaftsbildern bleibt Barabbas von der Grundkomposition her dem Realen nahe, wandelt die Wiedergabe aber in eine surreale verfremdete Landschaft um, die er im Sinne einer ganzheitlichen Sichtweise des Lebensablaufes interpretiert. Barabbas hat mit diesen Werken eine Ausdrucksform gefunden, die sich im Spannungsfeld von Abstraktem, Naturbezug und Spirituellem befindet. Die Natur wird umgedeutet und zu einer Metapher für existentielle Fragestellungen transformiert.

Einen Höhepunkt in dieser Hinsicht bedeuten die Werke „Milky Head" und „Travel through the $4^{th}$ Dimension" (Abb. 91+92) von 1991. Bei diesen explodiert eine Verflechtung von Schlingen, Wogen, Wellen, Linien und Formen in einem bizarren kosmischen Gewitter, eruptiv, dynamisch und ungeordnet. Die Unfassbarkeit des kosmischen Raumes wird in der formalen Struktur des Gemäldes reflektiert.

Die Entstehung der Welt, der Urknall, die Genesis: Barabbas fand angesichts der Größe der australischen Landschaft zu neuen Anknüpfungspunkten für jene Fragen, die ihn seit den sechziger Jahren beschäftigten. In diesen Kontext ist auch die Arbeit „$E = mc^2$" (Abb. 95) zu stellen, die er 1996 malte. Barabbas widmete dem Gemälde in einem Brief eine komplexe Analyse, die hier zur Gänze wiedergegeben sei:

*„Wie man hier sofort erkennen kann, habe ich ein Detail des Bildes ‚Genesis' (Big Bang) wieder verwendet, sozusagen um einen alten Gedanken ‚neu' zu bearbeiten. Die spezielle und weiters generelle Relativitätstheorie lässt sich natürlich ‚thematisch' kaum darstellen, aber darum ging/geht es mir nicht. Wichtig dabei ist, dass ich während des Malens intensiv darüber nachdachte und studierte. (Ich erhebe nicht den Anspruch, alles komplett verstanden zu haben, insbesondere wenn es zur Generellen Relativ. Theorie kommt.)*

- *Nichts, nicht einmal Zeit bleibt gleich, wenn sie von zwei verschiedenen Punkten aus gemessen wird – einer in Bewegung ist z. B.*

- *Inmitten des ‚angenommenen Urknalls' nehmen Partikel A (unendlich) & B (unendlich), Partikel C (unendlich) und alle Partikel (A, B & C usw.) zueinander eine andere Zeit (relativ zur eigenen) wahr.*

- *Nothing, not even time, remains the same when it is measured from two different vantage points – for example, when one is in motion.*
- *Amid the 'presumptive big bang,' particles A (infinite) & B (infinite), particle C (infinite), and all particles (A, B & C, etc.) perceive different relative times (relative to their own).*
- *And if you then also place mass and space in interrelation, things really get going!*

*Allow me to spin a yarn: let's assume that time came into existence with the big bang. What was 'before' was pre-time (which has nothing at all to do with time, but somehow that term will have to do). Then time is already infinitely measurable in the primal event, because from the moment time has been created, there's always been a smaller unit before, and that goes back until (at least hypothetically) we reach the point where 'pre-time' is. But certainly it's not so easy, and in fact virtually impossible, because from the presumptive big bang, time is immediately measurable as relative. And then there's the fact that energy and mass increase with motion. In other words:*

*$E = mc^2$ applies right away, in the big bang.*

*I've no idea whether what I thought to myself as I was painting is recognizable in the finished picture – I'm still too aware of my own thoughts to tell. And God knows I don't claim that I've presented a 'cosmopolitan' (mathematically correct) argument, I lack the specialized knowledge to do that; but as for so many others who've studied physics, astronomy, and cosmology, insight often comes through intuition rather than research.*

*What could I do but symbolize space, for example, by means of a dark blue. Please note how the second figure either transcends out of space or transmutes into space.*

*As regards the central figure:*

*First of all, both figures are of course once again the twin prophets of the Baha'i revelation. The first principle. The following may always be related back to this principle – revelation.*

*My ideas: the big bang may be understood as God's first revelation known to us (just as Adam is God's first prophet an account of whom has come down to us). In other words: we may give accounts of what we know of, think about it, construct theories.*

*Since before, now, and afterward are concepts of time, just as the first and the last, beginning and end, we develop a sense of time and hence also history.*

*But to come back to the picture:*

*1. The central figure extends a hand*

- Und wenn man nun auch noch Masse und Raum zueinander in Beziehung bringt, dann beginnt es erst so richtig!

Lass mich spinnen: Nehmen wir an, dass Zeit mit dem Urknall entstand und ‚davor' eben Vorzeit war (was mit Zeit überhaupt nichts zu tun hat, aber irgendwie muss diese Bezeichnung herhalten), so kann im Urereignis bereits unendlich Zeit gemessen werden, denn ab dem Moment, wo Zeit geschaffen wurde, gab es immer eine kleinere Einheit davor und das geht so lange zurück, bis wir (zumindest hypothetisch) zum Punkt kommen, wo ‚Vorzeit' ist. Doch dies ist auf keinen Fall so einfach, ja nahezu unmöglich, da ab dem angenommenen Urknall Zeit sofort relativ gemessen werden kann. Nun kommt auch noch dazu, dass Energie und Masse durch Bewegung zunehmen. Mit anderen Worten:

$E = mc^2$ gilt ab sofort im Urknall.

Ich habe keine Ahnung, ob das, was ich da so beim Malen gedacht habe, auch sichtbar geworden ist – dazu bin ich mir meiner eigenen Gedanken noch zu sehr bewusst. Auch erhebe ich um Himmels willen nicht den Anspruch, ‚kosmopolitisch' (mathematisch korrekt) argumentiert zu haben, dazu fehlt mir das Fachwissen, doch wie so viele andere, welche sich mit Physik, Astronomie und Kosmologie beschäftigt haben, kommen Erkenntnisse oft eher durch Intuition, denn durch Forschung.

Was blieb mir anderes übrig als z. B. Raum durch tiefes Blau zu visualisieren. Bitte beachte, wie die zweite Figur entweder aus dem Raum transzendiert oder in den Raum transmutiert.

Zur zentralen Figur:

Zuerst einmal, natürlich sind beide Figuren wieder einmal die Zwillingspropheten der Baha'i-Offenbarung. Das erste Prinzip. Das Folgende kann immer auf dieses Prinzip – Offenbarung – bezogen werden.

Meine Gedanken: der Urknall kann als die erste uns bekannte Offenbarung Gottes verstanden werden (so wie Adam der erste uns überlieferte Prophet Gottes ist). Mit anderen Worten: worüber wir wissen, können wir berichten, nachdenken und Theorien aufstellen.

Da Vorher, Jetzt und Nachher Zeitbegriffe sind, genauso wie das Erste und das Letzte, der Anfang und das Ende, entwickeln wir ein Zeitgefühl und somit auch Geschichte.

Aber zurück zum Bild:

1. Die zentrale Figur streckt die Hand aus

- als eine Geste der Überraschung,

- *as a gesture of surprise,*
- *in blessing,*
- *in surrender – self-abandonment,*
- *sowing, as the peasant in March, etc.*

*2. Just as man is born into this world head first, the same happens here: the prophet, man, the archetype, rises head first into the other, the new dimension and merges with it. Thus a new world is created, etc.*

*Then there's also: floating, sun, worlds expanding, etc.*

*The vertical red line is the 'umbilical cord,' the connection to the creator, but just as much what lets us be rational.*

*From here on, I'll leave you room for your own associations."*[34]

During his time in Australia, Barabbas's pictorial world grew into a universal cosmology that fused several sources of influence. Scientific insights, religious traditions, mythological explanations of the world are compressed to create an allegory of being and becoming. Not surprisingly, this imagery is very hard to decode for the beholder, and so the works resist unequivocal interpretation. Such ambiguity, however, would seem to be a characteristic feature of Barabbas's work and in fact the source of its particular appeal. It bears looking at again and again from a fresh perspective, which makes for an exciting experience.

Interestingly, it seems that, in the 1990s, narrative structure returns to the forefront of his pictures. Each tells a story, one that is highly personal in form and anchored in many cross-references. *"I should be a teller of fairy tales!",*[35] as Barabbas himself put it on one occasion. His penchant for storytelling, for confabulation and associations, is evident also in the titles he gives his pictures: "Mystical Encounter between Montezuma and Charles I at Funchal," "Bear, Sky Wallpapers with Threat," "The Jaw Harps of Tutankhamen," "Firmanent Machine," "Prayer Rug with Two Fried Eggs," "Three Space Probes Fly Through Mars Full of Holes": these are only some examples of his poetic sense of language and the eloquent magic of words.

Settling in Australia, Barabbas found a local gallery to represent him; he showed his early Australian pictures at AFFA and, later on, also at Bendigo Art Gallery in his new hometown. The Australian press showed consistent interest in his exhibitions, but true commercial success once again eluded him. His Australian gallerist offered one explanation: "Barabbas has become one of us, but there's still the music and the soul of Vienna in his art."[36]

In 1996, collectors and friends of Barabbas's art organized an exhibition at Galerie Peithner-Lichtenfels in Vienna. In Bendigo, the artist meticulously prepared the

- *segnend,*
- *sich selbst ausliefernd – hingebend,*
- *säend, wie der Bauer im März usw.*

*2. So wie der Mensch mit dem Kopf voran in diese Welt geboren wird, so geschieht das hier ebenso, dass der Prophet, der Mensch, der Archetyp, mit dem Kopf voran in die andere, neue Dimension abhebt und verbunden ist. Somit wird eine neue Welt geschaffen etc.*

*Dann gibt es da noch: Schweben, Sonne und sich ausdehnende Welten etc.*

*Die rote vertikale Linie ist die ‚Nabelschnur' zum Schöpfer, aber ebenso gut das, was uns rational sein lässt.*

*Ich lasse Dir von hier an Raum für eigene Assoziationen."*[34]

In der australischen Zeit entwickelte sich die Bildwelt Barabbas' zu einer universellen Kosmologie, die verschiedene Einflüsse verbindet. Erkenntnisse der Wissenschaft, religiöse Überlieferungen, mythologische Welterklärungen werden zu einer Allegorie des Seins und des Werdens komprimiert. Dass diese Bildwelten für den/die Betrachter/in kaum zu entschlüsseln und daher auch in ihrer Lesbarkeit widerständig sind, liegt nahe. Diese Ambiguität erscheint aber charakteristisch für Barabbas und macht auch einen besonderen Reiz seiner Arbeit aus. Immer neue Sichtweisen der Betrachtung erlauben ein spannendes Erleben der Werke.

Interessant erscheint, dass in den neunziger Jahren die narrative Struktur wieder deutlich in den Vordergrund tritt. Jedes Bild erzählt eine Geschichte, eine sehr persönlich geformte und in vielen Querverbindungen verankerte Geschichte. *„Ich sollte Märchenerzähler werden!"*,[35] formulierte Barabbas selbst dazu. Der Hang zum Erzählen, zum Fabulieren und Assoziieren wird auch an Barabbas' Bildtiteln deutlich: „Mystische Begegnung zwischen Montezuma und Karl I. in Funchal", „Bär, Himmeltapeten mit Drohung", „Die Maultrommel des Tutenchamun", „Firmamentmaschine", „Gebetsteppich mit zwei Spiegeleiern", „Drei Raumsonden durchfliegen den löchrigen Mars" sind nur einige Beispiele für einen poetischen Wortsinn und eine beredte Sprachmagie.

Barabbas gelang es in Australien, in einer lokalen Galerie Fuß zu fassen, und er präsentierte seine frühen australischen Bilder in der Galerie AFFA, später auch in der Bendigo Art Gallery in seinem neuen Heimatort. Seitens der australischen Presse fanden diese Ausstellungen durchwegs Interesse, doch der Durchbruch stellte sich auch in Australien nicht ein. Eine mögliche Begründung lieferte sein australischer Galerist: „Barabbas ist einer von uns geworden, aber da ist immer noch die Musik und die Seele von Wien in seiner Kunst."[36]

show. But in Vienna, too, the response to his art was tepid; the only exception was the essay by the art critic Maria Buchsbaum quoted several times in these pages. She identifies Barabbas's transcultural perspective and the individualism that defined his life's journey as the reason why his work struck beholders as inscrutable. His adopted country "became a source of inspiration to the artist, who had already in Vienna stood out for his transcultural views, although he did not disown the continuity of his creative impulses, which had their roots in Vienna. After ten years abroad, he has been virtually forgotten in his native country,"[37] the critic observed. And so Barabbas's paintings appear as the oeuvre of a traveler between worlds, never firmly moored to any place or tradition.

From the mid-1990s to the end of the millennium, impressions of nature are the dominant element in his work. "Aftermath (Nach der Flut)" (fig. 97), the artist noted, was created after a hike through the bush. The forest had been scorched by fire, and fresh shoots sprouted from the charred rubble. New life emerged "like Phoenix from the ashes."[38] What Barabbas saw in nature were questions of becoming and passing away, and so he focused his landscapes on moments that allowed him to articulate the passage of time. As a closer look at the painting shows, compositional structure is crucial to this expression.

Although nature's exuberant growth is captured in its sprawling and chaotic upward sweep, the picture is symmetrically structured. A vertical line leading up from the bottom of the painting to a circular element emphasizes the central axis, dividing the picture into two nearly identical segments. Barabbas introduces another division in the upper part of the painting, which allows him to visualize a distinctive sequence. The segmentation of the picture establishes a specific narrative structure, with the passage of time articulated by different structures in the individual segments. This compositional makeup is characteristic of the period of the artist's oeuvre extending from 1995 to the creative efforts of the final years.

Between 1992 and 2000, Barabbas increasingly turned to working on paper, partly out of indigence: he lacked the money to buy painting materials. Working in ink and brown earth tone washes, often in small formats, Barabbas explores the many faces of Australia's landscape. The graphic works demonstrate his mastery of composition and lineament. Examples include "Aftermath No. 3" (fig. 102) and "Models of Ideal Perfection" (fig. 101), which capture a detail of a scenery from various angles. By dividing up the sheet, Barabbas allows the beholder to experience the expanse of space and the trajectory of his gaze. The most conspicuous quality of these drawings, besides their sophisticated structure, is the acute and forceful use of the quill. He puts

1996 organisierten Sammler und Freunde von Barabbas eine Ausstellung in Wien in der Galerie Peithner-Lichtenfels. Barabbas bereitete die Ausstellung von Bendigo aus akribisch vor. Auch in Wien fand die Ausstellung jedoch – bis auf den bereits mehrfach zitierten Text der Kunstkritikerin Maria Buchsbaum – wenig Echo. Sie ortet die transkulturelle Auffassung von Barabbas und die Individualität seines Werdegangs als Ursache für seine Unzugänglichkeit. Seine Wahlheimat „wurde für ihn, der schon in Wien durch seine transkulturelle Auffassung aufgefallen war, zu einer Quelle der Inspiration, ohne dass er die Kontinuität seines in Österreich verwurzelten Schaffens verleugnete. Zehn Jahre Absenz haben ihn hier zu Lande fast in Vergessenheit gebracht",[37] meinte die Kritikerin. So stellt sich Barabbas in seiner Malerei als Grenzgänger zwischen den Welten dar, der sich mit seiner Arbeit nirgendwo verankerte.

In der zweiten Hälfte der neunziger Jahre bis zum Jahrtausendwechsel bestimmen Natureindrücke das Werk. Von „Aftermath (Nach der Flut)" (Abb. 97) berichtete der Künstler, dass es nach einem Spaziergang durch den Buschwald entstanden sei. Der Wald war verkohlt, und aus diesen Aschefragmenten wuchsen neue Triebe. „Wie ein Phönix aus der Asche" entstand Neues.[38] Barabbas sah in der Natur Fragen von Werden und Vergehen und konzentrierte seine Landschaftsbilder auf Momente, die den zeitlichen Ablauf zum Ausdruck bringen können. Wesentlich trägt dazu der Bildaufbau bei, wie ein näherer Blick auf das Gemälde zeigt.

Obwohl die wuchernde und wachsende Natur in ihrem ausladenden Aufstreben und in ihrer Ungeordnetheit erfasst wurde, ist das Bild symmetrisch aufgebaut. Eine Vertikale, die vom Bildgrund nach oben zu einem Kreisrund führt, betont die Mittelachse und teilt das Gemälde in zwei nahezu idente Bildabschnitte. Im oberen Bildbereich führt Barabbas ebenfalls eine Trennung ein. Dadurch entsteht die Möglichkeit, eine eigene Sequenz darzustellen. Die Aufteilung der Bildfläche erlaubt eine spezifische erzählerische Struktur, deren zeitlicher Ablauf sich in den einzelnen Bildabschnitten unterschiedlich aufbaut. Diese Bildstruktur charakterisiert die Werkphase von 1995 bis zu den letzten Schaffensjahren.

Zwischen 1992 und 2000 wandte sich der Künstler verstärkt der Arbeit auf Papier zu, auch aus materieller Not, es fehlte das Geld für Malmaterial. Mit oft kleinen Blättern, in Tusche mit braunen Erdtönen laviert, nähert sich Barabbas den vielen Gesichtern der australischen Landschaft. Die Grafiken zeigen Barabbas' Meisterschaft in Komposition und Lineament. Beispiele dafür sind „Aftermath Nr. 3" (Abb. 102) und „Models of Ideal Perfection" (Abb. 101), die verschiedene Blickwinkel auf ein Landschaftsdetail erfassen. Durch die Teilung der Fläche macht Barabbas die Ausdehnung des Raumes und den Ablauf des Blicks erfahrbar. Neben dem raffinierten Bildaufbau fällt bei den Grafiken besonders die intensive

hatchings and shadings on the paper with almost aggressive energy. It is as though the tensions within him were mounting.

*"The loss of my homeland and the engagement with the sceneries around here [...] have no doubt influenced me and hence also my art. Australia is different. Beauty doesn't present itself to the eye as readily as a lush spring meadow in the Wienerwald mountains does. Here, one must look for beauty, and more important, one must be willing to see it!"*[39]

After the turn of the millennium, he produced no more than few works on canvas. In one of the last paintings, created in 2002, it seems that the artist, looking back, is framing the legacy of his ideas, his vision of himself: "Odysseus" (fig. 117). Throughout his life, he had identified with Odysseus – a warrior, a seeker, who returned home after his wanderings, Odysseus may have struck Barabbas, a seeker as well, as an ideal version of himself. As the artist wrote, " – *Odysseus's dangerous and interminable travels on the way home, the return of the Prodigal Son, or our struggle to gain insight into the meaning of existence and our responsibility for a peaceful life for all human beings on earth ...*" The Paul Gauguin of the Tahiti years was another character Barabbas often cited as a romantic hero, a screen on which he projected his own life. *"Gauguin was and is my mentor!"*[40] he remarked. The artist recognized himself in Gauguin not only with his unending quest, but also with his failures in the social sphere and the transcultural Odyssey of his art.

Like the chief melody of a piece of music, moreover, "Odysseus" gathers up all specific traits of his artistic career in a single crescendo: vigorous color, elaborate ornamentation, expansive dimensions, and a structure that lets the beholder "experience" the passage of time; these compositional means are here united in a last culmination. In this work, Barabbas's quest for an integral painting – one integrated in every one of its aspects[41] – seems to have led him to a solution commensurate with his vision.

"The Center" (fig. 116), a work created in 2007, may be considered one of the last works in color on a sizable format. The picture may be looked at from all sides, since the painter turned it various ways as he worked on it, which lends new significance to the center. But interestingly enough, that very center has remained unpainted – the void, that is to say, has become a motif of sorts. In Barabbas's monumental "Big Bang" or "Genesis," painted in 1975, the yellow center was particularly significant, representing the tabernacle from which everything originates and toward which everything strives. *"Bringing from non-being into being"* – that was the aspiration of Barabbas's art. And of course he also knew the path in the opposite direction.

und kraftvolle Führung der Feder auf. Nahezu aggressive Strichlagen und Schraffuren werden zu Papier gebracht. Es ist, als ob sich die Anspannung verdichtet.

*„Der Verlust meiner Heimat und die Auseinandersetzung mit dieser Umgebung hatten […] sicherlich einen Einfluss auf mich und somit auf meine Kunst. Australien ist anders. Die Schönheit liegt nicht so offen da wie eine üppige Frühlingswiese im Wienerwald. Hier muss man die Schönheit suchen und vor allem, man muss sie sehen wollen!"*[39]

Nach dem Jahrtausendwechsel entstanden nur noch wenige Leinwände. Eine der letzten Arbeiten erscheint wie ein Blick zurück, ein Vermächtnis der Ideen und Selbstsicht des Künstlers: „Odysseus" (Abb. 117), 2002 entstanden. Barabbas hatte sich zeitlebens mit Odysseus identifiziert, Odysseus, ein Krieger, ein Suchender, der nach seinen Irrfahrten heimkehrte, mag ihm, dem Suchenden, als Ideal seiner selbst erschienen sein. Barabbas: *„– die gefährliche und langwierige Heimreise eines Odysseus, die Heimkehr des verlorenen Sohnes oder unser Ringen nach Erkenntnis über den Sinn des Daseins und unsere Verantwortung für ein friedvolles Leben aller Menschen auf Erden …"* Auch Paul Gauguin in Tahiti war eine oftmals zitierte Gestalt, die Barabbas als romantische Projektionsfigur seiner selbst diente. *„Gauguin war und ist mein Mentor!",*[40] stellte Barabbas fest. Der Künstler erkannte sich in ihm nicht nur in seiner permanenten Suche wieder, sondern auch in seinem Scheitern in der Gesellschaft wie in seinem artistischen Grenzgang.

Das Gemälde „Odysseus" versammelt zudem – wie die Hauptmelodie eines Musikstückes – alle Spezifika seines künstlerischen Werdegangs in einem Crescendo: die kraftvolle Farbe, die kunstvolle Ornamentik, die räumliche Ausdehnung und die „zeitliche" Erlebbarkeit; diese Kompositionsmittel finden sich in einer Kulmination vereinigt. Barabbas' Suche nach einer integralen Malerei – einer Malerei, die im Ganzen integriert ist[41] – scheint bei diesem Werk seinen Vorstellungen entsprechend an ein Ziel gelangt.

„Die Mitte" (Abb. 116) von 2007 kann als eine der letzten farbigen Arbeiten größeren Formats gelten. Das Bild ist von allen Seiten zu betrachten und wurde auch von verschiedenen Seiten aus gemalt. Die Mitte erlangt damit eine neue Bedeutung. Interessanterweise ist das Zentrum aber unbemalt belassen – die Leerstelle also ist gleichsam zum Motiv avanciert. Auch bei seinem Monumentalwerk „Big Bang" oder „Genesis" aus dem Jahr 1975 war die gelbe Mitte besonders bedeutend, stellte diese doch das Tabernakel dar, aus dem alles entsteht und wohin alles strebt. *„Aus dem Nichtsein ins Dasein zu bringen"* – dies war das Streben der Kunst von Barabbas. Und natürlich wusste er auch um den umgekehrten Weg.

1 Claus Mayrhofer Barabbas, letter to Rosemarie Sebek, March 31, 1989.
2 http://de.wikipedia.org/wiki/Avantgarde.
3 Alfred Schmeller, "Roter Apfel am Tannenbaum: Zu einer sehenswerten Ausstellung junger Künstler auf der Landstraße 74," Kurier, December 27, 1960.
4 Walter Malli, quoted in Semirah Heilingsetzer, Die Galerie "Zum roten Apfel" 1959–1965: Künstlerpositionen der 60er Jahre in Wien (Frankfurt am Main: Lang, 2003), 20.
5 Ahmad Pechoc, quoted ibid., 31.
6 Peter Baum, "Kunst in Österreich," in Tradition und Avantgarde: Kunst in Österreich 1945–1980, exh. cat. (Neuhaus: Museum Liaunig, 2010), 76.
7 Rosemarie Sebek in conversation with the author, February 17, 2012.
8 Heinrich Neumayer, "Tragische Masken und Phantasien aus der Tube," Österreichische Neue Tageszeitung, March 12, 1960, 4.
9 Heilingsetzer, Die Galerie „Zum roten Apfel", 35.
10 "My first exhibition at Galerie zum Roten Apfel took place in 1960, when I presented 'Tachist, Automatist' pictures. I've mentioned at some point [...] that I'm still a tachist-automatist at heart. That's my background, that's my method of painting with blindfolded or closed eyes," Barabbas noted in an email to his long-time friend and collector Fritz Jelinek. Given the exact technique of his later paintings, however, the remark would seem to refer primarily to a variation of his pictorial invention.
11 Wolfgang Hilger, "Recollections and Remarks: A Subjective Look at the Viennese Art Scene of the 1960s," in Die sechziger Jahre: Eine phantastische Moderne, Sammlung der Kulturabteilung der Stadt Wien – MUSA, ed. Berthold Ecker and Wolfgang Hilger (Vienna: Springer, 2011), 22.
12 Alfred Schmeller, in Kurier, November 15, 1963.
13 Maria Buchsbaum, "Barabbas: Das Ornamentale als Inhaltsträger," Vernissage 16, no. 8 (October 1996): 4–7.
14 See Andreas Felber's contribution to the present volume.
15 Ibid.
16 "The latest thing in Vienna's underground: Overground" was the headline the Express ran over an article by Michael Jeannée on October 29, 1969.
17 Georg Fischhof on an invitation card for an exhibition of Barabbas's work at Paulanergasse 9/19, Vienna, December 2, 1970.
18 Claus Mayrhofer Barabbas, email to Rosemarie Sebek, October 24, 2007.
19 Claus Mayrhofer Barabbas, original manuscript, collection of Fritz Jelinek.
20 Rosemarie Sebek in conversation with the author, August 12, 2012.
21 See http://en.wikipedia.org/wiki/Bahá'í_Faith.
22 Buchsbaum, "Barabbas."
23 Erwin Melchart, "Das Riesenbild von Wien," Neue Kronen Zeitung, August 10, 1975.
24 Ibid.
25 Rosemarie Sebek, "The Big Bang," unpublished manuscript, 1.
26 Claus Mayrhofer Barabbas, letter to Fritz Jelinek, November 15, 1995.
27 Claus Mayrhofer Barabbas, letter to Fritz Jelinek, September 7, 2007.
28 Claus Mayrhofer Barabbas, email to Rosemarie Sebek, August 7, 2004.
29 Ibid.
30 Buchsbaum, "Barabbas."
31 Ibid.
32 Fritz Jelinek in conversation with the author, December 2011.
33 Claus Mayrhofer Barabbas, letter to Fritz Jelinek, May 24/25,1996.
34 Ibid.
35 Ibid.
36 David Thomas, quoted in: Sebek, "The Big Bang," 29.
37 Maria Buchsbaum, "Barabbas."
38 Claus Mayrhofer Barabbas, letter to Fritz Jelinek, May 24/25,1996.
39 Claus Mayrhofer Barabbas, email to Rosemarie Sebek, September 19, 2004.
40 Claus Mayrhofer Barabbas, letter to Fritz Jelinek, May 24/25,1996
41 Claus Mayrhofer Barabbas, work diary, entry dated May 20, 1988.

1 Claus Mayrhofer Barabbas, Brief an Rosemarie Sebek, 31.3.1989.
2 http://de.wikipedia.org/wiki/Avantgarde.
3 Alfred Schmeller, Roter Apfel am Tannenbaum. Zu einer sehenswerten Ausstellung junger Künstler auf der Landstraße 74, in: Kurier, 27.12.1960.
4 Walter Malli, zit. in: Semirah Heilingsetzer, Die Galerie „Zum roten Apfel" 1959–1965. Künstlerpositionen der 60er Jahre in Wien, Frankfurt/Main 2003, S. 20.
5 Ahmad Pechoc, in: Heilingsetzer, Die Galerie „Zum roten Apfel", S. 31.
6 Peter Baum, Kunst in Österreich, in: Tradition und Avantgarde. Kunst in Österreich 1945–1980, Ausstellungskatalog Museum Liaunig, Neuhaus 2010, S. 76.
7 Rosemarie Sebek im Gespräch mit der Autorin, 17.2.2012.
8 Heinrich Neumayer, Tragische Masken und Phantasien aus der Tube, in: Österreichische Neue Tageszeitung, 12.3.1960, S. 4.
9 Heilingsetzer, Die Galerie „Zum roten Apfel", S. 35.
10 „Meine erste Ausstellung in der Galerie zum Roten Apfel war im Jahr 1960 mit ‚Tachistischen, Automatistischen' Bildern. Ich habe [...] einmal erwaehnt, dass ich immer noch ein Tachist-Automatist at Heart bin. Das ist mein Hintergrund, das ist meine Methode mit verbundenen oder geschlossenen Augen zu malen", stellt Barabbas in einer E-Mail vom 22. Februar 2002 an Fritz Jelinek, langjähriger Freund und Sammler, fest, doch scheint aufgrund der exakten Malweise späterer Tage mit dieser Bemerkung eher eine Variante der Bildfindung angesprochen zu sein.
11 Wolfgang Hilger, Erinnerungen und Anmerkungen. Subjektives zu Wiens Kunstbetrieb in den sechziger Jahren, in: Berthold Ecker/ Wolfgang Hilger (Hg.), Die sechziger Jahre. Eine phantastische Moderne, Sammlung der Kulturabteilung der Stadt Wien – MUSA, Wien 2011, S. 23.
12 Alfred Schmeller, in: Kurier, 15.11.1963.
13 Maria Buchsbaum, Barabbas. Das Ornamentale als Inhaltsträger, in: Vernissage, 16. Jg., Nr. 8, Oktober 1996. S. 4–7.
14 Vgl. dazu den Beitrag von Andreas Felber in diesem Band.
15 Siehe ebd.
16 „Letzter Schrei im Wiener Underground: Overground" war die Schlagzeile im „Express" am 29.10.1969 von Michael Jeannée.
17 Georg Fischhof auf einer Einladungskarte zu einer Ausstellung von Barabbas in Wien, Paulanergasse 9/19, am 2.12.1970.
18 Claus Mayrhofer Barabbas, E-Mail an Rosemarie Sebek, 24.10.2007.
19 Claus Mayrhofer Barabbas, Originalmanuskript aus der Sammlung Fritz Jelinek.
20 Rosemarie Sebek im Gespräch mit der Autorin, 12.8.2012.
21 http://de.wikipedia.org/wiki/Bahai.
22 Buchsbaum, Barabbas.
23 Erwin Melchart, Das Riesenbild von Wien, in: Neue Kronen Zeitung, 10.8.1975.
24 Ebd.
25 Rosemarie Sebek, The Big Bang, unveröffentlichtes Manuskript, S. 1.
26 Claus Mayrhofer Barabbas, Brief an Fritz Jelinek, 15.11.1995.
27 Claus Mayrhofer Barabbas, Brief an Fritz Jelinek, 7.9.2007.
28 Claus Mayrhofer Barabbas, E-Mail an Rosemarie Sebek, 7.8.2004.
29 Ebd.
30 Buchsbaum, Barabbas.
31 Ebd.
32 Fritz Jelinek im Gespräch mit der Autorin, Dezember 2011.
33 Claus Mayrhofer Barabbas, Brief an Fritz Jelinek, 24./25.5.1996.
34 Ebd.
35 Ebd.
36 David Thomas, zit. in: Sebek, The Big Bang, S. 29.
37 Maria Buchsbaum, Barabbas.
38 Claus Mayrhofer Barabbas, Brief an Fritz Jelinek, 24./25.5.1996.
39 Claus Mayrhofer Barabbas, E-Mail an Rosemarie Sebek, 19.9.2004.
40 Claus Mayrhofer Barabbas, Brief an Fritz Jelinek, 24./25.5.1996
41 Eintragung in das Werktagebuch, 20.5.1988.

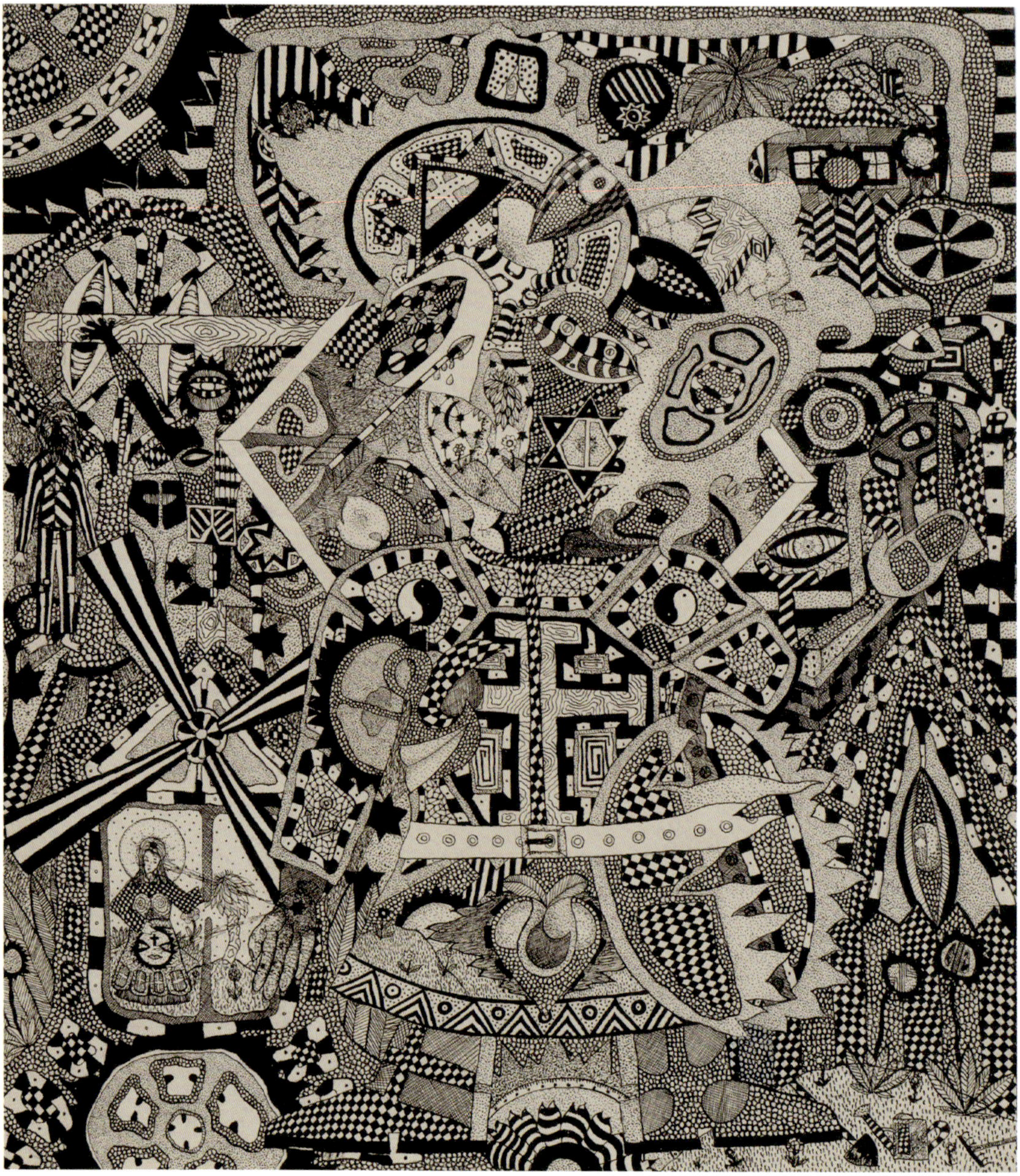

23
Mariä Verkündigung, 1963
Tusche auf Papier, 28 x 25 cm
Annunciation to the Blessed Virgin Mary, 1963
drawing ink on paper, 28 x 25 cm

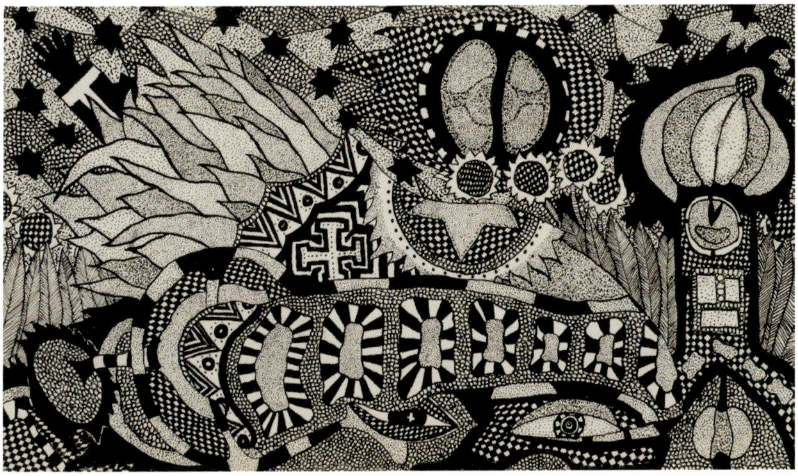

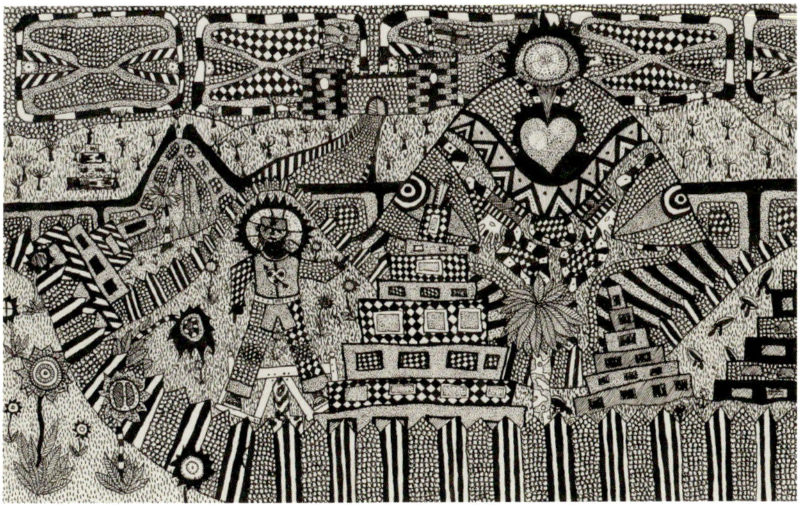

24
Urchristlicher Tintenfisch in Nachbars Garten, 1962
Tusche auf Papier, 11,2 x 19,3 cm
Early Christian Squid in the Neighbor's Garden, 1962
drawing ink on paper, 11,2 x 19,3 cm

25
Prophet Jeremia, 1962
Tusche auf Papier, 15,3 x 24,4 cm
Prophet Jeremiah, 1962
drawing ink on paper, 15,3 x 24,4 cm

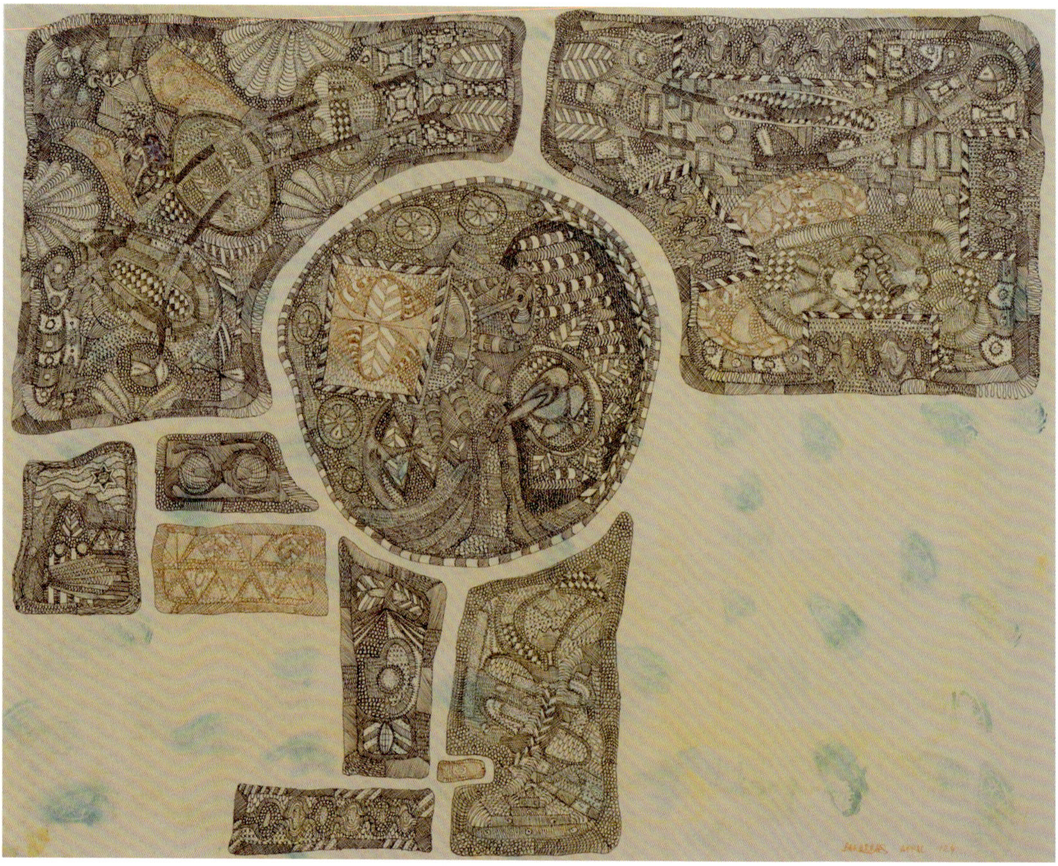

26

O.T., 1968-1969
Tusche und Kartoffelstempel auf Karton, 57 x 62 cm
Untitled, 1968-1969
drawing ink and potato stamp on cardboard, 57 x 62 cm

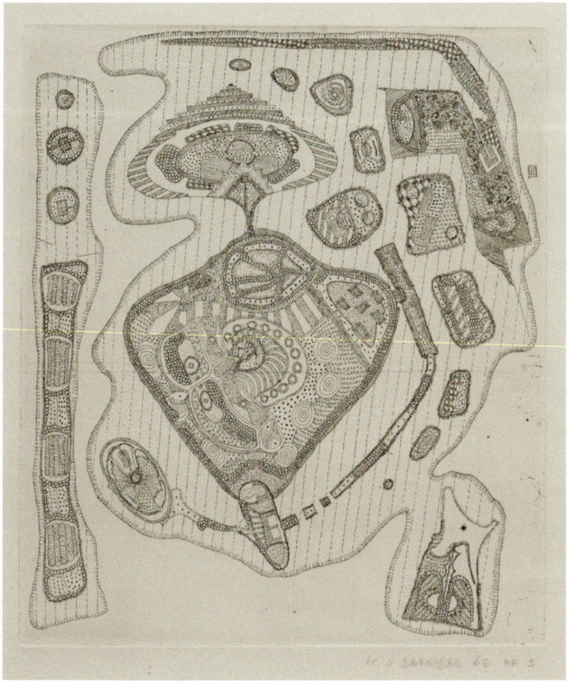

27
Sonnentanz einer Sicherheitsmumie, 1966
Radierung, 33 x 29 cm
Sun Dance of a Security Mummy, 1966
etching, 33 x 29 cm

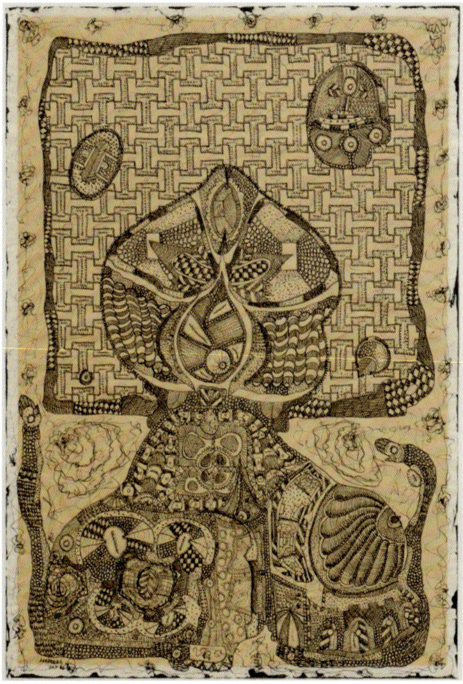

28
Lennire II, 1966
Tusche auf Papier, 45 x 31,4 cm
Lennire II, 1966
drawing ink on paper, 45 x 31,4 cm

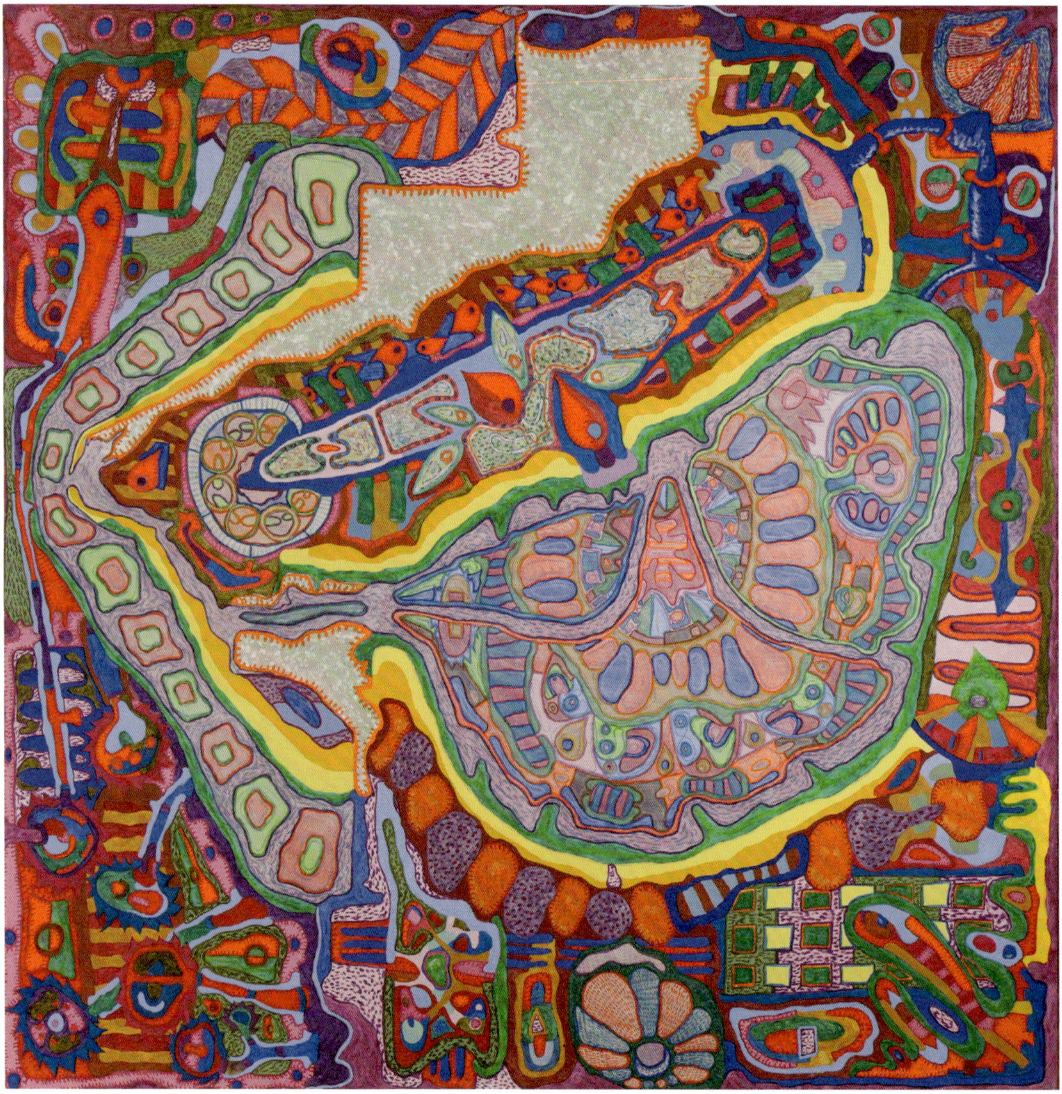

29
Mallis Insel, undatiert (Mitte 1960er Jahre)
Öl, Kasein, Eitempera auf Leinwand, 200 x 200 cm
Malli's Island, undated (mid-1960s)
oil, casein, egg tempera on canvas, 200 x 200 cm

30
Gebetsteppich mit zwei Spiegeleiern, undatiert (Mitte 1960er Jahre)
Öl, Kasein, Eitempera auf Leinwand, 200 x 130 cm
Prayer Rug with Two Fried Eggs, undated (mid-1960s)
oil, casein, egg tempera on canvas, 200 x 130 cm

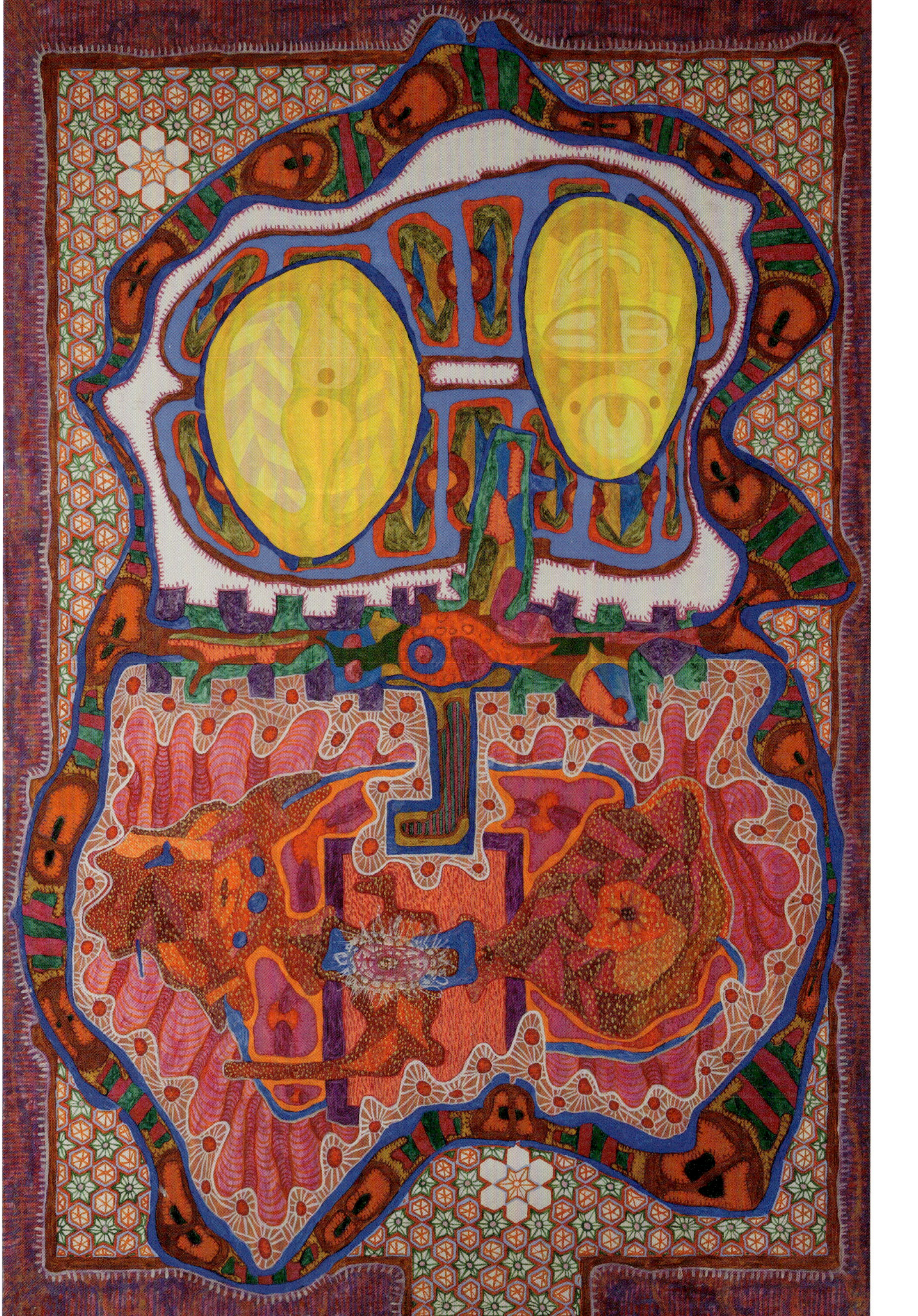

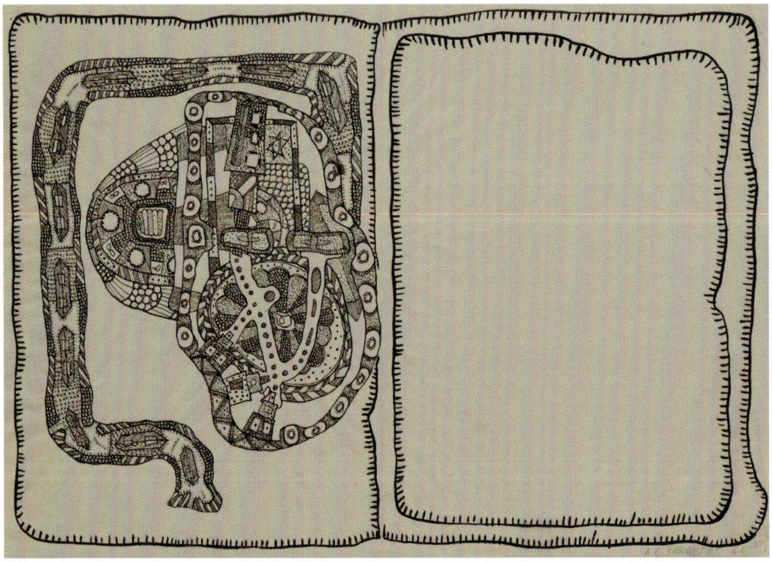

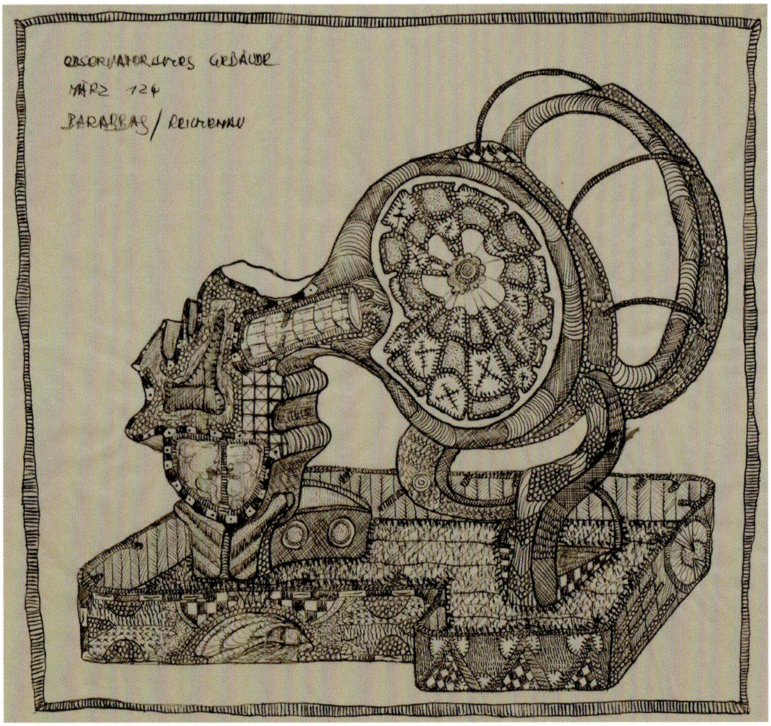

31
O.T., 1966
Tusche auf Transparentpapier, 31 x 45 cm
Untitled, 1966
drawing ink on tracing paper, 31 x 45 cm

32
Observatorium-Gebäude, 1968
Tusche auf Transparentpapier, 32 x 44 cm
Observatory Building, 1968
drawing ink on tracing paper, 32 x 44 cm

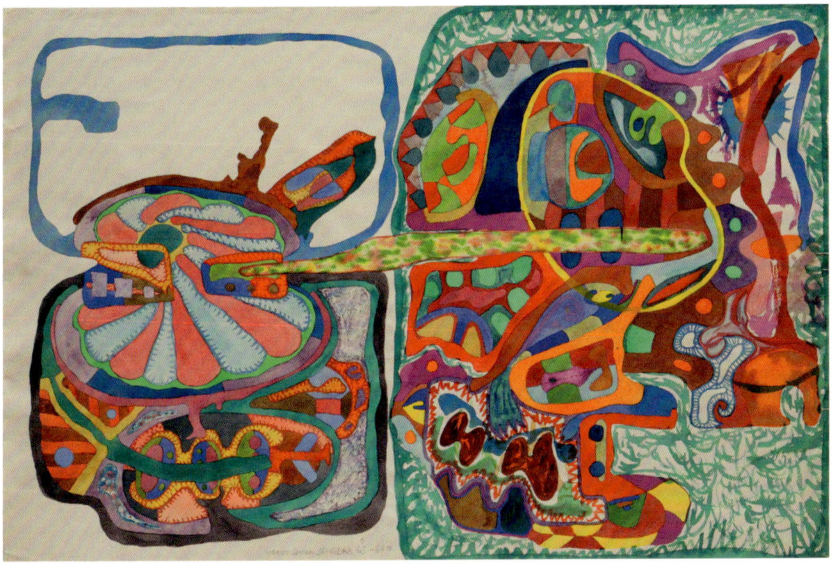

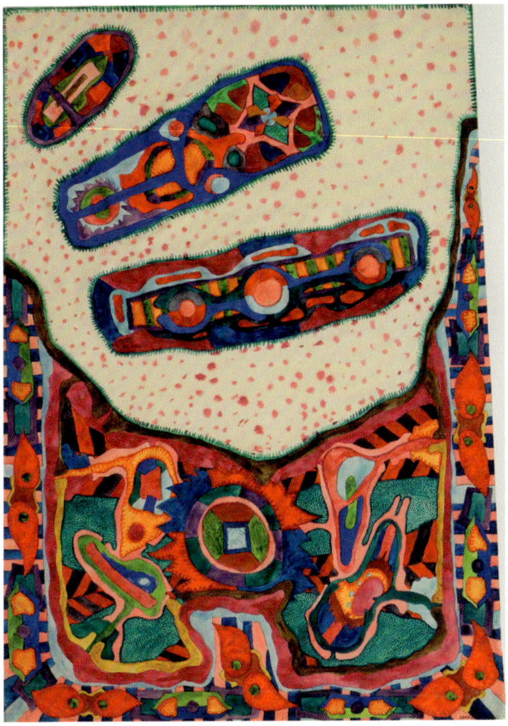

33
O.T., 1965-1967
Aquarell auf Papier, 52 x 80 cm
Untitled, 1965-1967
watercolor on paper, 52 x 80 cm

34
Drei Raumsonden durchfliegen den löchrigen Mars, 1965
Aquarell auf Papier, 80 x 55,5 cm
Three Space Probes Fly Through Mars Full of Holes, 1965
watercolor on paper, 80 x 55,5 cm

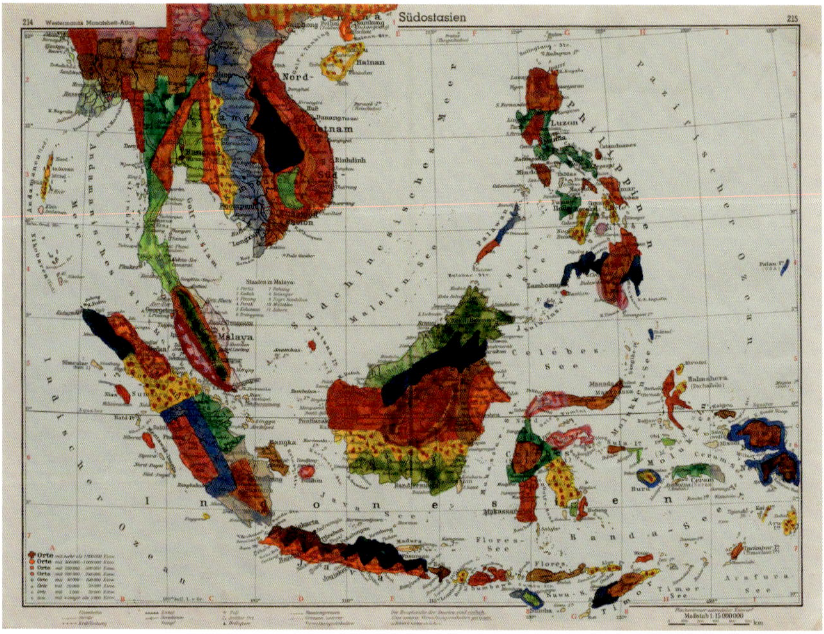


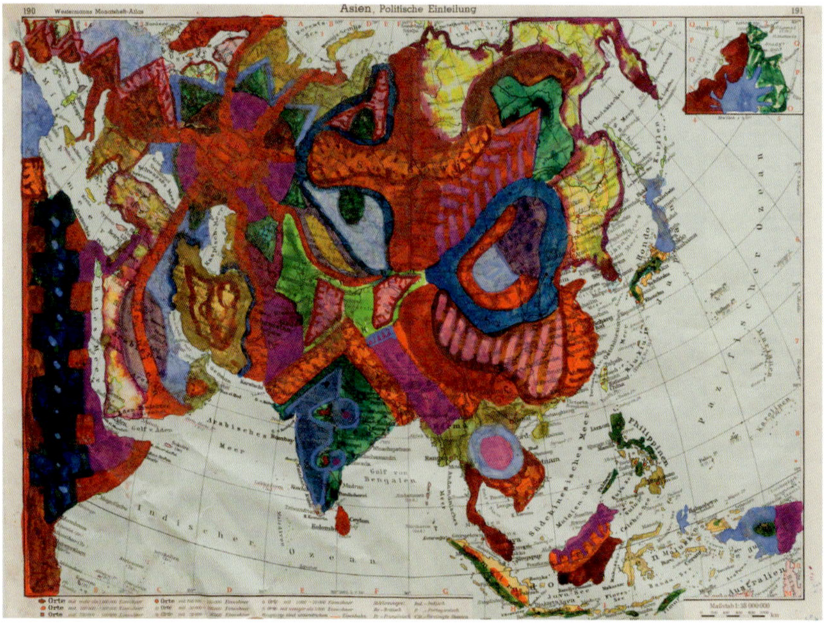


35
Südostasien, 1967
Wasserfarbe auf Landkarte, 24 x 33,5 cm
South East Asia, 1967
watercolor on map, 24 x 33,5 cm

36
Asien, 1967
Wasserfarbe auf Landkarte, 24 x 33,5 cm
Asia, 1967
watercolor on map, 24 x 33,5 cm

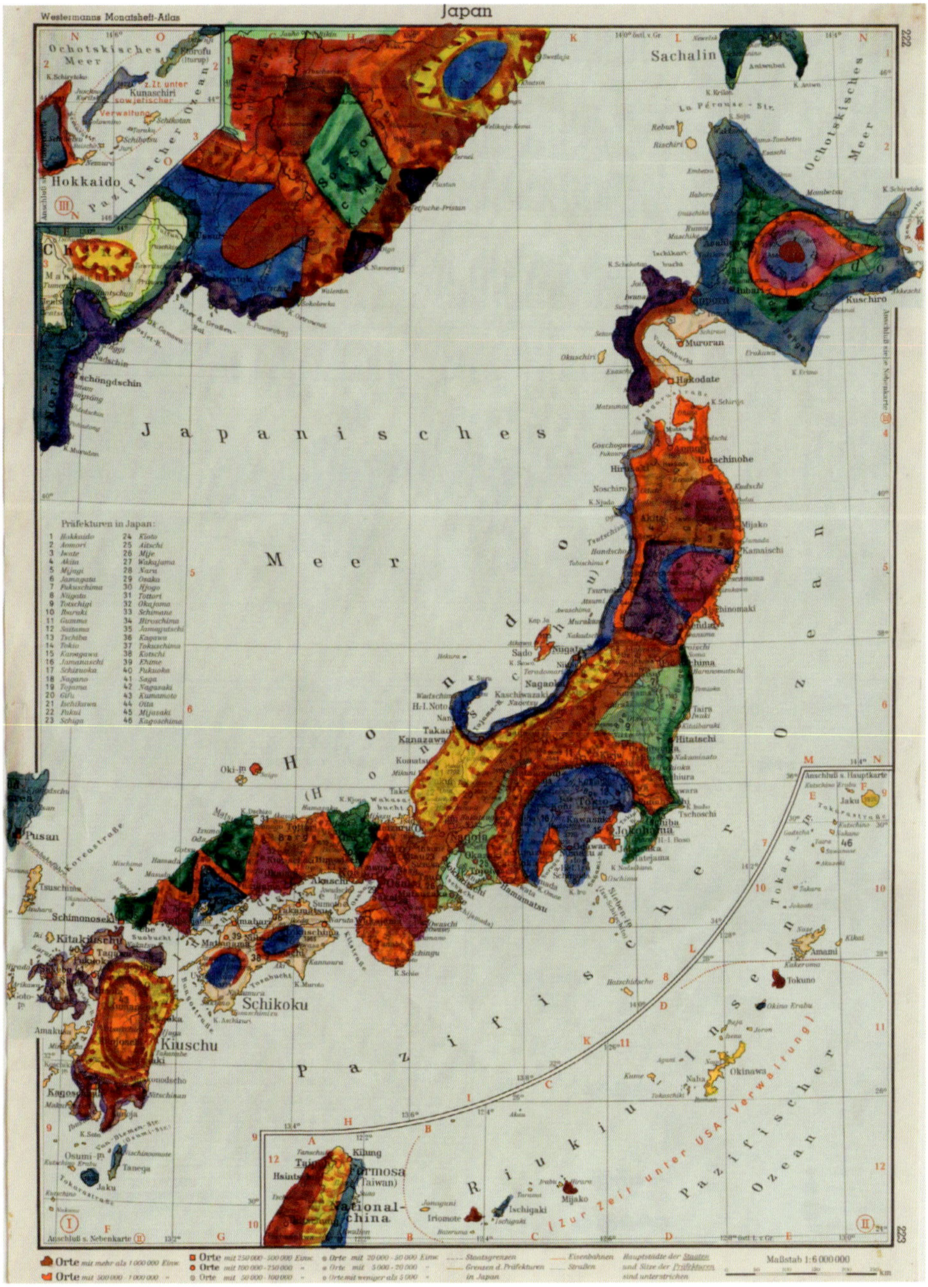


37
Japan, 1966
Wasserfarbe auf Landkarte, 33,5 x 24 cm
Japan, 1966
watercolor on map, 33,5 x 24 cm

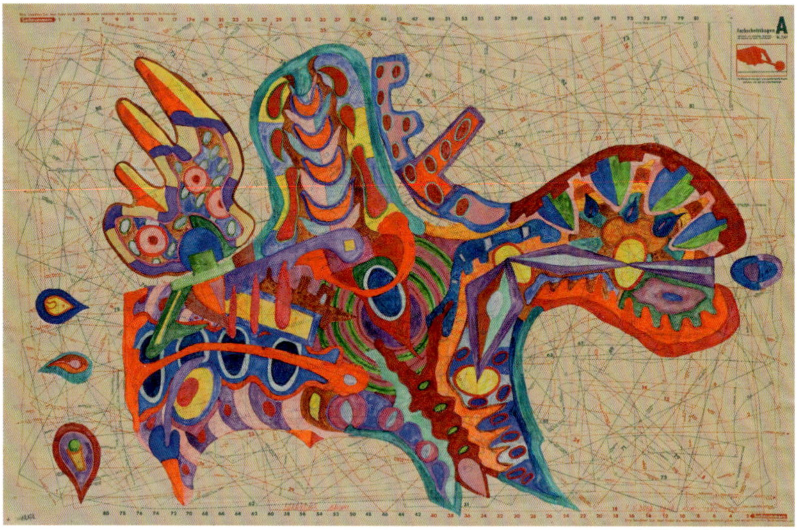

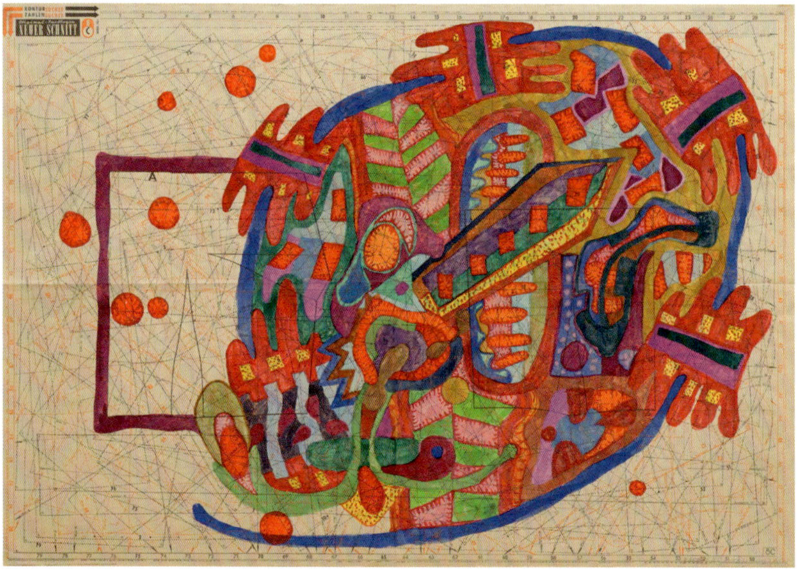

38
O.T., 1967
Wasserfarbe auf Schnittbogen, 59 x 87 cm
Untitled, 1967
watercolor on pattern sheet, 59 x 87 cm

39
O.T., 1967
Wasserfarbe auf Schnittbogen, 59 x 87 cm
Untitled, 1967
watercolor on pattern sheet, 59 x 87 cm

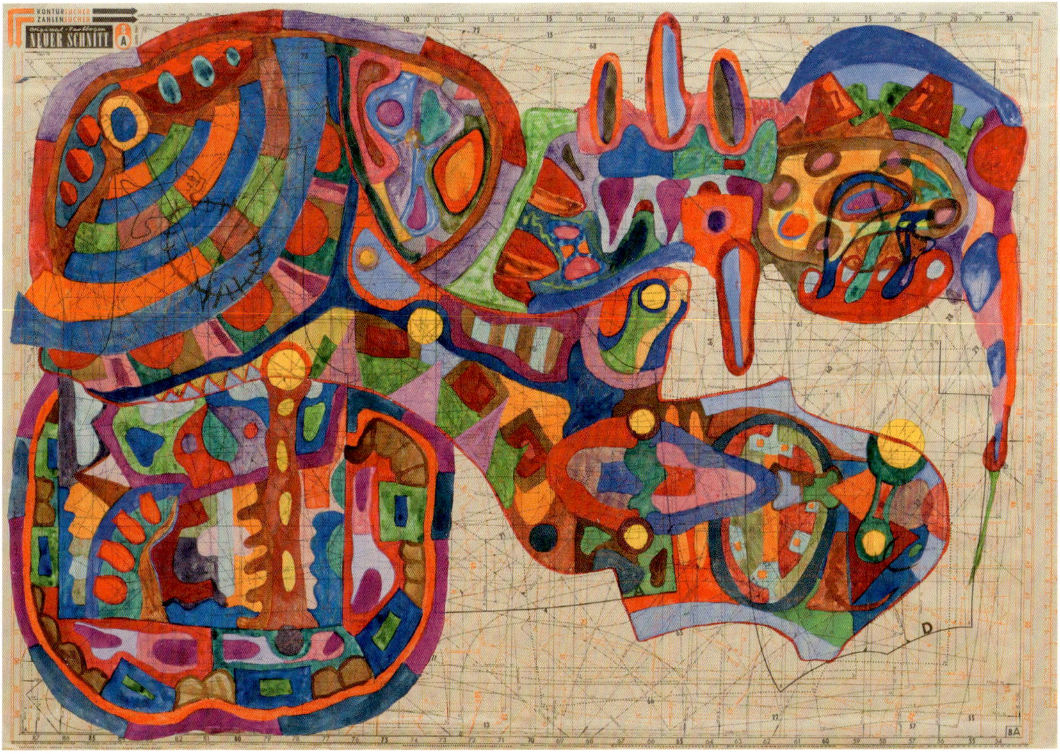


40
O.T., 1967
Wasserfarbe auf Schnittbogen, 59 x 87 cm
Untitled, 1967
watercolor on pattern sheet, 59 x 87 cm

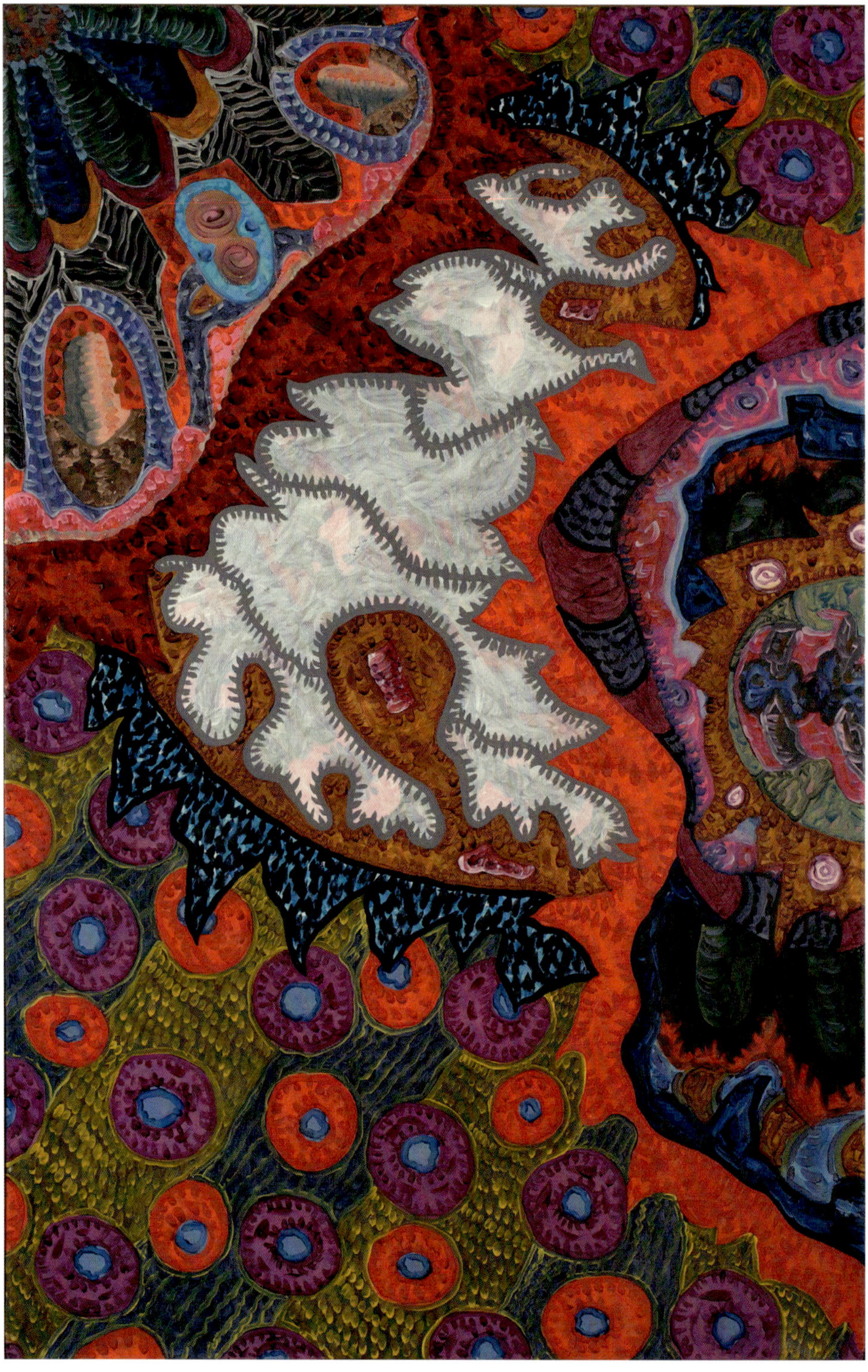

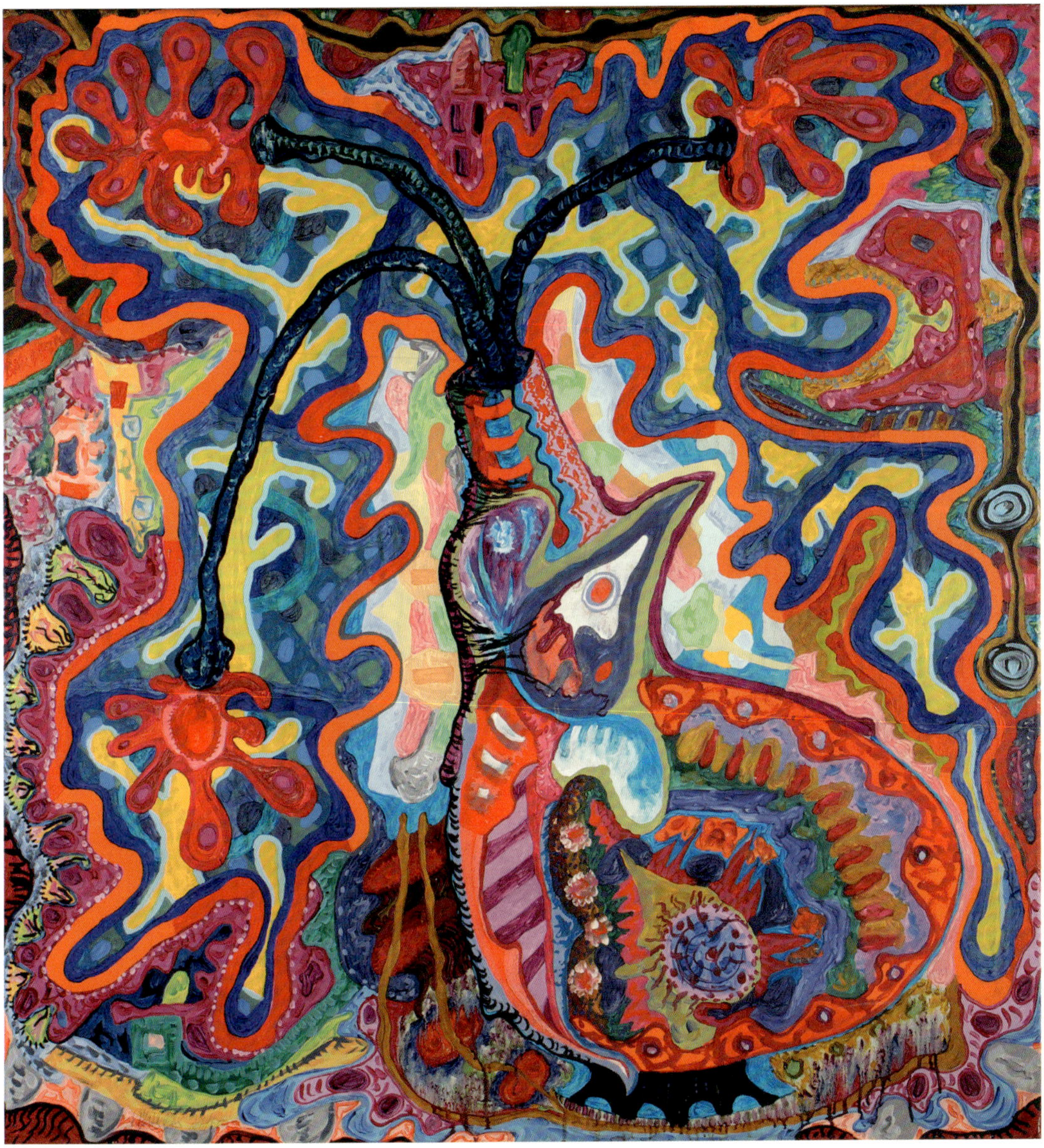

41
Black Power Nr. II, 1969
Öl auf Leinwand, 105 x 68,5 cm
Black Power No. II
oil on canvas, 105 x 68,5 cm

42
Sonny Rollins, 1968
Öl auf Leinwand, 105 x 100,5 cm
Sonny Rollins, 1968
oil on canvas, 105 x 100,5 cm

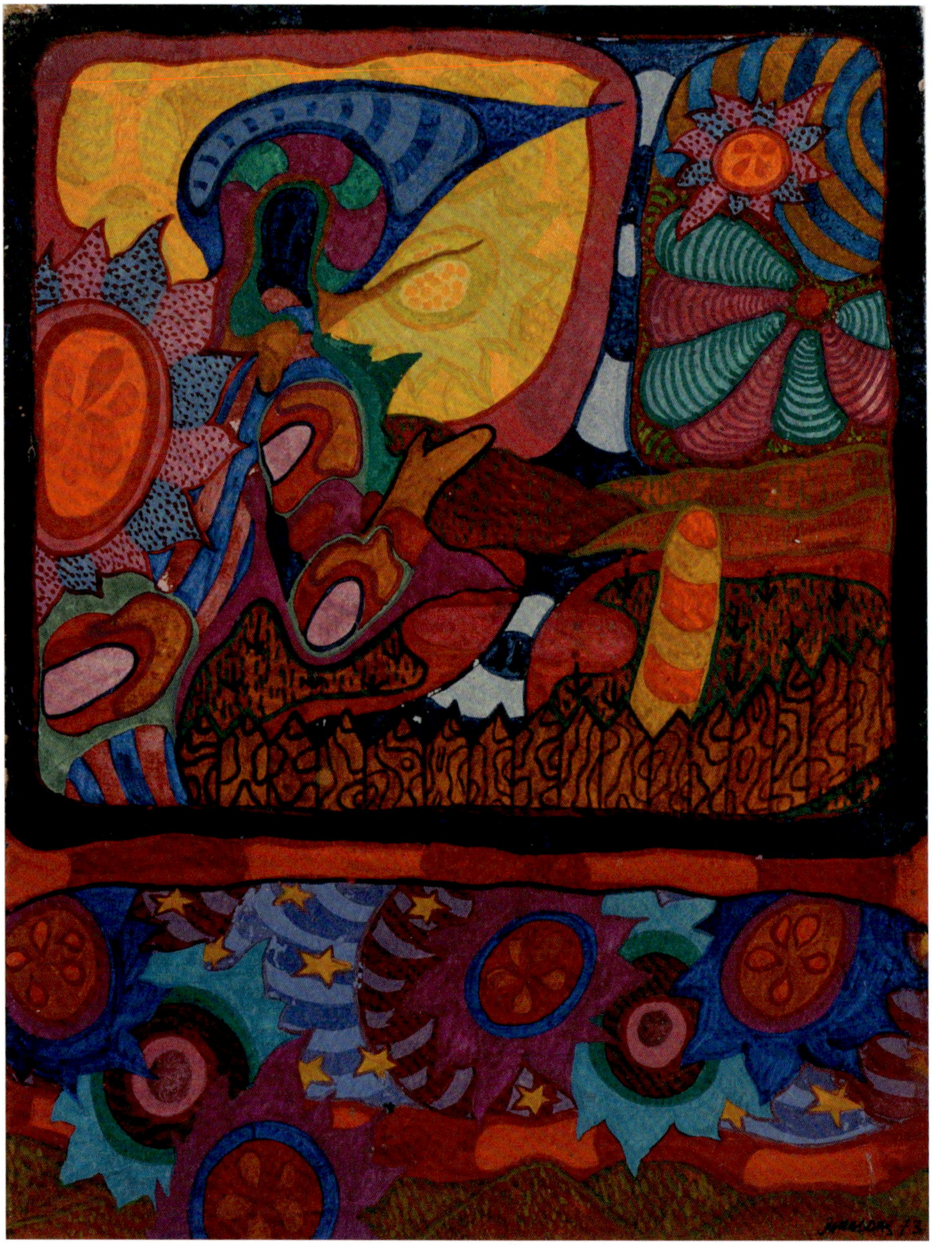

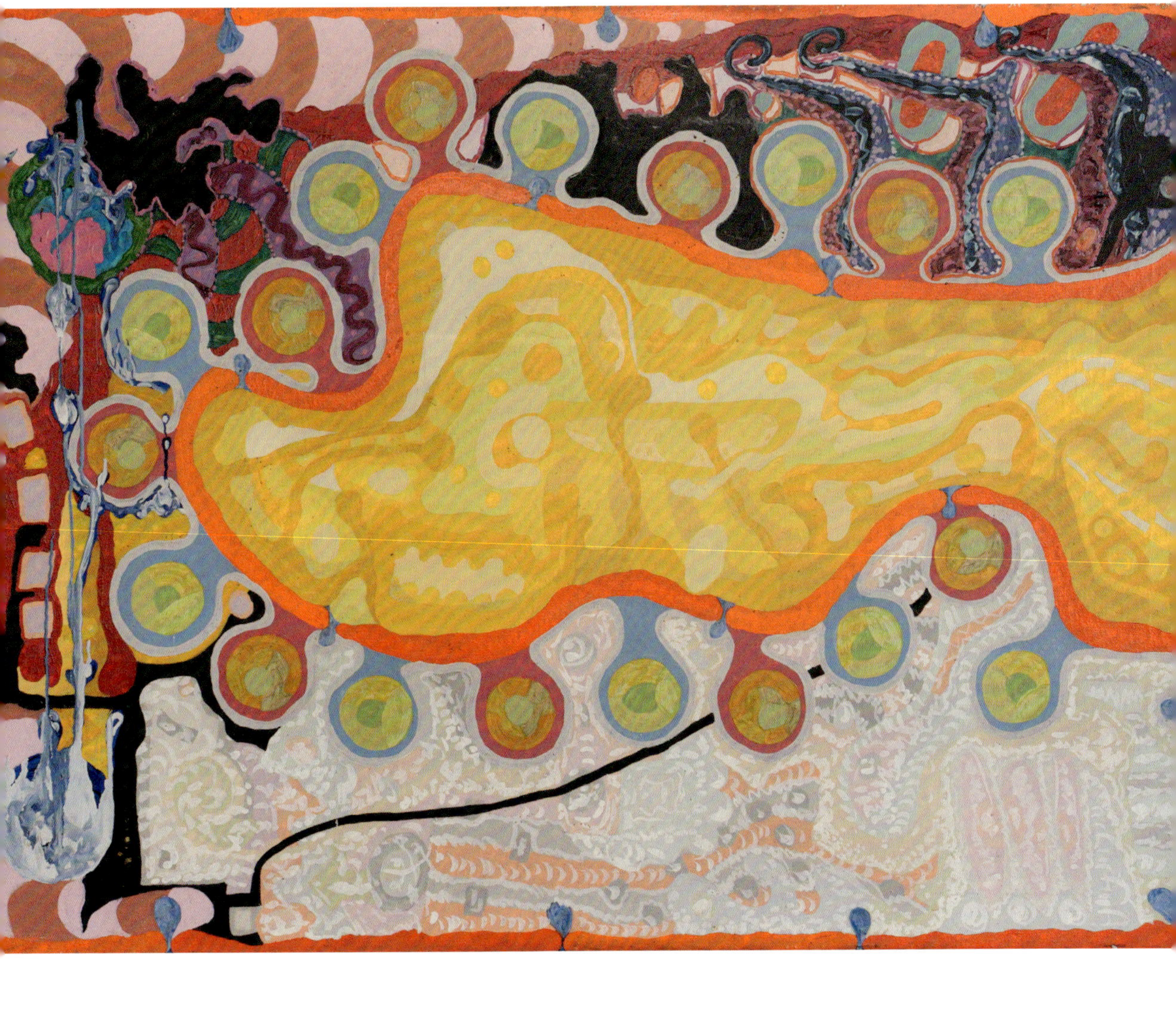

43
O.T., undatiert (ca. 1960)
Mischtechnik auf Spanplatte, 30,5 x 23 cm
Untitled, undated (ca. 1960)
mixed technique on particleboard, 30,5 x 23 cm

44
O.T., undatiert (ca. 1970)
Mischtechnik auf Leinwand, 71 x 92 cm
Untitled, undated (ca. 1970)
mixed technique on canvas, 71 x 92 cm

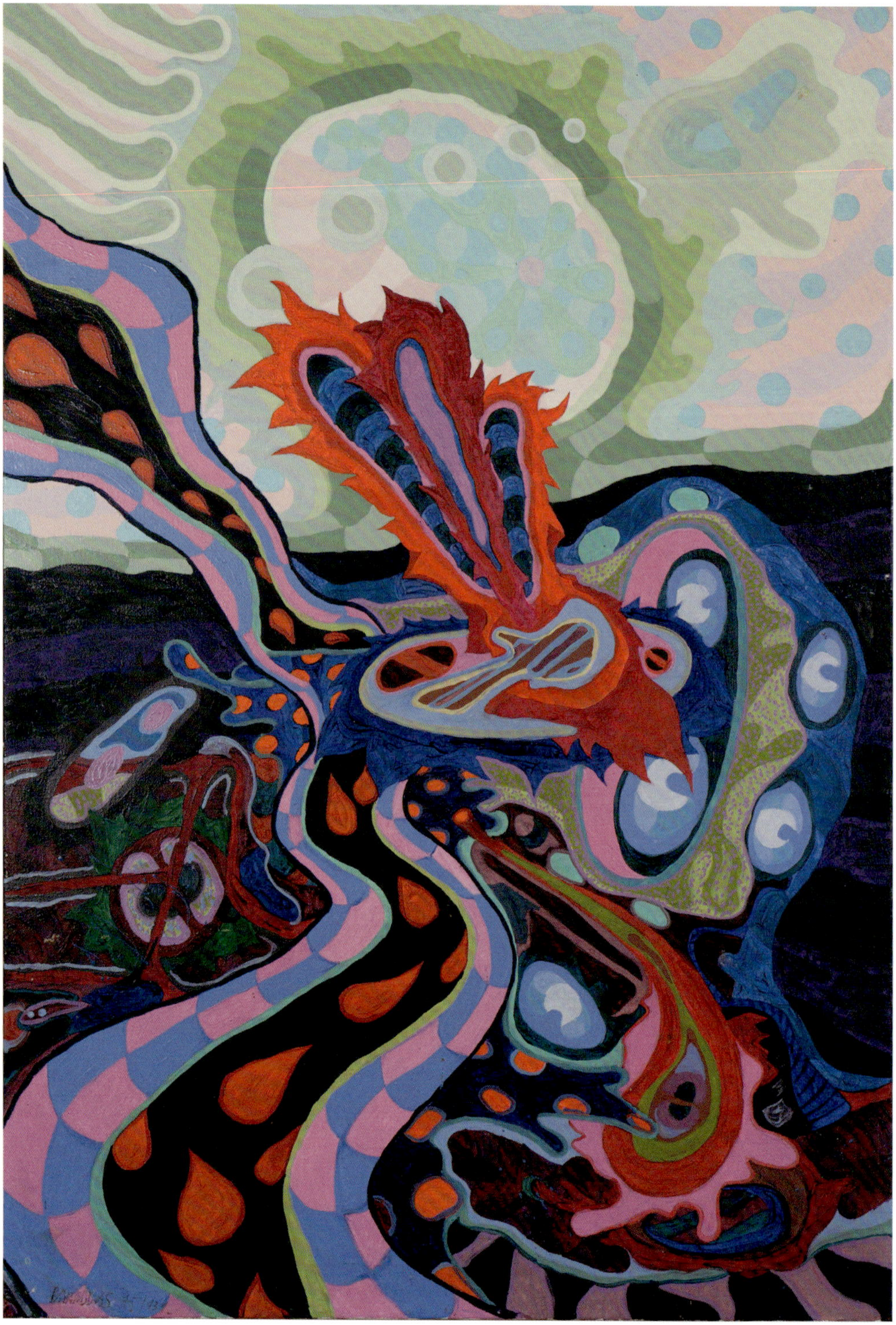

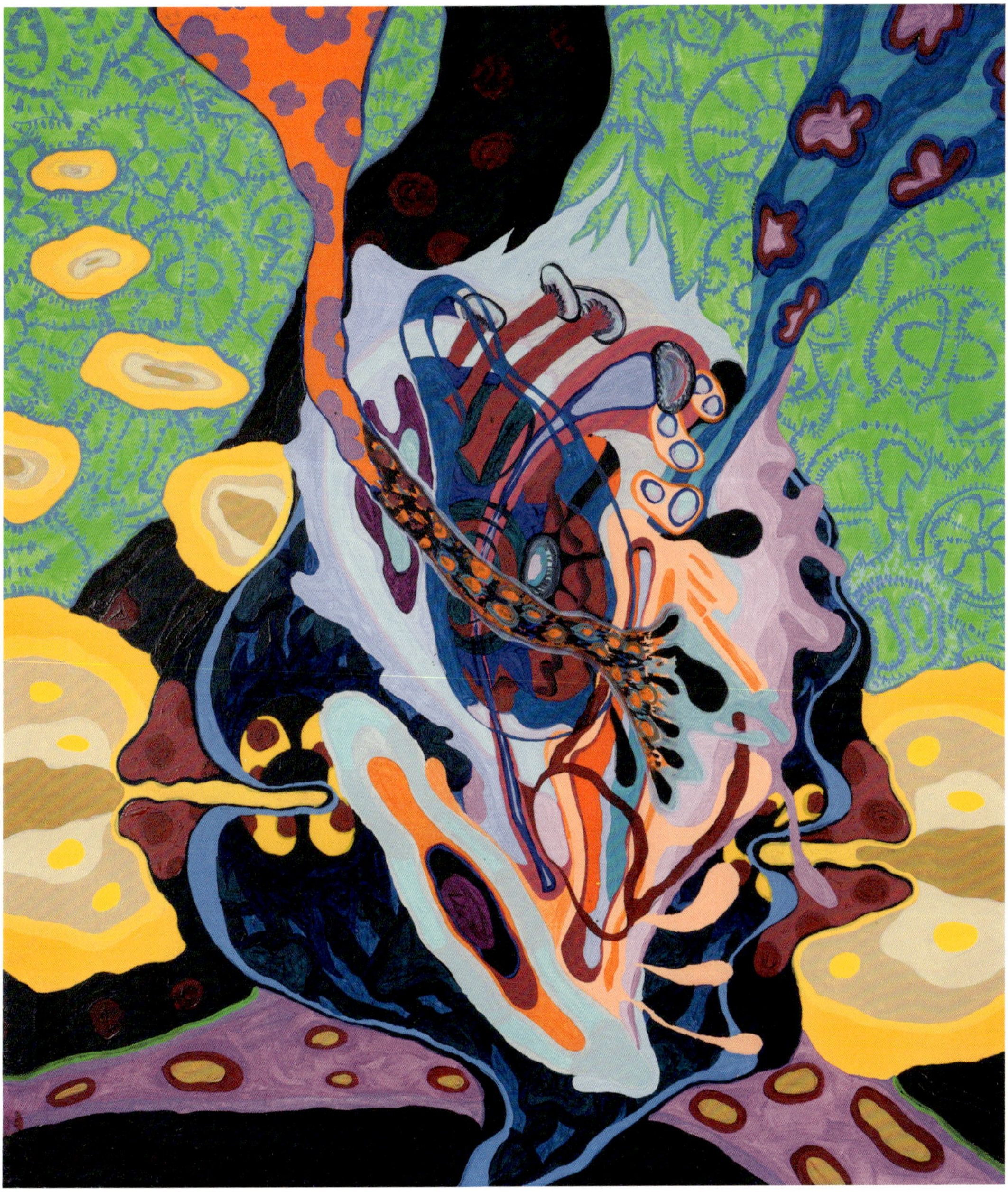

45
Milchstraße mit weißem Loch, 1975
Mischtechnik auf Leinwand, 100 x 70 cm
Milky Way with White Hole, 1975
mixed technique on canvas, 100 x 70 cm

46
Mystische Begegnung zwischen Montezuma und Karl I. in Funchal, 1975
Mischtechnik auf Leinwand, 85 x 75 cm
Mystical Encounter between Montezuma and Charles I at Funchal, 1975
mixed technique on canvas, 85 x 75 cm

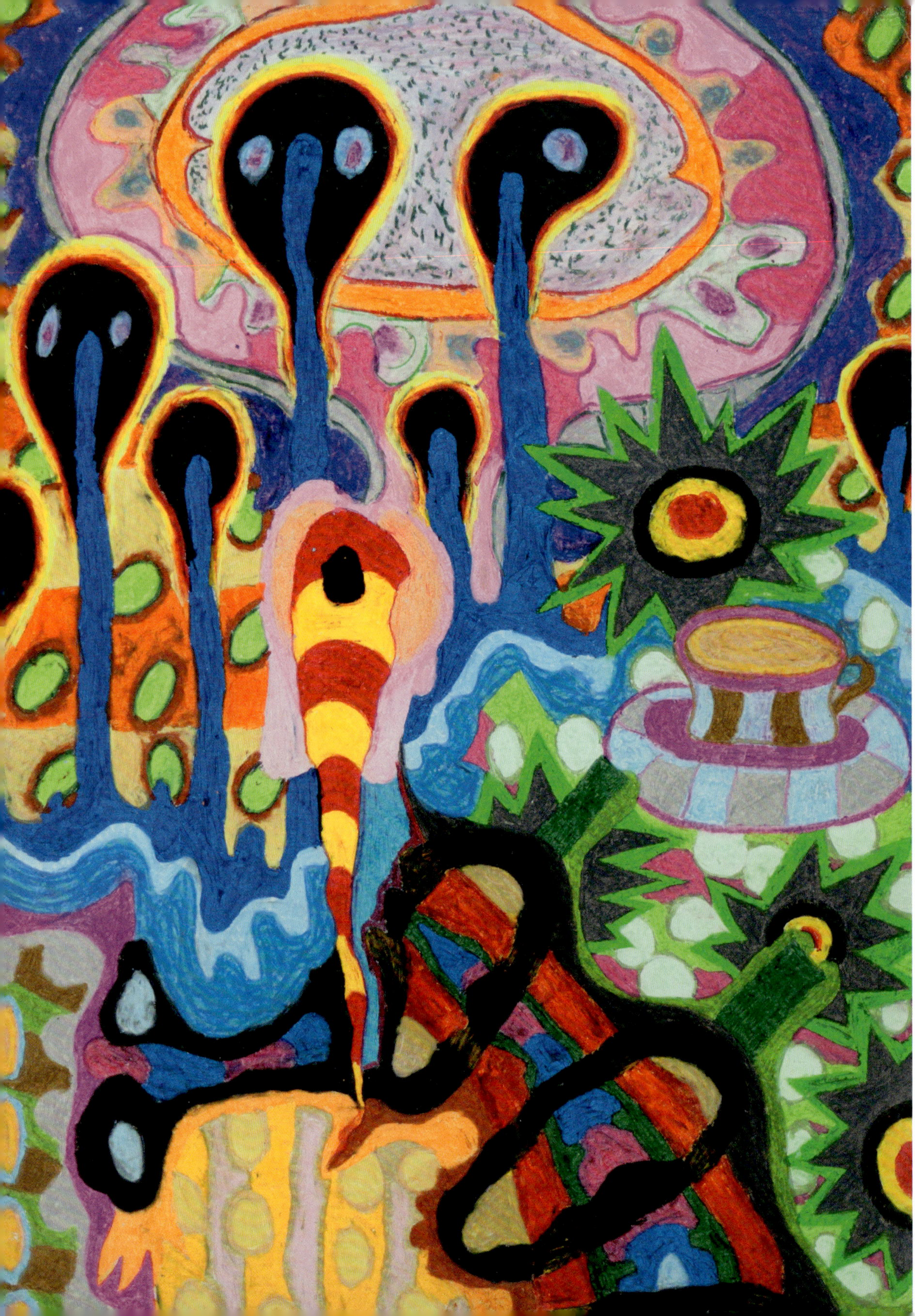

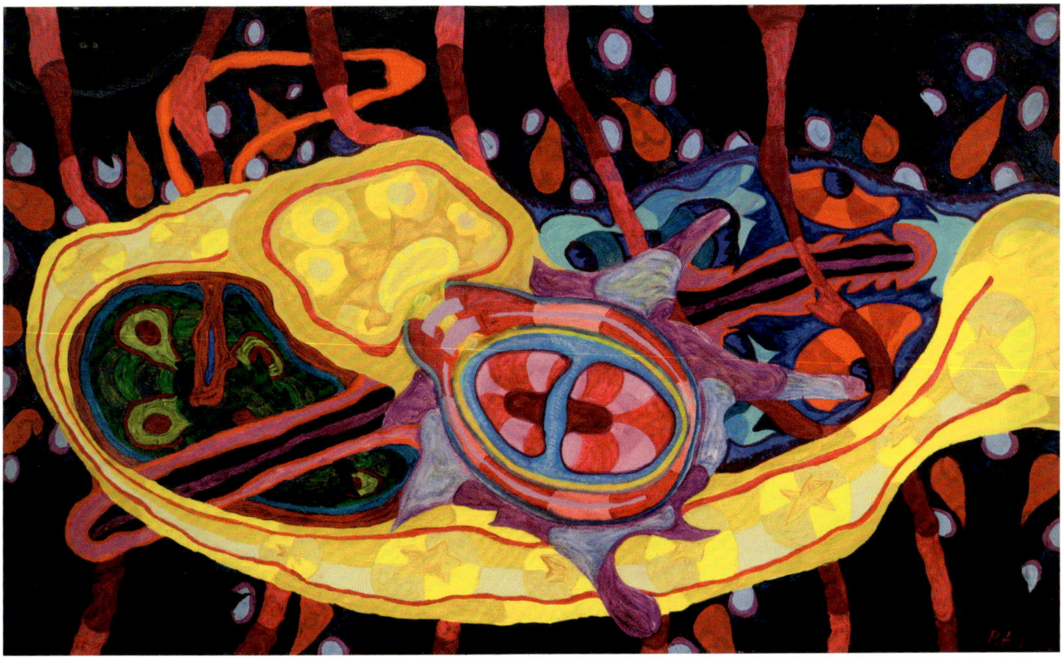

47
Panama, 1971
Pastell und Öl auf Papier, 80 x 62,6 cm
Panama, 1971
pastel and oil on paper, 80 x 62,6 cm

48
Astral Travelin, 1973
Aquarell, Öl auf Leinwand, 110 x 140 cm
Astral Travelin, 1973
watercolor, oil on canvas, 110 x 140 cm

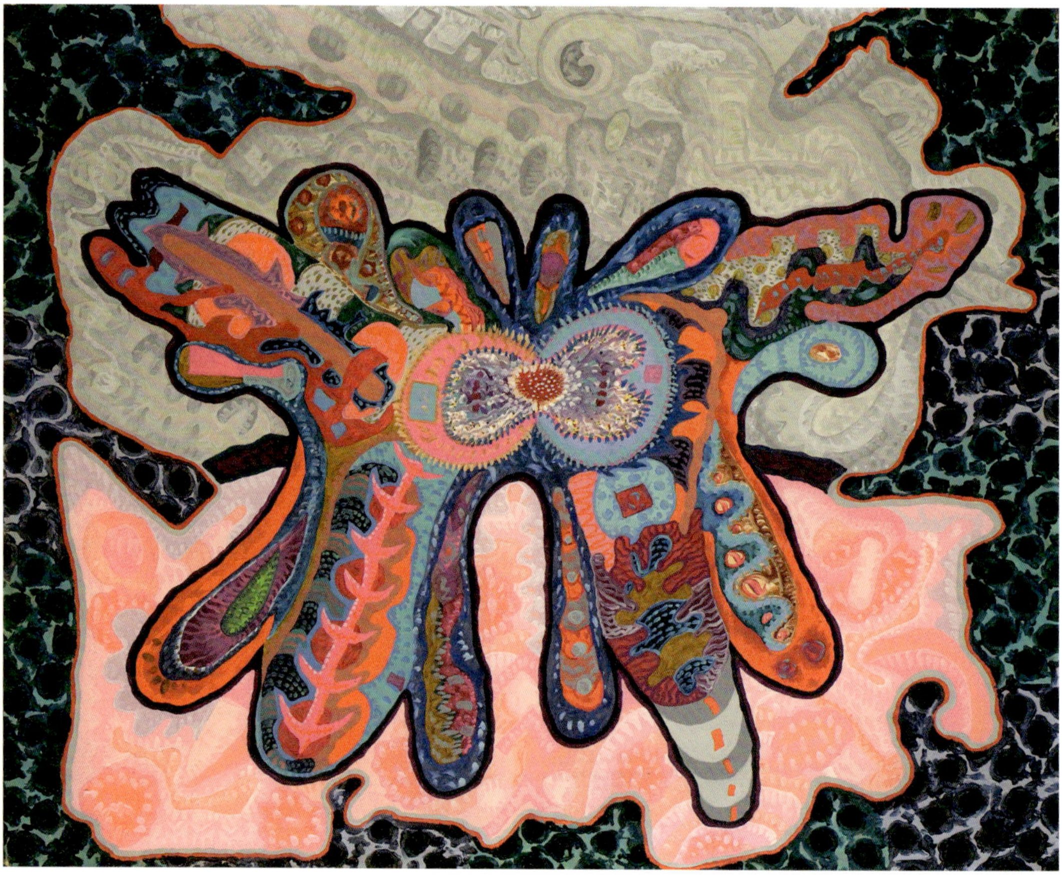

49
Baha, 1968
Öl auf Leinwand. 80 x 100,5 cm
Baha, 1968
oil on canvas, 80 x 100,5 cm

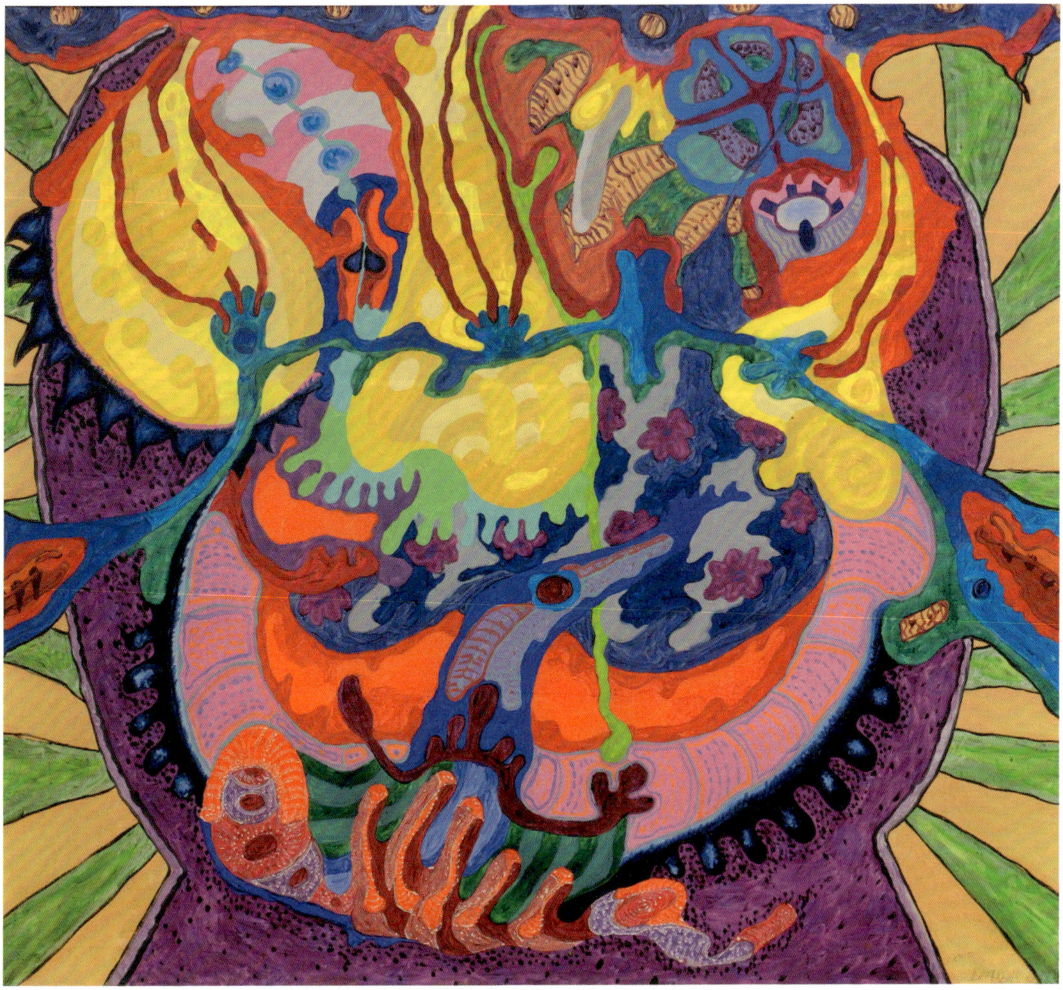

50
Audubon Ubiquist, 1974
Öl auf Leinwand, 90 x 100 cm
Audubon Ubiquist, 1974
oil on canvas, 90 x 100 cm

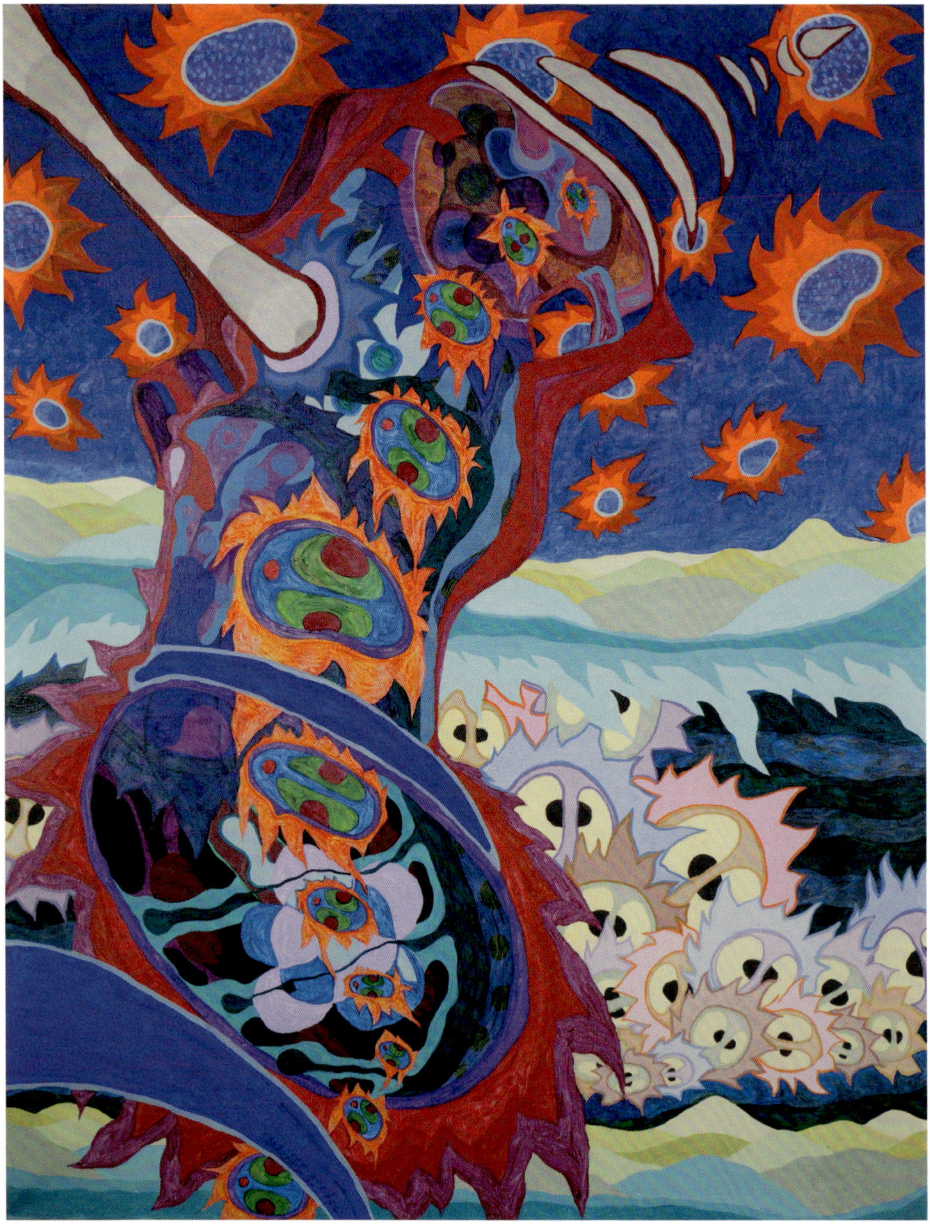

51
Al Khaf, undatiert (ca. 1970)
Öl auf Leinwand, 120 x 95 cm
Al Khaf, undated (ca. 1970)
oil on canvas, 120 x 95 cm

52
Bär, Himmeltapeten mit Drohung, 1975
Öl auf Leinwand, 100 x 80 cm
Bear, Sky Wallpapers with Threat, 1975
oil on canvas, 100 x 80 cm

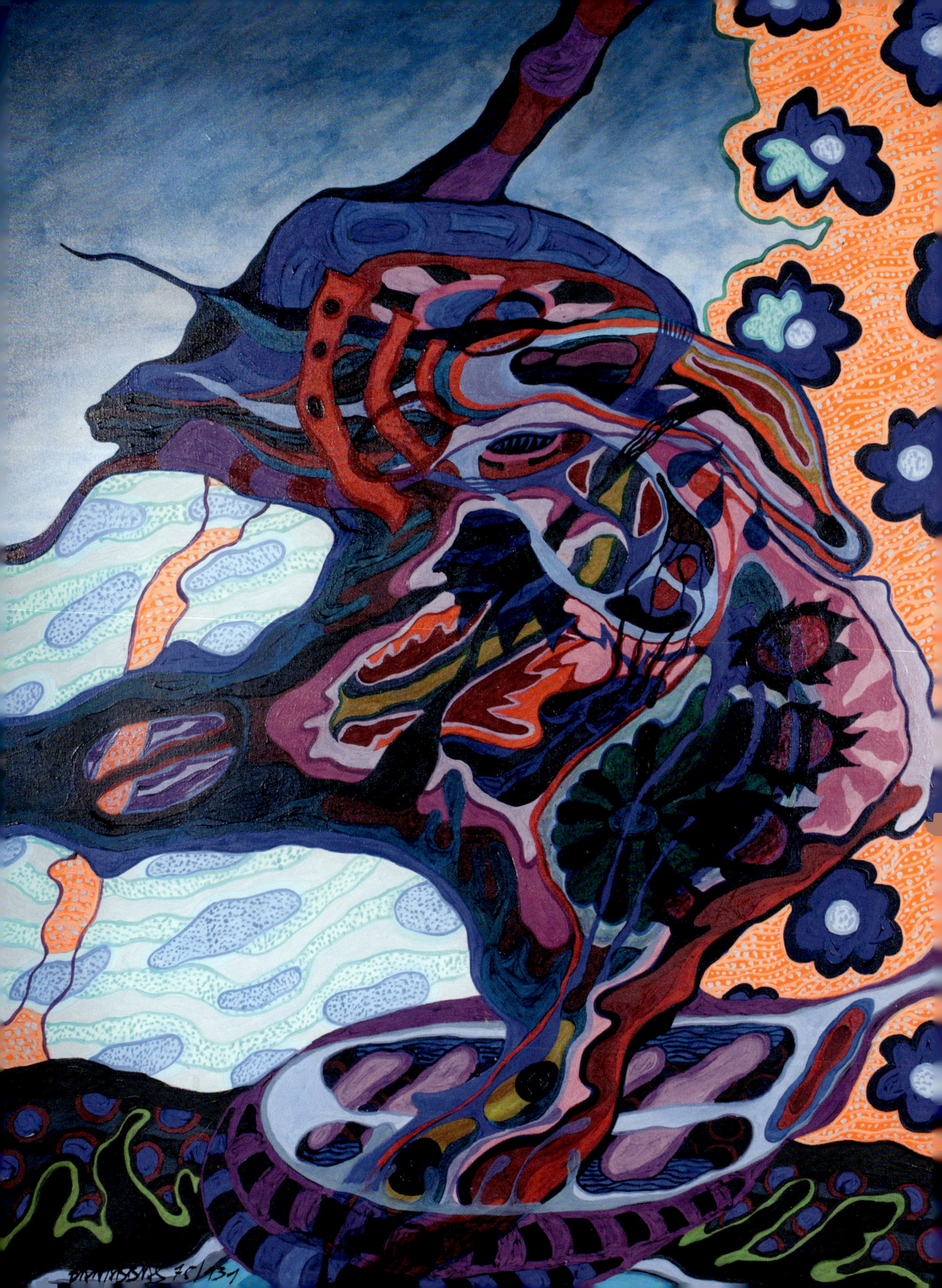

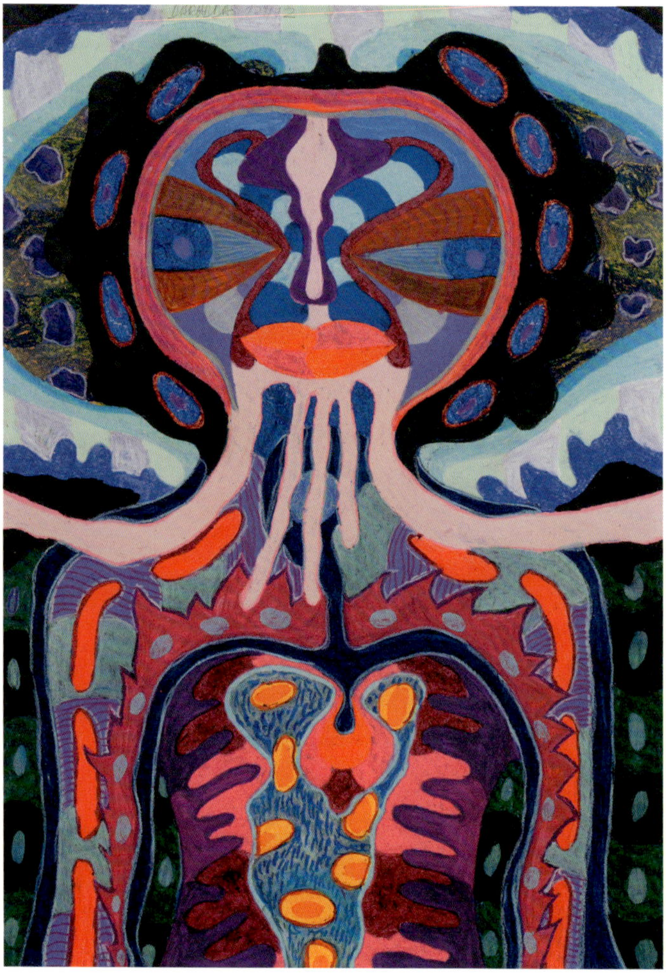

53
Archangel, 1972
Mischtechnik auf Papier, 85 x 60 cm
Archangel, 1972
mixed technique on paper, 85 x 60 cm

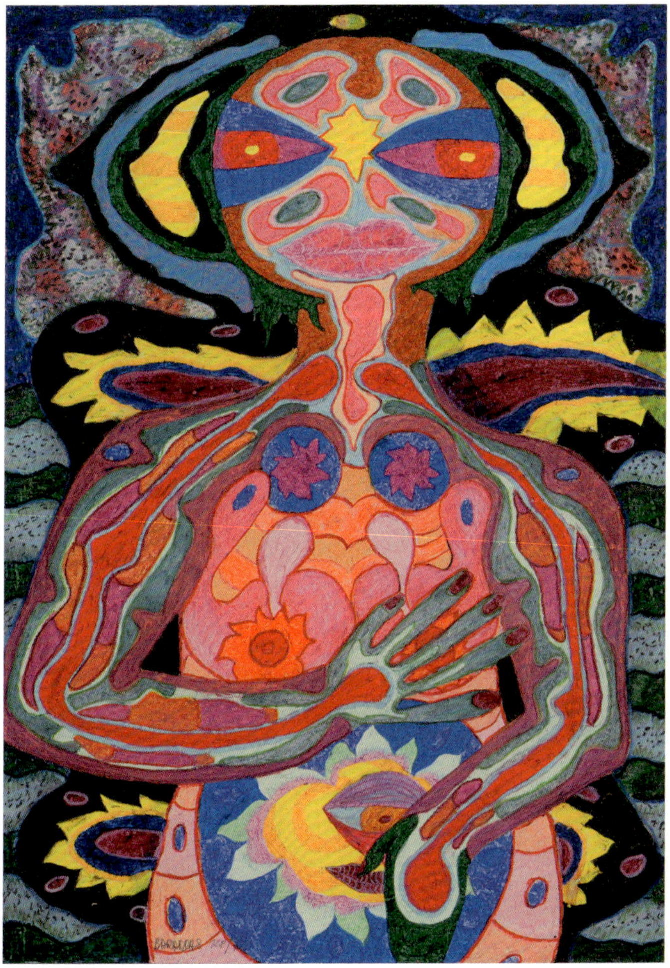

54
Archangel, 1972
Mischtechnik auf Papier, 85 x 60 cm
Archangel, 1972
mixed technique on paper, 85 x 60 cm

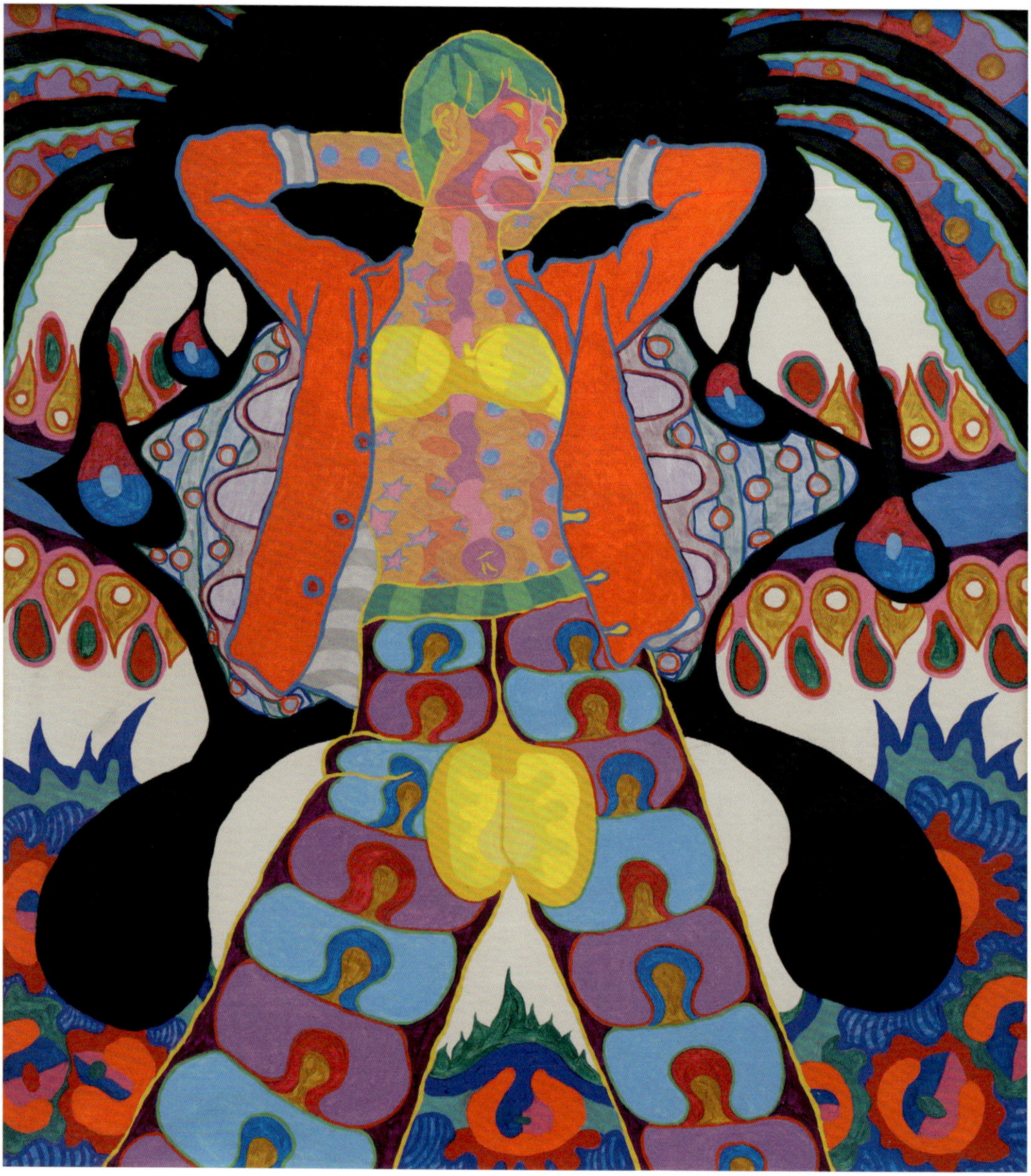

55
O.T., undatiert (erste Hälfte 1970er Jahre)
Öl auf Leinwand, 111,5 x 101,5 cm
Untitled, undated (first half of the 1970s)
oil on canvas, 111,5 x 101,5 cm

56
First Moves, 1975
Mischtechnik auf Leinwand, 100 x 70 cm
First Moves, 1975
mixed technique on canvas, 100 x 70 cm

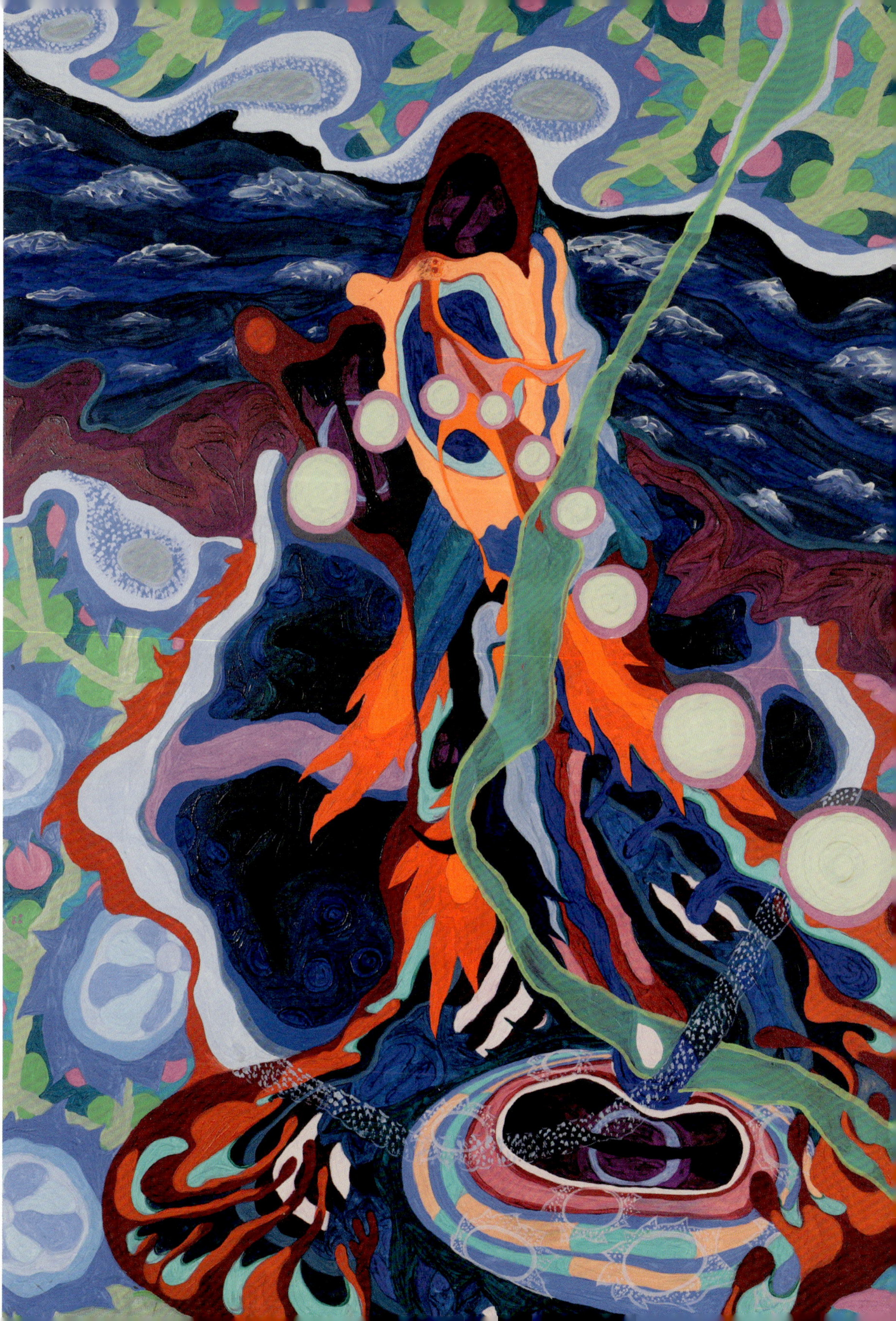

# BARABBAS, SHE & I

*Manfred M. Lang*

*"My aim in my art is to lose intention."*

How do I write about an artist whom I didn't know personally but could have known, even should have known? After all, my birth year is almost the same as his. One an artist, the other a gallery owner. He was a bit out there, and so am I. So it would've been only natural. Of course, I'd heard his name, and heard of some of his escapades as well. And yet we never actually met. All I can say in retrospect is: what a shame, a real shame.

So how do I write about BARABBAS, a stranger to me and, the more I study him, ever more a stranger? From a distanced vantage point? With sober technical elegance? By inventing a new artist from whole cloth, and let him turn in his grave? Or do I just leave a trail of admiring slime? Do I write as one for whom Barabbas's art is an open book, even though it has seven seals? Or do I approach the matter more modestly and turn to HER for help?

Do I start with Claus Mayrhofer, which is to say, with who he was before he became Barabbas? Do I focus on his worldly life? On his four women, his three daughters, his son; on his various bizarre habits, his sudden and hurried disappearance to Bali and Australia? Do I write about his unconditional and honest friendships, about the relationship with his first wife, the *"mother of my daughters,"* as he called HER, a relationship he maintained to his death?

Or should I be dutiful and give a chronological description and analysis of one picture after another in the exhibition at MUSA?

I think I'll write a little of everything. That may not be what academic professionalism demands, what you expect from a serious preface, but perhaps it'll help you get to know Barabbas and his art a bit better.

If you add up all the stories and funny anecdotes people have shared with me, it seems safe to say that Barabbas the artist was an individualist through and through, an artist driven by a primal urge. Or as Erwin Melchart described him on one occasion: "He was one of the queerest Bohemians of the Viennese scene in the 1960s, running through drab gray streets steeped in the musty and prissy atmosphere of Vienna's postwar reconstruction era as the long-haired terror incarnate of the middle classes, dressed in garish green pants, painting colorful pictures and ... playing bizarre free jazz."

# BARABBAS, SIE & ICH

Manfred M. Lang

*„Was ich in meiner Kunst anstrebe, ist, die Absicht zu verlieren."*

Wie schreibe ich über einen Künstler, den ich persönlich nicht kannte, den ich aber hätte kennen können, wenn nicht sogar müssen? Schließlich liegen unsere Geburtsjahre knapp beieinander. Der eine Künstler, der andere Galerist. Er ein bissl ausgezuckt und ich nicht minder. Da wär's doch nahegelegen. Natürlich kannte ich seinen Namen, bekam auch einiges von seinen Eskapaden mit. Trotzdem haben wir uns nie kennengelernt. Rückblickend kann ich nur sagen: schade, sehr schade.

Also wie schreibe ich über den BARABBAS, dieses für mich unbekannte – und je mehr ich mich mit ihm beschäftige, immer unbekanntere – Wesen? Distanziert? Fachlich-sachlich elegant? Indem ich einen gänzlich neuen Künstler erfinde, egal ob er sich im Grab umdreht oder nicht? Oder ziehe ich einfach nur eine bewundernde Schleimspur? Schreibe ich als einer, für den die Kunst des Barabbas ein offenes Buch ist, obwohl es doch sieben Siegel hat? Oder gehe ich's eher bescheiden an und halte mich an SIE?

Fange ich mit dem Claus Mayrhofer an, also mit dem, der er war, bevor er Barabbas wurde? Schreibe ich schwerpunktmäßig über sein profanes Leben? Über seine vier Frauen, über seine drei Töchter, über seinen Sohn, über seine diversen Skurrilitäten, sein plötzliches und eiliges Entschwinden nach Bali und Australien? Schreibe ich über seine bedingungslosen, ehrlichen Freundschaften, über seine bis zu seinem Tod gepflegte Beziehung zu seiner ersten Frau, der *„Mutter meiner Töchter"*, wie er SIE nannte?

Oder soll ich ein Bild nach dem anderen, das in der Ausstellung im MUSA hängt, im Katalog abgebildet ist, brav und chronologisch beschreiben und analysieren?

Ich glaube, ich schreibe von allem ein bissl was. Das mag wissenschaftlich – also so, wie es sich eigentlich für ein ernstzunehmendes Vorwort gehört – nicht sehr professionell sein, aber dafür lernt man Barabbas und seine Kunst vielleicht besser kennen.

Wenn man alle Erzählungen und Schnurren, die mich erreicht haben, zusammenzählt, dann kann man ruhigen Gewissens sagen, der Barabbas war ein durch und durch individualistischer Künstler, ein künstlerisches Urviech sozusagen. Oder, wie ihn Erwin Melchart einmal beschrieb: „Er war einer der schrägsten Bohemi-

As a painter, draftsman, musician, Barabbas was pretty singular in Vienna. And he was an art sponge – there was nothing that didn't draw his interest, that he didn't incorporate into his own artistic intuition. Be it folklore, pop art, Mexican or Native American folk art, naïve art, Surrealism, abstraction, art brut – Barabbas respected everything for what it was and let everything become part of his artistic universe. No underground phenomenon was too strange or too insignificant for him to lift it to his personal *"overground,"* as he once called it. And so he produced what Maria Buchsbaum has described as the Barabbasian "revolutionary utopian visions" that would define his entire life as an artist. "They flowed from the religious attitude underlying the complex of his pictorial themes, in which he matched Christian, Buddhist, and Islamic symbolism to his own psychedelic ornamentation, unreally heightened by gold and silver."

Let's leave it at that for a prelude and move on to Barabbas, the human being behind the artist, with whom everything seemed to happen on an impulse, chaotically, archaically, haphazardly and disorderly, and let's start with his life – with a brief biography whose most significant stages SHE compiled.

Claus Mayrhofer was born in Vienna in 1943. We don't really need to know whether he was well-behaved and neat or wild and truculent as a child. Since his was a good middle-class family, he was presumably brought up to be well-behaved. In other respects, he was probably a child like other children.

The first giant step toward his life as an artist came when Barabbas was fifteen – he met Padhi Frieberger, who introduced him to the Vienna arts scene around Galerie nächst St. Stephan: *"At the age of fifteen, I quite simply realized that I was an artist. This recognition came when I was confronted with other artists."* A little later, he dropped out of school and adopted the alias Barabbas.

Over the years, he would also add a number of monograms, as Barabbas once explained in a letter to Fritz Jelinek: *"In the early 1990s, I started signing more and more of my pictures as follows: CMay, Claus, CB, but I also still used BARABBAS, etc. The reason is very simple: because I was making more and more drawings and some were fairly small, BARABBAS sometimes looked too long, especially once I added the year, etc. I then gradually adopted this way of signing my works for my oil paintings as well. BVC – CBI – number ... it's a code. For the rest, all these names are mine anyway."*

His first key artistic experience was a painting action Georges Mathieu held at the Theater am Fleischmarkt in 1959. Afterwards, Mathieu gave him the leftover paints as a gift, attesting to his talent for networking in the art world.

ens der Wiener Szene in den sechziger Jahren, der als leibhafter Bürgerschreck im Wien der Nachkriegszeit, im muffig-braven Wiederaufbauklima, mit langen Haaren und in giftgrünen Hosen durch die grauen tristen Straßen lief, bunte Bilder malte und ... bizarren Freejazz spielte."

Barabbas war als Maler, Zeichner, Musiker in Wien ziemlich singulär. Und er war ein Kunstschwamm – es gab nichts, was ihn nicht interessiert hätte, was er nicht seiner eigenen künstlerischen Intuition einverleibt hätte. Ob Folklore, Pop-Art, mexikanische oder indianische Volkskunst, Naive Kunst, Surrealismus, Abstraktion, Art Brut – Barabbas ließ alles gelten und ließ alles in sein künstlerisches Universum einfließen. Nichts Undergroundiges war im fremd oder unbedeutend genug, um es nicht an seinen individuellen *„Overground"* zu holen, wie er es einmal ausdrückte. Und es entstanden, wie es Maria Buchsbaum nannte, die Barabbas'schen „revolutionären Utopien", die sein gesamtes Künstlerleben prägten. „Es entsprach der religiösen Grundhaltung seiner Bildthematik, darin er christliche, buddhistische und islamische Symbolik seiner – mit Gold und Silber irreal gehöhten – psychedelischen Ornamentik zuordnete."

Lassen wir das zunächst als Präludium so stehen und wechseln zu Barabbas, dem Menschen hinter dem Künstler, bei dem alles scheinbar so impulsiv, so chaotisch, so archaisch, so zufällig und ungeordnet zuging, und fangen wir mit der Biografie an. Mit einer Kurzbiografie, deren wichtigste Stationen SIE zusammengestellt hat.

Geboren wurde Claus Mayrhofer 1943 in Wien. Ob er als Kind brav und ordentlich oder wild und aufsässig war, hat uns eigentlich nicht wirklich zu interessieren. Da er aus einem gutbürgerlichen Haus stammte, wurde er wohl brav erzogen. Sonst war er wahrscheinlich ein Kind wie so viele andere auch.

Dass Barabbas mit 15 Jahren Padhi Frieberger kennenlernte, der ihn mit der Wiener Kunstszene rund um die Galerie nächst St. Stephan bekannt machte, war bereits der erste Riesenschritt in Richtung Künstlerdasein: *„Mit fünfzehn Jahren erkannte ich ganz einfach, dass ich Künstler bin, und zwar durch die Konfrontation mit anderen Künstlern."* Kurz darauf schmiss er die Schule hin und legte sich den Künstlernamen Barabbas zu.

Im Laufe der Zeit kam auch noch eine Menge von Monogrammen dazu, wie Barabbas einmal in einem Brief an Fritz Jelinek erklärte: *„In den frühen 90er Jahren begann ich, immer öfter meine Bilder folgendermaßen zu signieren: CMay, Claus, CB, aber auch noch BARABBAS etc. Der Grund ist ganz einfach: Da ich immer mehr und mehr Zeichnungen machte und manche auch relativ klein sind, wirkte BARABBAS manchmal zu lang, noch dazu mit der Jahreszahl usw. Nach und nach übernahm ich*

Barabbas first exhibited his work, pictures in the style of *art informel*, at Galerie zum roten Apfel in 1960, and soon became a member of the group "Zum roten Apfel." With Walter Malli, Richard Pechoc, and Karl Anton Fleck, he founded the legendary "Masters of Unorthodox Jazz." An so he moved smoothly and uncompromisingly between the rhythm of free jazz and the pulsing rhythm of colors and shapes that gave his pictures their ecstatic appeal.

From 1964 to 1969, he lived in Reichenau an der Rax in his parents' villa. Regular visitors included Fuchs, Malli, Pechoc, and Stangl; with temporary roommates like Othmar Zechyr, they turned the villa into a rural idyll where everything breathed art.

Between 1970 and 1981, Barabbas was a member of the group "Der Kreis." It was also during this period that he created the painting "Big Bang," also titled "Genesis," a monumental work measuring roughly 1980 sq ft (12 by 165 ft) that was displayed in 1975 as part of his grand retrospective at the Künstlerhaus.

After an extended stay in New York (1977) and the subsequent black period in his painting, he disappeared in 1986, moving via Bali – partly because he felt drawn to the country, partly because he wanted to escape Austria – to Australia, where he lived until his death in 2009.

We don't know for sure whether Barabbas was ever seized by real homesickness for Austria. There are frequent overtones to suggest as much in his various Australian diary notes, although he repeatedly emphasized to himself that nothing but vexations awaited him in Vienna.

SHE and his friend Fritz Jelinek in Vienna were often the addressees of his grand confessions – he would give accounts of his life and artistic work. Many letters contained reports of his financial calamities: *"I'm making small and very small works on paper – so at least each one of them is a picture. That way, I can save paper ... but I'll be running out of ink soon ... no turpentine, no primer, few brushes, and the ochers are used up ..."* The financial hardship that marked his life in Australia is also a central subject in many of his diary notes. In others, Barabbas sensitively and sometimes painstakingly examined his artistic ambitions, his compositional inventions, and his practices. These observations include observations and insights that would have done Barabbas honor if he'd been an art philosopher – that, I admit, did surprise me.

To give a few examples:

*"Last night, today's morning was the future, and now the period at the end of this sentence is the future."*

*dann auch diese Art zu signieren bei meinen Ölbildern. BVC – CBI – Nummer … ist ein Code. Außerdem sind alle diese Namen ja ohnedies meine."*

Sein erstes künstlerisches Schlüsselerlebnis war eine Malaktion von Georges Mathieu 1959 im Theater am Fleischmarkt. Dass ihm danach Mathieu gleich die übriggebliebenen Farben schenkte, spricht für sein Talent zum künstlerischen Netzwerken.

1960 stellte Barabbas erstmals mit seinen informellen Bildern in der Galerie zum roten Apfel aus, kurz darauf wurde er bereits Mitglied der Gruppe „Zum roten Apfel" – und gründete mit Walter Malli, Richard Pechoc und Karl Anton Fleck die legendären „Masters of Unorthodox Jazz". Und so wechselte er bruch- und kompromisslos zwischen dem Rhythmus des Freejazz und dem pulsierenden Farb- und Formrhythmus seiner ekstatisch wirkenden Bilder hin und her.

Von 1964 bis 1969 lebte er in Reichenau an der Rax in der Villa seiner Eltern. Häufige Gäste waren Fuchs, Malli, Pechoc, Stangl, die gemeinsam mit zeitweiligen Mitbewohnern wie Othmar Zechyr die Villa zur ländlichen und kunstintensiven Idylle machten.

1970 bis 1981 war Barabbas Mitglied der Gruppe „Der Kreis". In dieser Zeit entstand auch sein monumentales, knapp 200 m$^2$ (ca. 3,5 x 50 m) großes Gemälde „Big Bang", auch „Genesis" genannt, das 1975 in seiner großen Retrospektive im Künstlerhaus gezeigt wurde.

Nach einem längeren Aufenthalt in New York (1977) und seiner darauffolgenden schwarzen Malperiode verschwand er 1986 – halb zog es ihn, halb floh er hin – über Bali nach Australien, wo er bis zu seinem Tod 2009 blieb.

Ob Barabbas je echtes Heimweh nach Österreich gepackt hat, wissen wir nicht so genau. In seinen diversen australischen Tagebuchnotizen klang das oftmals durch, obwohl er sich immer wieder bestätigte, dass ihn in Wien nur Unbill erwarten würde.

SIE und sein Freund Fritz Jelinek in Wien waren sehr oft die Adressaten seiner menschlichen und künstlerischen Lebenszeichen. Häufig waren es Berichte über seine finanziellen Kalamitäten: *„Ich mache kleine und kleinste Arbeiten auf Papier – immerhin ist jedes dann ein Bild. Auf diese Weise kann ich Papier sparen … doch mit der Tinte geht es bald zu Ende … kein Terpentin, keine Grundiermasse, wenig Pinsel und die Ocker sind alle …"* Seine finanzielle Not in Australien stand auch immer wieder im Mittelpunkt seiner Tagebuchnotizen. Darüber hinaus äußerte sich Barabbas sensibel und auch penibel über seine künstlerischen Ambitionen, seine Bildfindungen und Arbeitsvorgänge. Dass dabei Formulierungen und Statements

*"An artist is always a bit like a magician, more or less honest, seasoned, inspired, but always magical, even if he avails himself of the craftsman's bag of tricks."*

*"The artist is illogical, but he relies on logical means for illogical answers."*

*"The artist is rational where that is the easy path to the answer, but irrational where necessary."*

*"I'm not interested in using art to demonstrate my ego – rather, I want to realize what is there but not yet seen."*

Barabbas had always had a particularly profound and intensely felt bond with nature, and especially with mountains, as the following email to HER, dated October 25, 2007, illustrates:

*"Mountains are something sensual. You see them in the distance, hike to their summits, and then gaze into the distance. You are among boulders, among rocks, and there's a different vibration to the air than, say, by the sea. Boulders sing. Mountains sing. The rock sings, and so does the shape, depending on the time of day and the weather, etc. In Bali, I lived directly at the foot of the active volcano known as Gunung Agung (Great Mountain). It murmurs its song to itself, you might say, a sort of recitation. Very present and dignified.*

*It's not the wind I mean, nor the rumbling of rocks and their crackling in the cold or the heat, though that's certainly part of it; what I'm alluding to is the quiet song that, we might say, the inner ear perceives, a song that then also gives rise, for example, to the music of the Alps and of the Andes, the seething of the ever-present great volcanic mountain in Balinese music, or an expansiveness that can be heard, for instance, in Gustav Mahler. Everything, in fact, sings and vibrates in one way or another, even people. And that's why there is music and painting, and art most generally, in the first place."*

Just as jazz is governed by a kind of order and clarity, Barabbas's works of art, with all their ostensible randomness, are everything but merely spontaneous and impulsive.

Yet reducing Barabbas to his profound emotionality and spontaneity doesn't do him justice. His painting style, for example, which seems so haphazard and explosive, is professionalized and implemented using very carefully chosen painting and graphic materials. The artist closely studies the different techniques and materials of painting. For instance, he writes about his preference for mixing alkyd resin with oil: *"the advantage is that alkyd is highly elastic ... rendering the surface much more elastic ..."* With ink, he likewise has a clear vision of what he wants – his favorite is Herbin black pearl: *"It is the blackest ink. It is*

zu finden sind, die einem Kunstphilosophen Barabbas zur Ehre gereicht hätten, war für mich dann doch überraschend.

Hier einige Beispiele:

*„Gestern Abend war der heutige Morgen Zukunft, und jetzt ist der Punkt am Ende des Satzes Zukunft."*

*„Ein Künstler ist immer etwas wie ein Zauberer, mehr oder weniger ehrlich, routiniert, inspiriert, aber immer magisch, auch wenn er sich der handwerklichen Trickkiste bedient."*

*„Der Künstler ist unlogisch, bedient sich aber logischer Mittel für unlogische Antworten."*

*„Der Künstler ist rational dort, wo es der einfache Weg zur Antwort ist, aber irrational, wo es notwendig ist."*

*„Es geht mir nicht um die Demonstration meines Egos in der Kunst, sondern vielmehr um die Verwirklichung dessen, was vorhanden ist, aber noch nicht gesehen wird."*

Zur Natur und vor allem zu den Bergen hatte Barabbas immer schon eine besonders innige und intensive Beziehung, wie in nachfolgendem E-Mail vom 25. Oktober 2007 an SIE zu lesen ist:

*„Berge sind etwas Sinnliches. Man sieht sie von der Ferne, steigt hinauf und sieht in die Ferne. Man befindet sich zwischen den Felsen, dem Gestein und die Luft vibriert anders als z. B. am Meer. Felsen singen. Berge singen. Das Gestein singt und die Form ebenfalls, je nach der Tageszeit und dem Wetter usw. Auf Bali wohnte ich direkt am Fuß des aktiven Vulkans namens Gunung Agung (Großer Berg). Er murmelt seinen Gesang sozusagen vor sich hin, so eine Art Rezitation. Sehr präsent und würdig.*

*Ich meine hier nicht den Wind, oder das Poltern von Steinen und das Knacken in der Kälte oder Hitze, das gehört sowieso auch dazu, hingegen spiele ich auf den stillen Gesang an, den sozusagen das innere Ohr wahrnimmt und der dann auch z. B. die Alpenmusik und die der Anden hervorbringt, das Brodelnde des immer anwesenden großen Vulkan-Berges in der balinesischen Musik, oder eine Weite, die z. B. bei Gustav Mahler hörbar wird. Eigentlich singt und vibriert alles auf diese oder jene Weise, auch Menschen. Und deshalb gibt es Musik und Malerei, ja die Kunst überhaupt."*

Genauso wie Jazz einer Ordnung und Klarheit unterworfen ist, genauso sind die Kunstwerke von Barabbas in ihrer scheinbaren Zufälligkeit alles andere als bloß spontan und impulsiv.

Wenn man Barabbas jetzt nur auf seine tiefe Emotionalität und Spontanität festlegt, würde man ihm nicht gerecht werden. Sein so zufällig und explosiv er-

*of superior quality and used throughout Europe by notaries for signatures on documents. That's because of one particular quality: instead of fading over the centuries, it grows darker."* Barabbas grinds his own inks from hard Chinese ink sticks, and he says about his quills that *"I cut my own goose, duck, peafowl, etc. feathers. The technical preparation is a minor science unto itself, and all I want to say is that no quill is exactly the same. With some quills, I use hot sand to harden them, with others, I use water, and there are yet other methods, such as cutting them untreated. Any quill from the bird's wing is slightly curved, and making the right cut requires ... well, courage."*

The paper he used and its preparation were essential to Barabbas:

*"I prefer watercolor or drawing paper that's not too thick (heavy), which is to say, that has no more than 200 gsm. It also shouldn't be too rough. The Hahnemühle paper I use is my roughest paper ... For some watercolors and drawings, I don't stretch the paper too tightly because (unlike the academic tradition) I use the slight arching the pictures develop to lend them another dimension generated by variations in the lighting conditions (also depending on the time of day).*

*I employ different methods of stretching the paper and designing the format.*

*A) Soaking the water in paper and stretching it using gummed adhesive tape. This produces very even paper, without arching or bumps. It is advisable to drain the paper well and let it dry just a bit (rolling it out also helps) ...*

*B) Stretching the dry paper using gummed adhesive tape and, once the tape has dried, using a sponge to wet the paper.*

*C) Moistening the paper on the reverse using a sponge and stretching the dry obverse using gummed adhesive tape.*

*D) Using self-adhesive tape (masking tape) on dry paper, which leaves a sharp edge once you remove the tape. I often combine this with method (C), but use masking tape instead of gummed paper tape ...*

*I also use liquid rubber (called masking fluid in the English-speaking world). This rubber solution covers the paper, and once it has dried, you can rub it off, leaving blank spots where the paper was covered. I just have to watch out that the rubber doesn't stay on the paper for too long – let's say, a week in the winter, a few days in the summer – or it'll get sticky again and difficult or even impossible to rub off. This method lets me produce uneven edges, among other things, but I also use this fluid inside the drawing or watercolor.*

scheinender Malstil zum Beispiel wird mit genau überlegten Mal- und Zeichenmaterialien professionalisiert und ausgeführt. Er setzt sich intensiv mit den verschiedenen Maltechniken und -materialien auseinander. So schreibt er, dass er am liebsten Alkydharz mit Öl vermischt: *„Der Vorteil ist, dass Alkyd sehr elastisch ist, ... was die Oberfläche wesentlich elastischer macht ..."* Auch bei Tinte hat er klare Vorstellungen – er verwendet am liebsten Herbin-Perlschwarz: *„Sie ist die schwärzeste Tinte. Sie ist von hoher Qualität und wird europaweit von Notaren für Unterschriften an Dokumenten verwendet. Dies wegen ihrer Eigenschaft, dass sie, anstelle über Jahrhunderte auszubleichen, nachdunkelt."* Chinesische Hartreibtusche reibt sich Barabbas selbst an, und über seine Federn sagt er: *„Federn von Gänsen, Enten, Pfauen etc. schneide ich mir selbst. Die technische Vorbereitung ist eine kleine Wissenschaft an sich und ich will nur sagen, dass keine Feder gleich ausfällt. Manche Federn härte ich mit Hilfe von heißem Sand, andere mit Wasser und es gibt noch andere Methoden wie z. B. sie unbehandelt zu schneiden. Jede Flügel-Feder hat eine leichte Kurve und den Schnitt richtig anzubringen erfordert ... naja, Mut."*

Wesentlich waren für Barabbas das verwendete Papier und seine Bearbeitung:

*„Ich bevorzuge nicht zu dickes (starkes) Aquarell- und Zeichenpapier, mit anderen Worten nicht über 200 gsm. Auch soll es nicht zu rau sein. Das Hahnemühlepapier, welches ich verwende, ist das raueste Papier ... Bei manchen Aquarellen und Zeichnungen spanne ich das Papier nicht zu straff auf, da ich (im Gegensatz zur akademischen Tradition) den Bildern dadurch, da sie sich leicht wölben, eine weitere Dimension verleihe, die durch den variierenden Lichteinfall (auch der Tageszeiten) entsteht.*

*Ich verwende verschiedene Methoden des Aufspannens und der Formatgestaltung.*

*A) Das Papier in Wasser einweichen und mit gummiertem Klebestreifen aufspannen. Das Papier wird auf diese Weise sehr glatt, ohne Wölbungen oder Buckel. Hier ist es ratsam, das Papier zuvor abrinnen und etwas antrocknen zu lassen (auswalzen hilft auch) ...*

*B) Das Papier trocken mit gummierten Klebestreifen aufspannen und, nachdem die Klebestreifen getrocknet sind, das Papier mit einem Schwamm nässen.*

*C) Das Papier auf der Rückseite mit einem Schwamm benetzen und die trockene Vorderseite mit gummierten Klebestreifen aufspannen.*

*D) Selbstklebende Klebestreifen (Maskierband) auf dem trockenen Papier verwenden, was dann beim Abspannen einen scharfen Rand hinterlässt. Hier verwende ich dann auch oft Methode C), aber anstelle gummierten Papierbands verwende ich Maskierband ...*

*The paper is often too white for my taste, and I don't like tinted paper very much. So I use coffee, tea, diluted ground ink, or graphite and coal dust, and in the graphic works of the early 1980s, I also boiled cigarette butts to tint the paper…*

That brings me to his pictures. They're not easy to experience and to get a sense of, to feel and to truly understand; it takes all the senses you have at your disposal. Their opulence is often overwhelming and intoxicating, because they are the products of a positively inexhaustible and boisterously expansive pictorial act.

Barabbas wasn't unaware of the massive impact of his pictures:

*"Visitor! Keep in mind that my pictures take time.*

*Imagine that nothing distracts you and you look at my picture again and again… an almost cosmic effect will emerge.*

*But you can't do that because you're distracted by other stimuli and by desires as well. Still, even the mere idea of your understanding what I mean will clarify some things to you for the future."*

Of course, I might continue with descriptions of various pictures in which I would throw around quotes about comparable art and give a more or less off-key sketch of Barabbas's international significance. But that's not my intention – I'd rather let Barabbas speak for himself, because I want to bring out the intensity, profound reflection, and dedication he brought to the engagement with his art. To my mind – and, I believe, any beholder of his pictures will find the same – that's more authentic and meaningful than any interpretation by a third party.

To let Barabbas speak for himself, I've selected two pictures that are of eminent artistic quality and for which we have personal notes from the artist's hand that demonstrate the intellectual acuity and focus of his work.

The first of these pictures bears the title "Time Cycle" (fig. 89); Barabbas described it as follows:

*"This picture is my father's life and his death. Because I couldn't be there for his burial, I buried him in this picture. The 'tree' on the left spreads out and bends and explodes in life. Between the tree on the left and the one striving upward, there is a dark green lawn – his grave. Then I laid my father in it and painted over it. Yet a new tree grows out of this grave ( – into infinity).*

*But there's another interpretation there – my identification.*

*As you can see, the new tree grows in front and out of a gate = BAB – praised be its threshold!*

*Auch verwende ich flüssigen Gummi (engl. masking-fluid). Diese Gummilösung deckt das Papier ab und kann, wenn er getrocknet ist, später abgerieben werden und das zuvor abgedeckte Papier bleibt blank. Ich muss nur aufpassen, dass der Gummi nicht zu lange am Papier gelassen wird, sagen wir eine Woche im Winter und ein paar Tage im Sommer, ansonsten wird er wieder klebrig und ist sehr schwer bis unmöglich abzureiben. Diese Methode erlaubt mir u. a. einen unregelmäßigen Rand, aber ich verwende dieses Fluid auch innerhalb der Zeichnung oder des Aquarells.*

*Oft ist mir das Papier zu weiß und getöntes Papier mag ich weniger. So verwende ich Kaffee, Tee, verdünnte Reibtusche oder Graphit und Kohlestaub und verwendete bei den Grafiken der frühen 80er Jahre auch ausgekochte Zigarettenstummel, um das Papier zu tönen …"*

Damit komme ich zu seinen Bildern. Sie sind nicht einfach zu erleben und zu empfinden, zu erfühlen und zu durchdringen, da bedarf es schon aller Sinne, die einem zur Verfügung stehen. Denn die Opulenz ist oft überwältigend und berauschend, weil aus einem schier unerschöpflichen und übermütigen Malakt entstanden.

Barabbas war sich der Wucht seiner Bilder durchaus bewusst:

*„Besucher! Bedenke, dass meine Bilder Zeit in Anspruch nehmen.*

*Stell Dir vor, dass nichts Dich ablenkt und Du schaust immer wieder und wieder auf mein Bild … dann entsteht ein nahezu kosmischer Effekt.*

*Das ist Dir aber nicht möglich, da Du von anderen Reizen, ja auch Wünschen abgelenkt wirst. Aber wenigstens die Vorstellung davon, dass Du begreifst, was ich meine, wird Dir einiges für Deine Zukunft klar machen."*

Ich könnte hier natürlich diverse Bildbeschreibungen anfügen, mit Kunstvergleichszitaten um mich werfen und den nationalen und internationalen Stellenwert von Barabbas mehr oder weniger verquer herausarbeiten. Aber das ist nicht meine Intention – ich lasse lieber Barabbas selbst zu Wort kommen, denn ich will zeigen, mit welcher Intensität, mit welchen Überlegungen und mit welchem Engagement er sich mit seinen Bildern auseinandergesetzt hat. Das ist für mich und, wie ich glaube, für jeden Betrachter seiner Bilder authentischer und sinnvoller als jede Fremdinterpretation.

Ich habe, um Barabbas selbst sprechen zu lassen, zwei Bilder ausgesucht, die von sehr hoher künstlerischer Qualität sind und zu denen es persönliche Anmerkungen von Barabbas gibt, die zeigen, wie intensiv er sich mit seinen Arbeiten auch gedanklich beschäftigt hat.

*The tree on the left – myself – man – bows before the gate = BAB in order to partake of the insight of Saint Bayan (one of his books of revelation) and reach BAHA'U'LLAH – o Glory of Glories! His name sits upon a throne in the heavens above all! If all that strikes you as laying it on rather thickly, I can understand, but that's the way I think, and words are often more difficult than glazes – ha, ha!"*

Regarding the second picture entitled "$E = mc^2$" – Elisabeth Voggeneder is going into detail within her text (51, fig. 95) - we read the following in his notes:

*"As you can see at first glance, I've reused a detail in the picture 'Genesis' in order to 'rework an old idea,' as it were.*

*Of course, the special and then the general theory of relativity pose virtually insurmountable obstacles to 'thematic' depiction, but that's not what I was/am interested in. What's important is that I pondered the matter and studied it with great focus as I was painting. (I don't claim that I've understood everything completely, especially when it comes to the general theory of relativity.)"*

Do I now know more about Barabbas, even though I never met him? Do I now understand his intentions, can I read his thoughts and desires from his pictures? Can that be done, and it should it even? Will I be able to see a picture he didn't write anything about from his eyes? I'd like to – that much I admit.

But perhaps it's better and more meaningful to try and find my way through his visual universe entirely by myself – or even better, to lose my way in it, to wander aimlessly, and to look for his cosmos, his fantasies, within myself? However that may be – one thing surely isn't going to work: looking past his pictures with a generous attitude.

Let me conclude by paying homage. It was important for me to have met HER. SHE – Rosemarie Sebek – his first wife and the mother of his daughters. Without her determination to keep the memory of the artist Barabbas alive, without her untiring activities and her dedication to collecting everything necessary and worth knowing about him and to buttress his oeuvre with all that requires, Barabbas would surely have been forgotten.

Thanks to her, the present catalogue and the retrospective at the Künstlerhaus and MUSA will demonstrate persuasively that Barabbas is an eminently important Austrian artist of the second half of the twentieth century.

(All quotations from Barabbas are taken from unpublished diary notes and letters provided to me by Ms. Rosemarie Sebek.)

Das erste dieser Bilder nannte er „Time Cycle" (Abb. 89) und beschrieb es folgendermaßen:

*„Dieses Bild ist das Leben meines Vaters und sein Tod. Da ich bei seinem Begräbnis nicht dabei sein konnte, begrub ich ihn in diesem Bild. Der linke ‚Baum' spreizt und biegt und explodiert im Leben. Zwischen dem linken und dem aufstrebenden Baum ist eine dunkelgrüne Rasenfläche – sein Grab. Dann habe ich meinen Vater hinein gelegt und darüber gemalt. Doch aus diesem Grab wächst ein neuer Baum (– in die Unendlichkeit). Doch da ist noch eine andere Ausdeutung – meine Identifikation. Wie man sieht, wächst der neue Baum vor und aus einem Tor = BAB – gepriesen sei seine Stufe!*

*Der linke Baum – ich – der Mensch – beugt sich vor dem Tor = BAB, um durch die Erkenntnis des Hl. Bayan (eines seiner Offenbarungsbücher) hin zu BAHA'U'LLAH – oh Herrlichkeit der Herrlichkeiten – zu gelangen. Sein Name thront am Himmel über allem! Wenn Dir das alles zu dick aufgetragen vorkommt, dann kann ich das auch verstehen, aber ich denke eben auf solche Weise und Worte sind oft schwerer als Lasuren – ha, ha!"*

Über das zweite Bild, auf das Elisabeth Voggeneder bereits in ihrem Text detailliert eingeht und das den Titel „$E = mc^2$" trägt (S. 51, Abb. 95), liest man in seinen Aufzeichnungen unter anderem:

*„Wie man hier sofort erkennen kann, habe ich ein Detail des Bildes ‚Genesis' wieder verwendet, sozusagen um einen ‚alten Gedanken neu' zu bearbeiten.*

*Die spezielle und weiters generelle Relativitätstheorie lässt sich natürlich ‚thematisch' kaum darstellen, aber darum ging/geht es mir nicht. Wichtig dabei ist, dass ich während des Malens intensiv darüber nachdachte und studierte. (Ich erhebe nicht den Anspruch, alles komplett verstanden zu haben, insbesondere wenn es zur Generellen Relativ. Theorie kommt.)"*

Weiß ich jetzt mehr von Barabbas, obwohl ich ihn nie kennengelernt habe? Verstehe ich jetzt seine Intentionen und kann ich aus seinen Bildern seine Gedanken und Wünsche dazu herauslesen? Wird mir das, soll mir das überhaupt gelingen? Werde ich ein Bild, über das er nichts geschrieben hat, mit seinen Augen sehen können? Wollen tät' ich schon ganz gern – ich geb's zu.

Aber vielleicht ist es besser und sinnvoller, mich ganz allein in seiner Bilderwelt zurechtzufinden – oder besser noch zu verlieren, zu verirren und seinen Kosmos, seine Phantasien in mir zu suchen? Wie auch immer – eines geht sicher nicht: über seine Bilder zügig drüberzuschauen.

Abschließend noch eine Reverenzerklärung. Es war für mich wichtig, SIE kennengelernt zu haben. SIE – Rosemarie Sebek – seine erste Frau und die Mutter seiner Töchter. Ohne ihren Willen, den Künstler Barabbas präsent zu halten, ohne ihre unermüdlichen Aktivitäten, alles Notwendige und Wissenswerte über ihn zu sammeln und sein Werk mit allen nur möglichen Notwendigkeiten zu untermauern, wäre Barabbas sicher dem Vergessen anheimgefallen.

Ihr, diesem Katalog und der retrospektiven Ausstellung im Künstlerhaus und im MUSA wird es gelingen, nachzuweisen, dass Barabbas einer der ganz wichtigen österreichischen Künstler der zweiten Hälfte des 20. Jahrhunderts ist.

(Sämtliche Zitate von Barabbas entstammen unveröffentlichten Tagebuchnotizen und Briefen, die mir von Frau Rosemarie Sebek zur Verfügung gestellt wurden.)

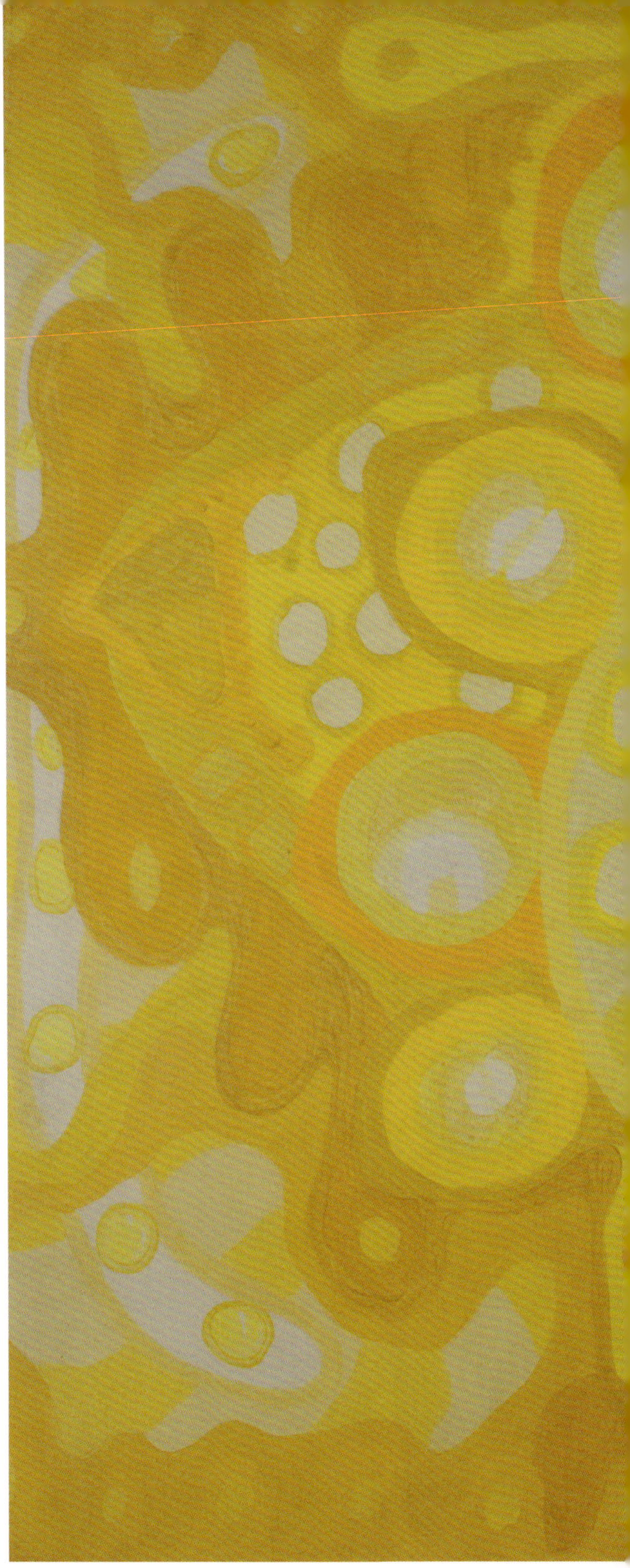

57
Aztekensonne, 1967
Mischtechnik auf Leinwand, 55 x 70 cm
Aztec Sun, 1967
mixed technique on canvas, 55 x 70 cm

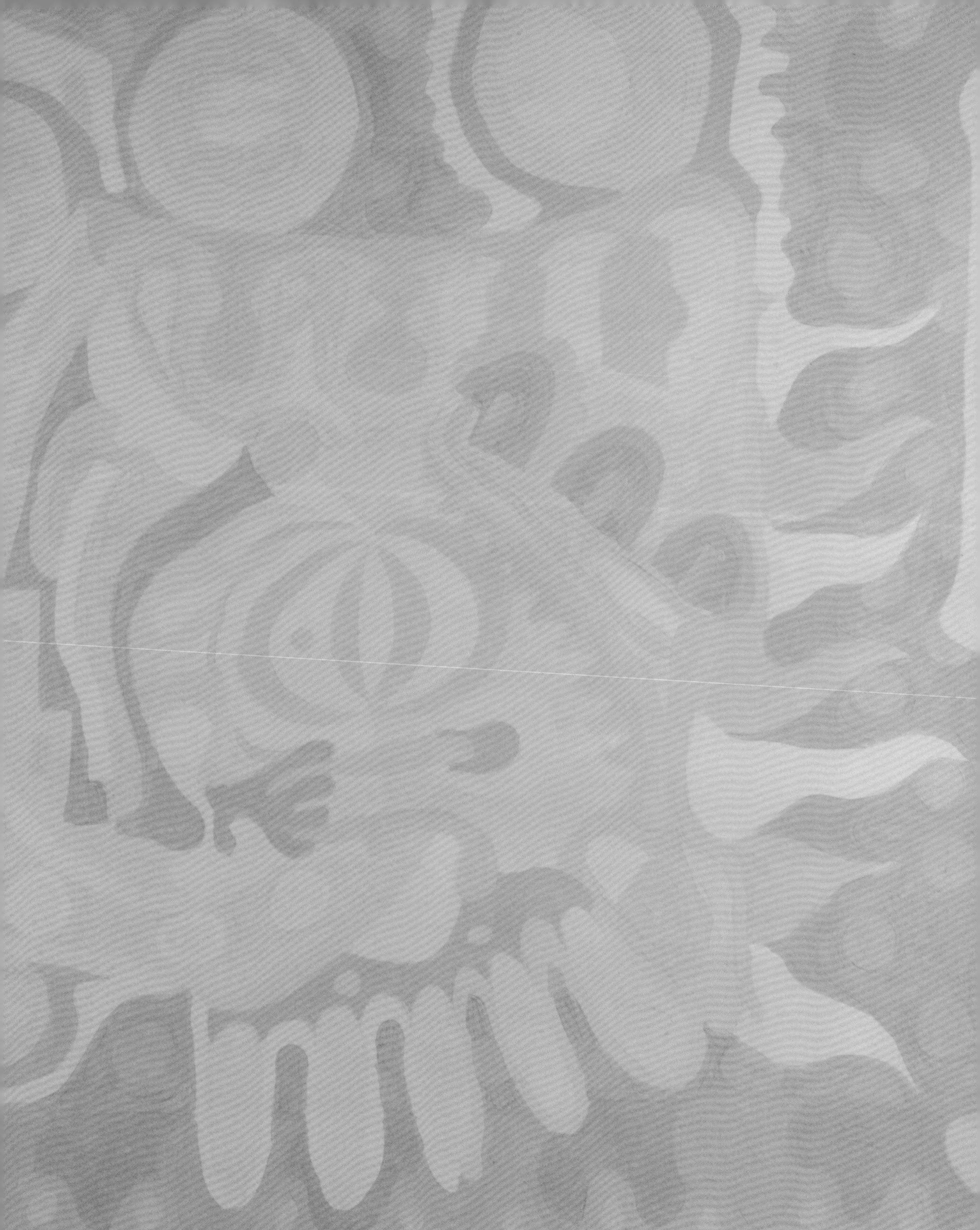

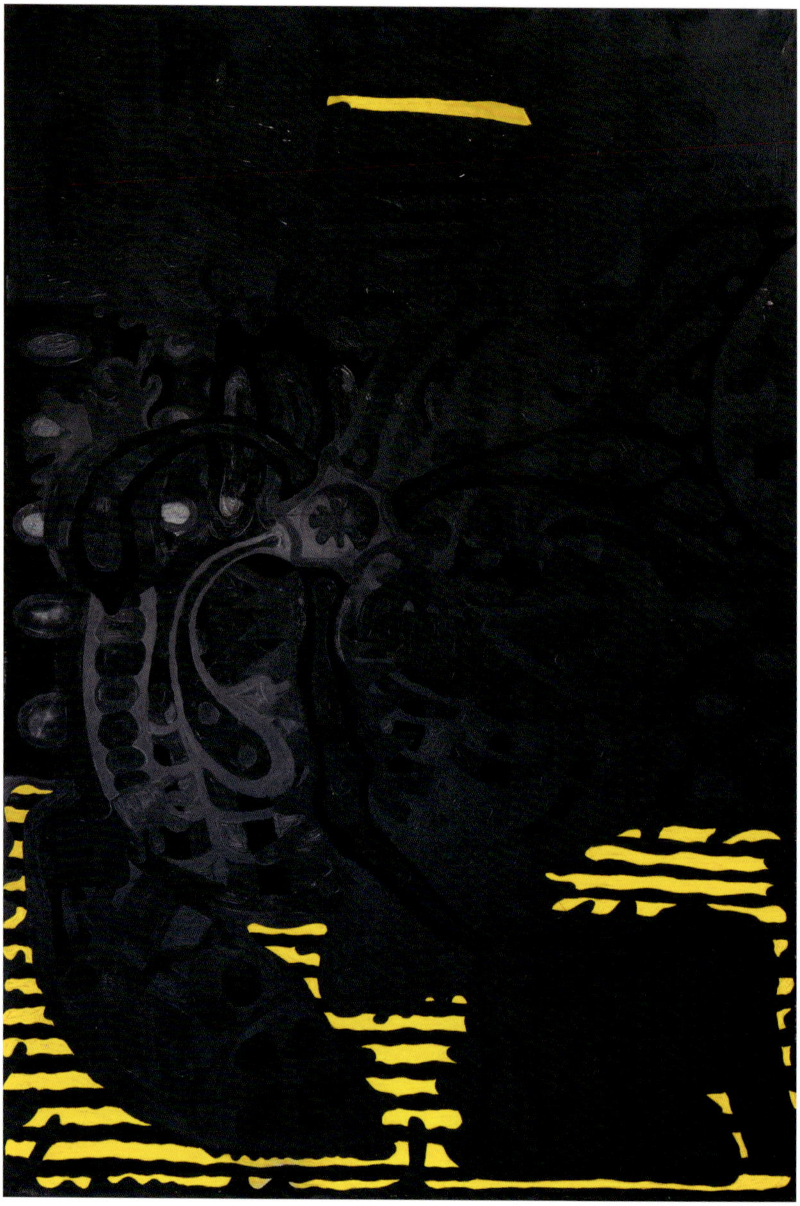

58
Psychopathic Petrol, Juni 1969
Harz, Wachs, Öl auf Leinwand, 160 x 110 cm
Psychopatic Petrol, June 1969
resin, wax, oil on canvas, 160 x 110 cm

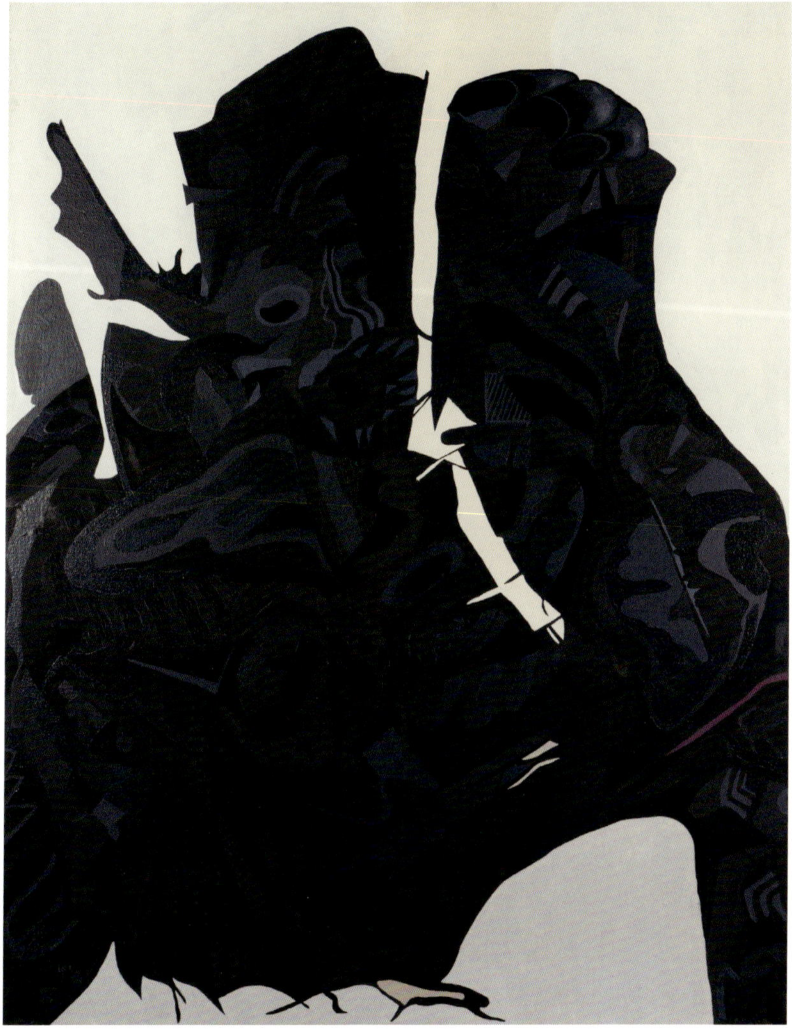

59
O.T., 1979
Mischtechnik auf Leinwand (schwarz-weiß), 100 x 80 cm
Untitled, 1979
mixed technique on canvas (black and white), 100 x 80 cm

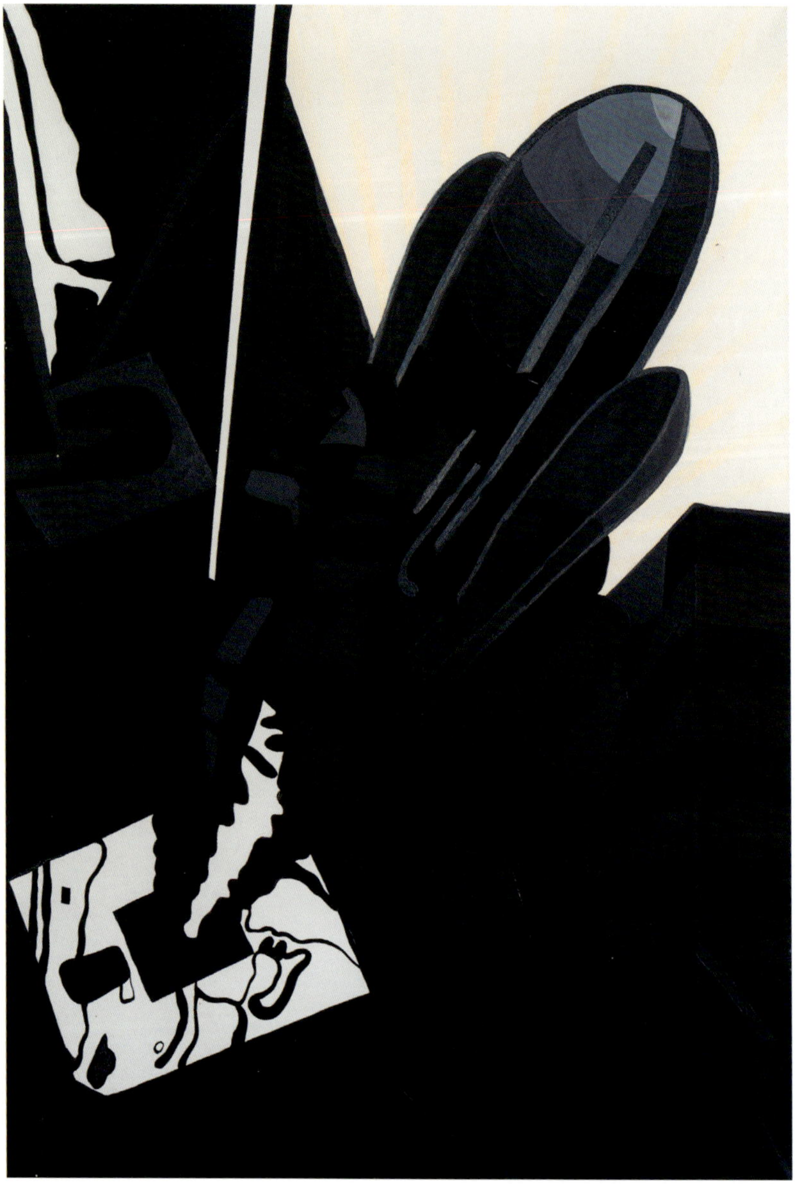

60
Space Shuttle, 1982
Mischtechnik auf Leinwand, 100 x 70 cm
Space Shuttle, 1982
mixed technique on canvas, 100 x 70 cm

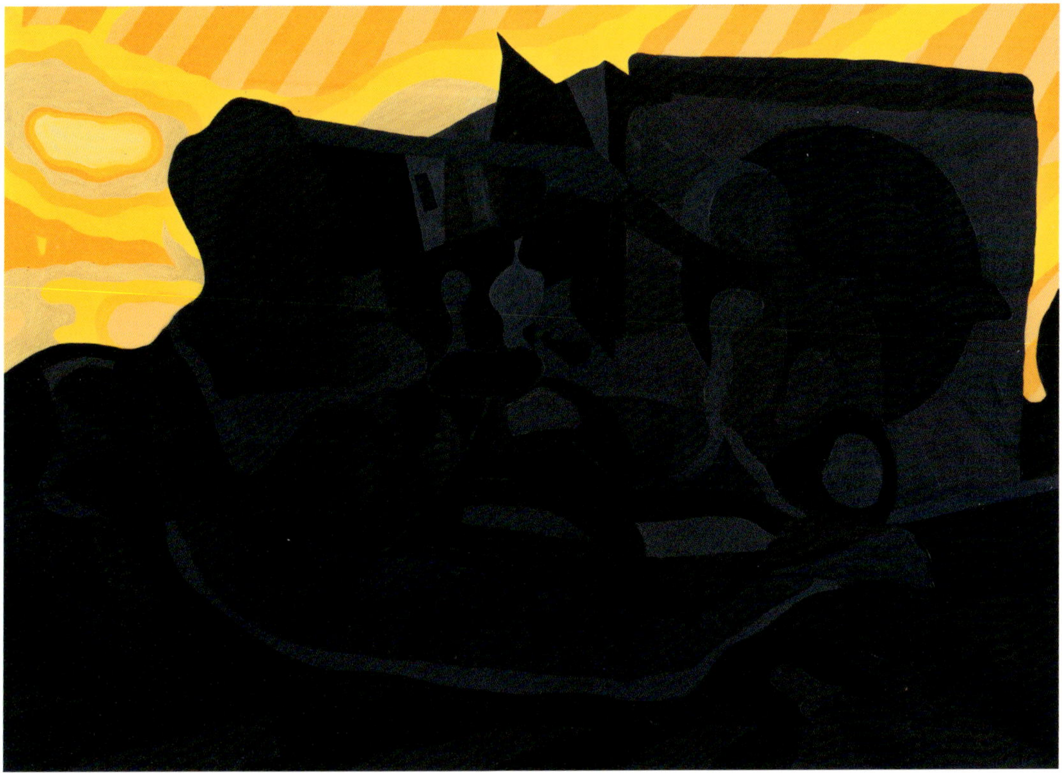

61
O.T. (für Burgi), undatiert (ca. 1980er Jahre)
Mischtechnik auf Leinwand, 70 x 100 cm
Untitled (for Burgi), undated (ca. 1980s)
mixed technique on canvas, 70 x 100 cm

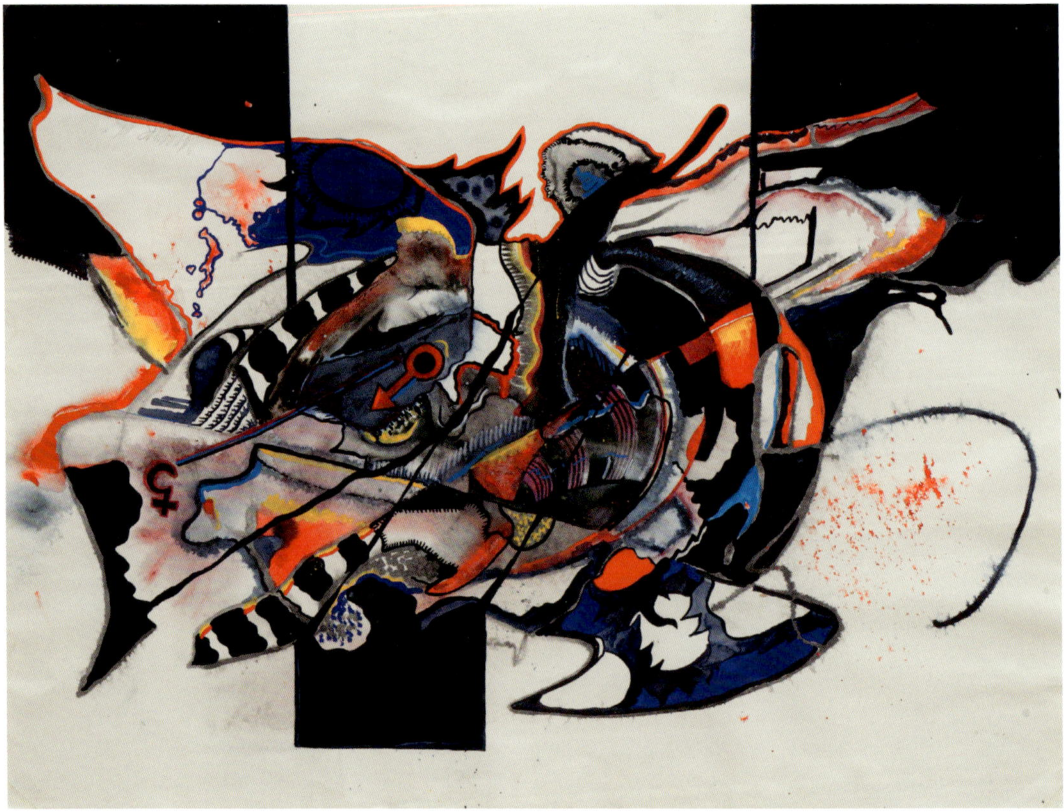

62
Mars-Saturn-Quadrat, 1981
Mischtechnik auf Papier, 56,1 x 75,6 cm
Mars Saturn Square, 1981
mixed technique on paper, 56,1 x 75,6 cm

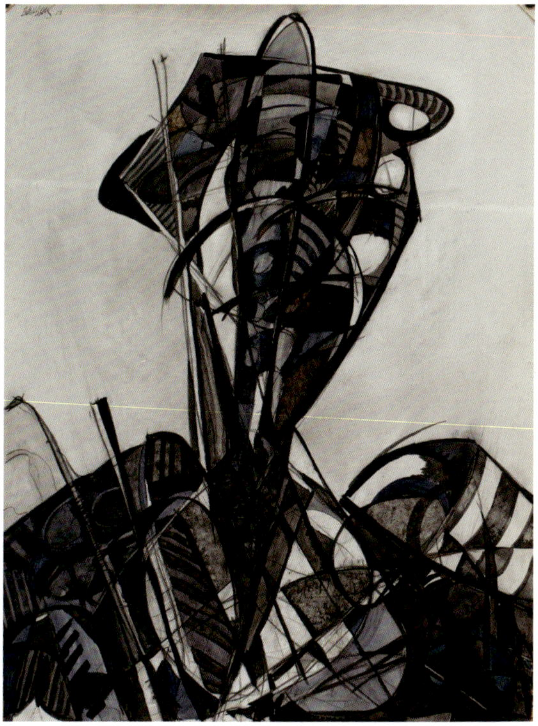

63
Mama Ocollo, 1983
Mischtechnik auf Papier, 90 x 70 cm
Mama Ocollo, 1983
mixed technique on paper, 90 x 70 cm

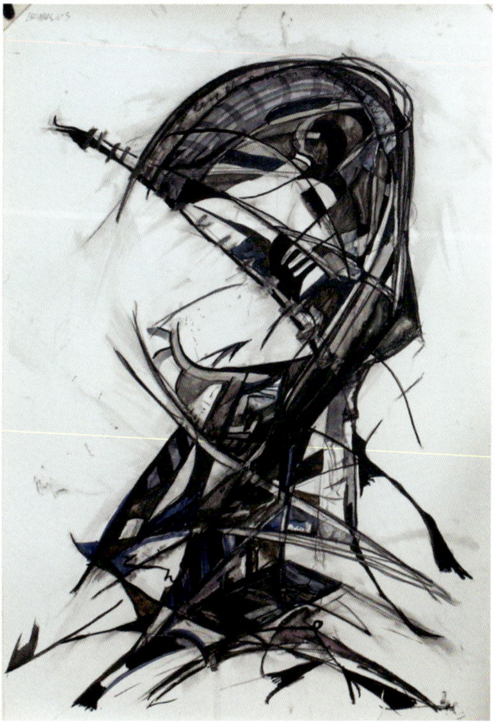

64
O.T., 1983
Mischtechnik auf Papier, 90 x 70 cm
Untitled, 1983
mixed technique on paper, 90 x 70 cm

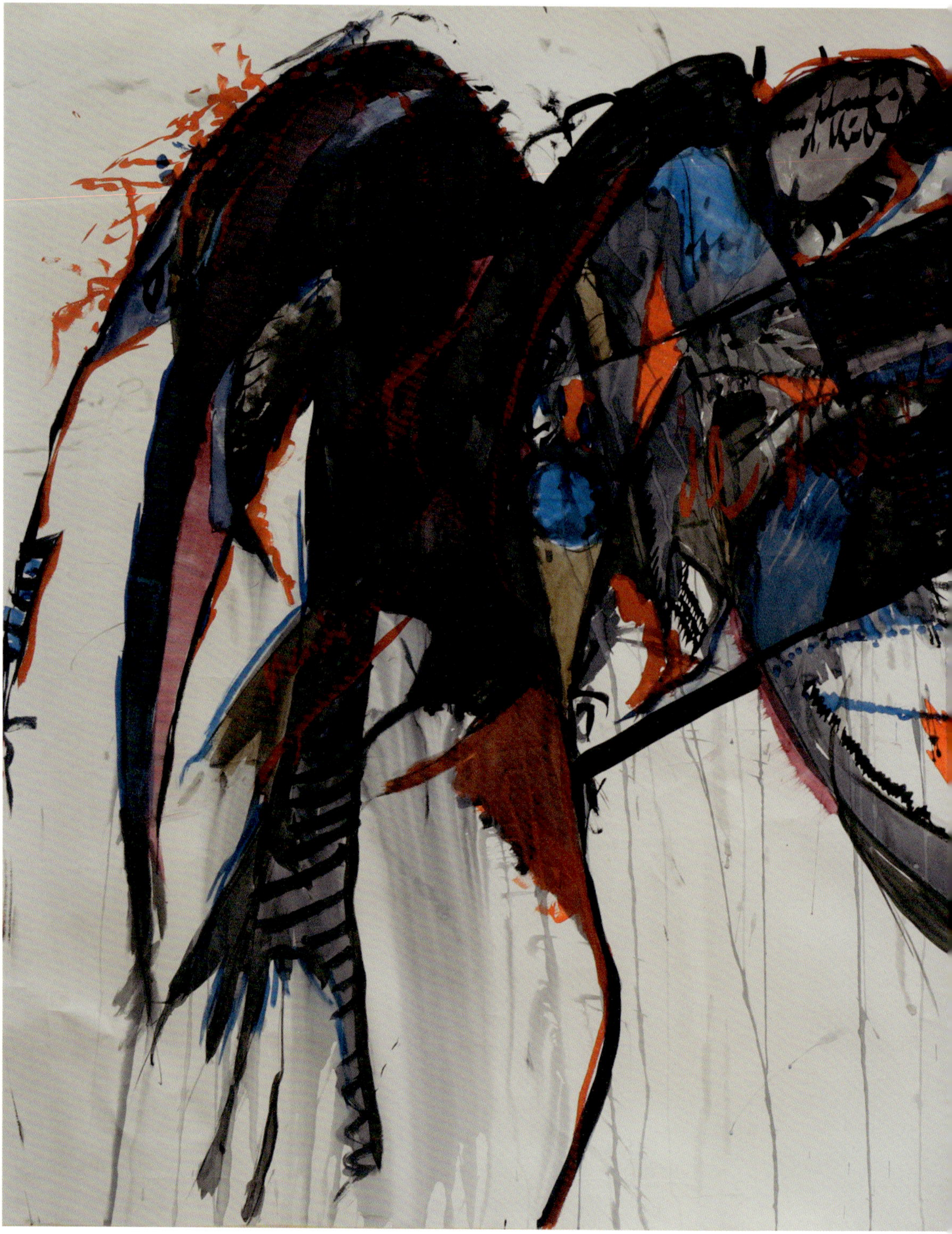

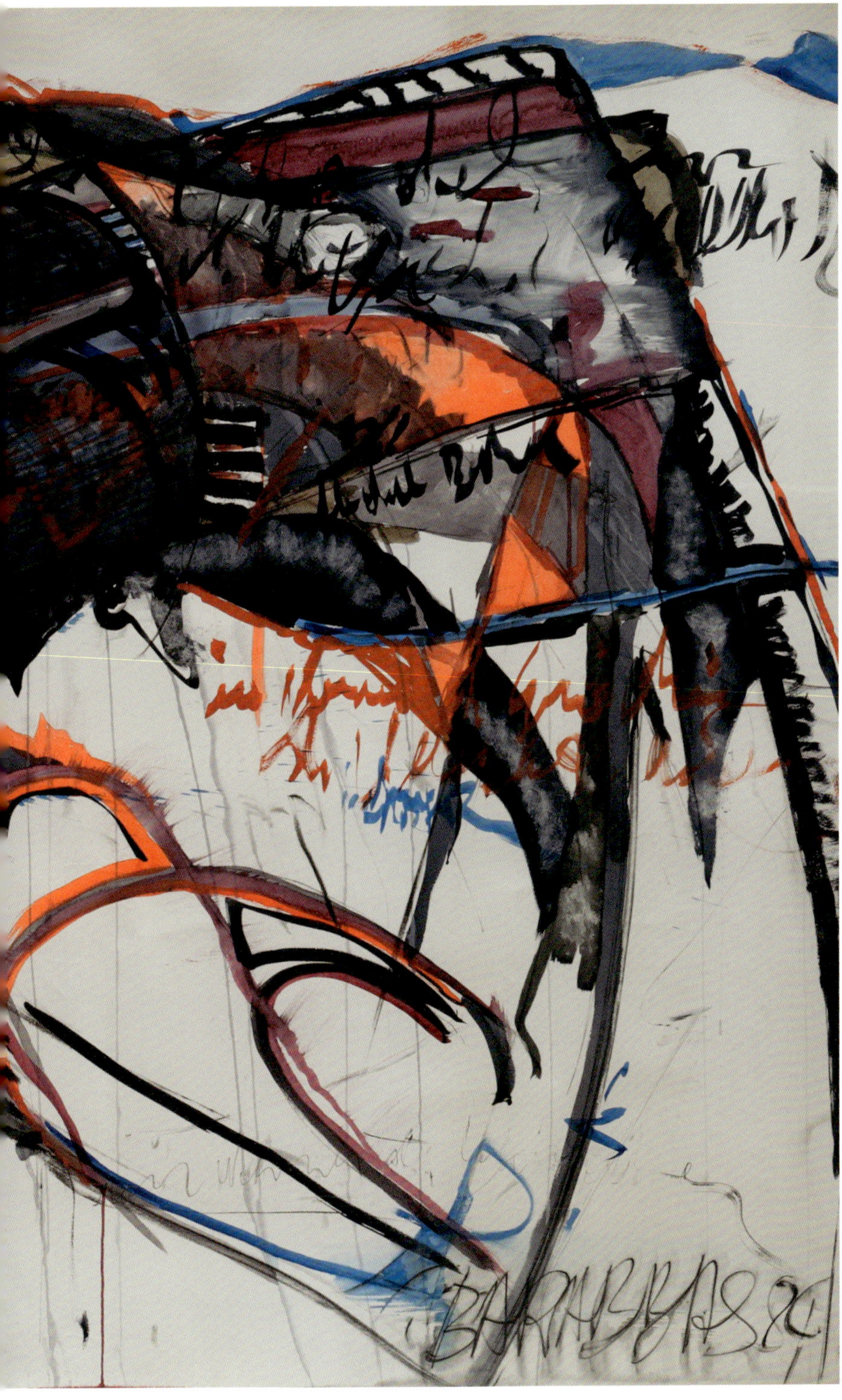

65
Im Namen des ..., 1984
Mischtechnik auf Papier,
120 x 185 cm
In the Name of the ..., 1984
mixed technique on paper,
120 x 185 cm

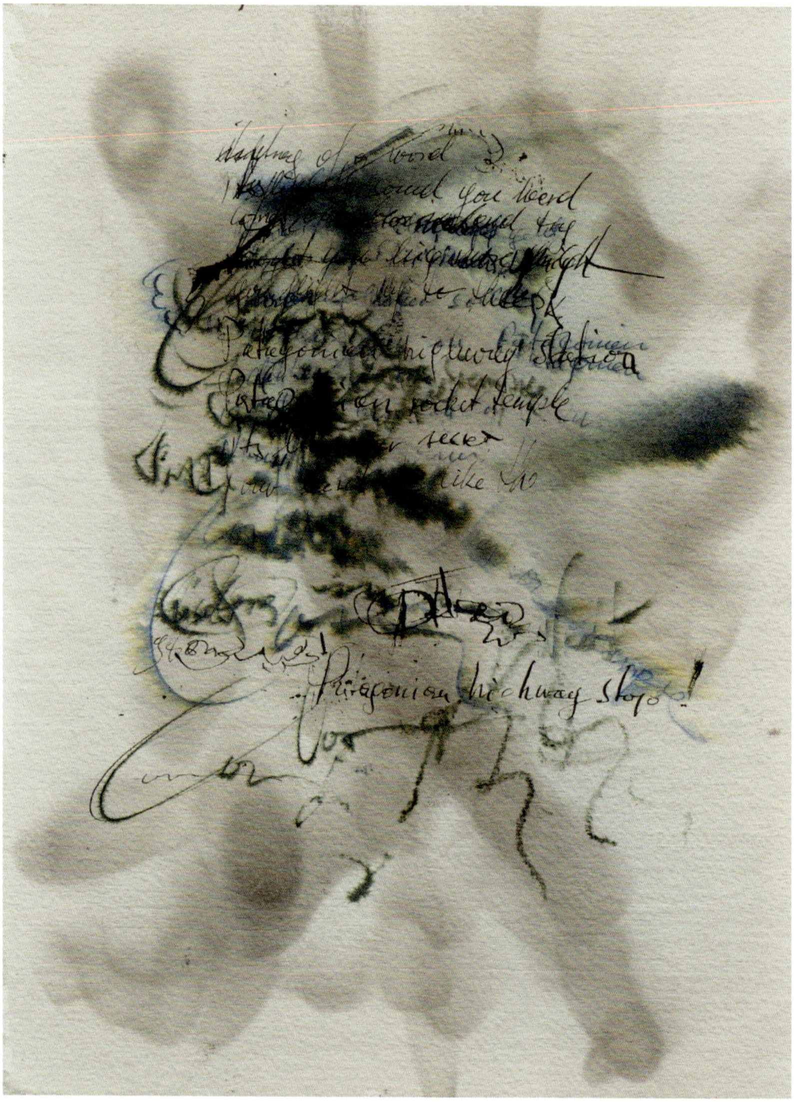

66
Skript 1, 1988
Mischtechnik auf Papier, 30,6 x 23 cm
Script 1, 1988
mixed technique on paper, 30,6 x 23 cm

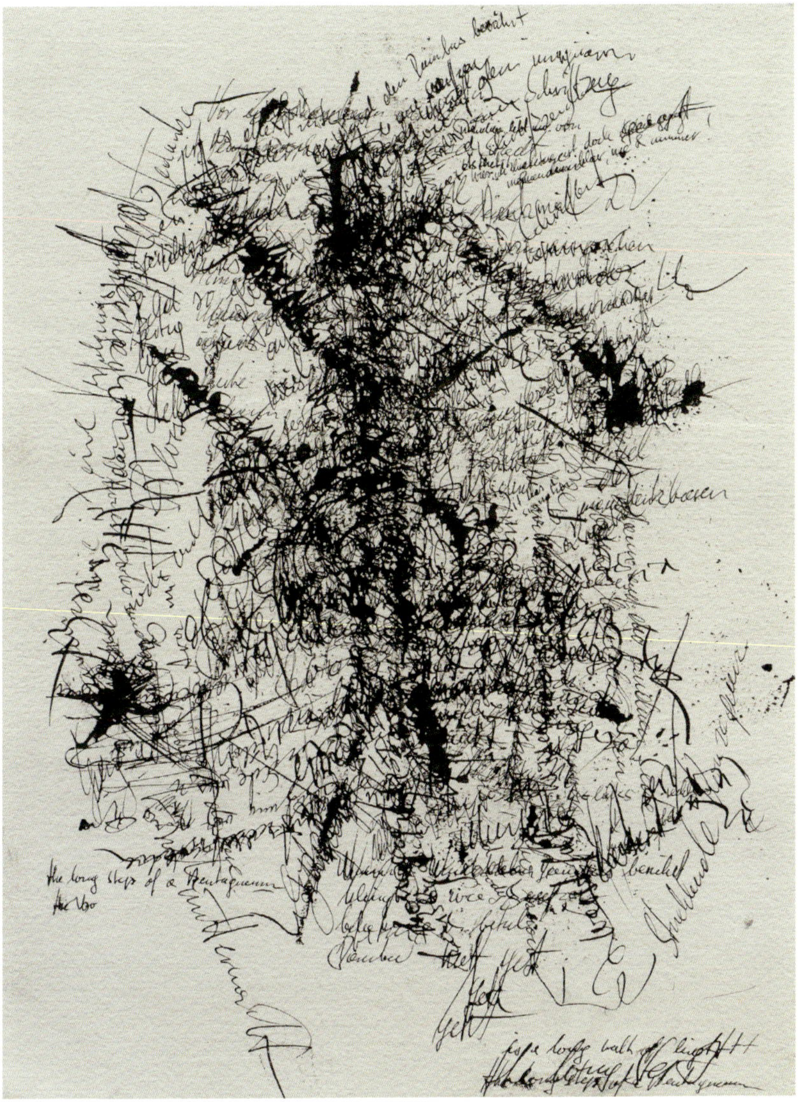

67
Skript 2, 1988
Tusche auf Papier, 30,6 x 23 cm
Script 2, 1988
drawing ink on paper, 30,6 x 23 cm

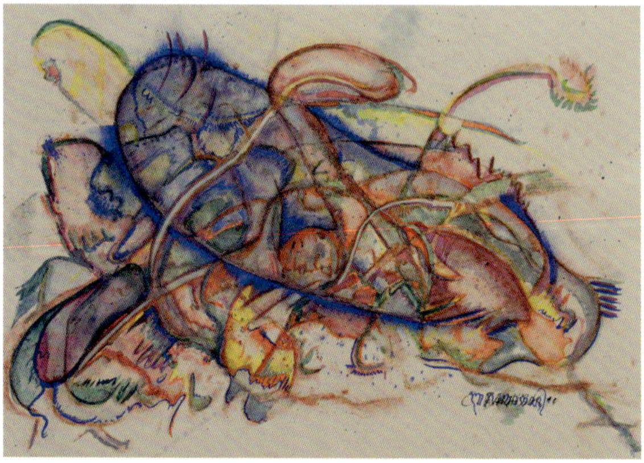

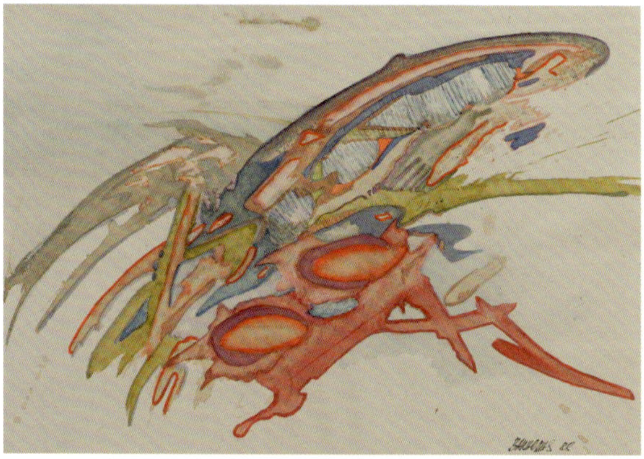

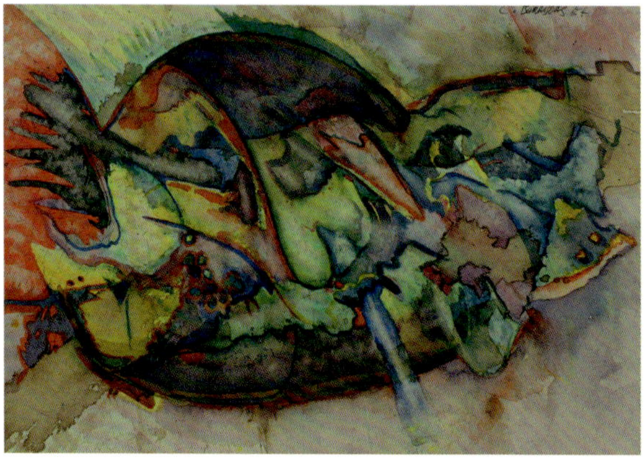

68
2. Juni 88, 1988
Aquarell auf Papier, 35 x 49,5 cm
June 2, 88, 1988
watercolor on paper, 35 x 49,5 cm

69
O.T., 1988
Aquarell auf Papier, 35 x 48,5 cm
Untitled, 1988
watercolor on paper, 35 x 48,5 cm

70
O.T., 1987
Aquarell auf Papier, 35 x 49,5 cm
Untitled, 1989
watercolor on paper, 35 x 49,5 cm

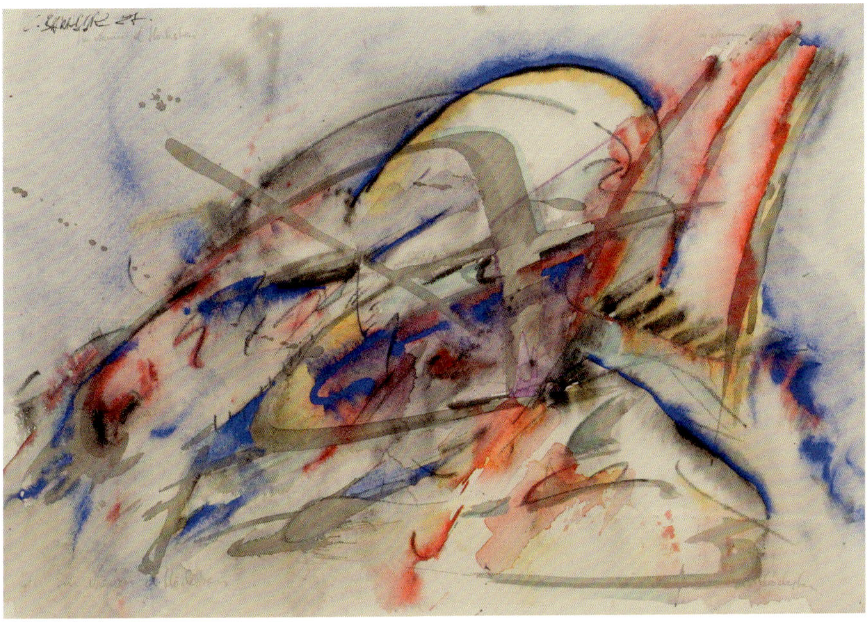

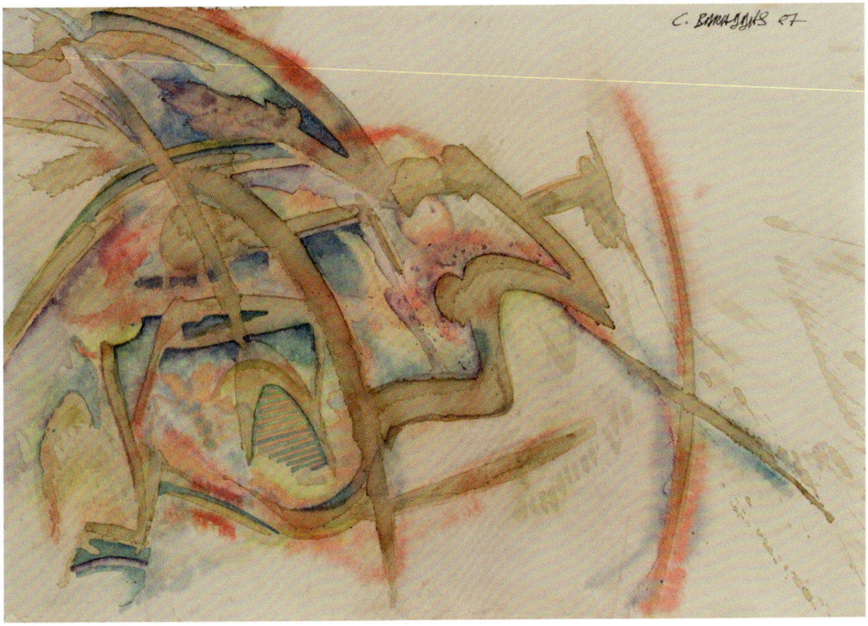

71
Im Namen des Höchsten, 1989
Aquarell auf Papier, 35 x 48,5 cm
In the Name of the Most High, 1989
watercolor on paper, 35 x 48,5 cm

72
O.T., 1989
Aquarell auf Papier, 35 x 48,5 cm
Untitled, 1989
watercolor on paper, 35 x 48,5 cm

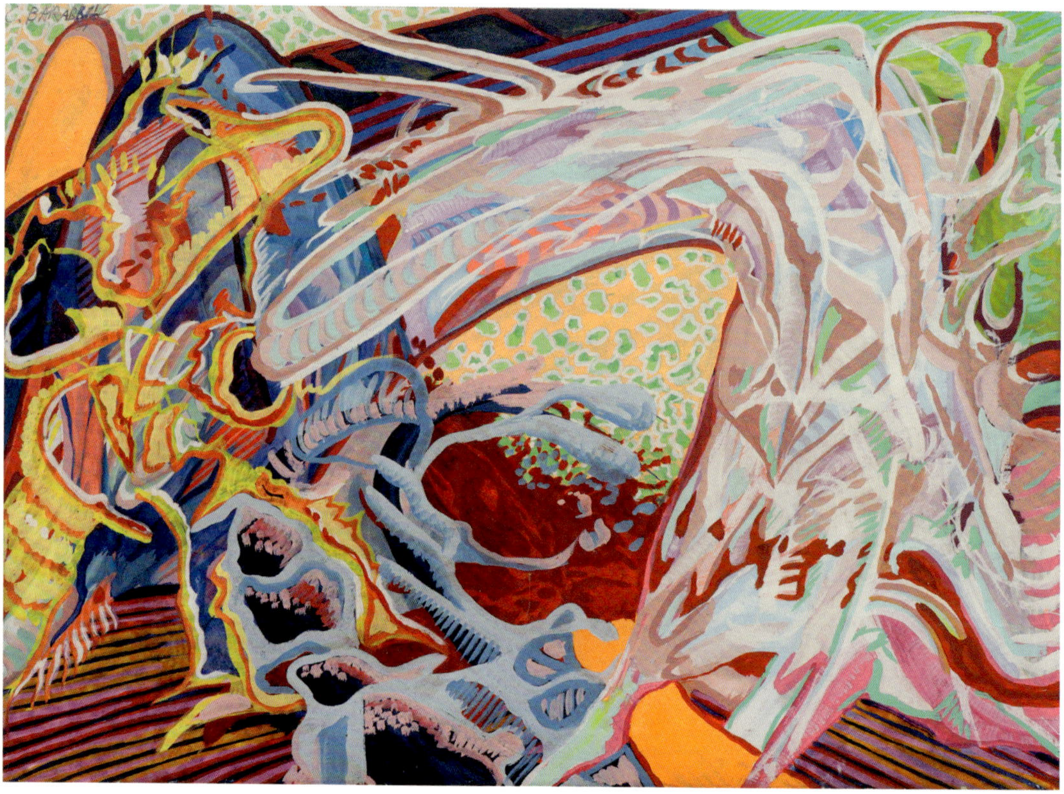

73
Bergtor, 1985
Tempera, Öl auf Leinwand, 54 x 75 cm
Mountain Gate, 1985
tempera, oil on canvas, 54 x 75 cm

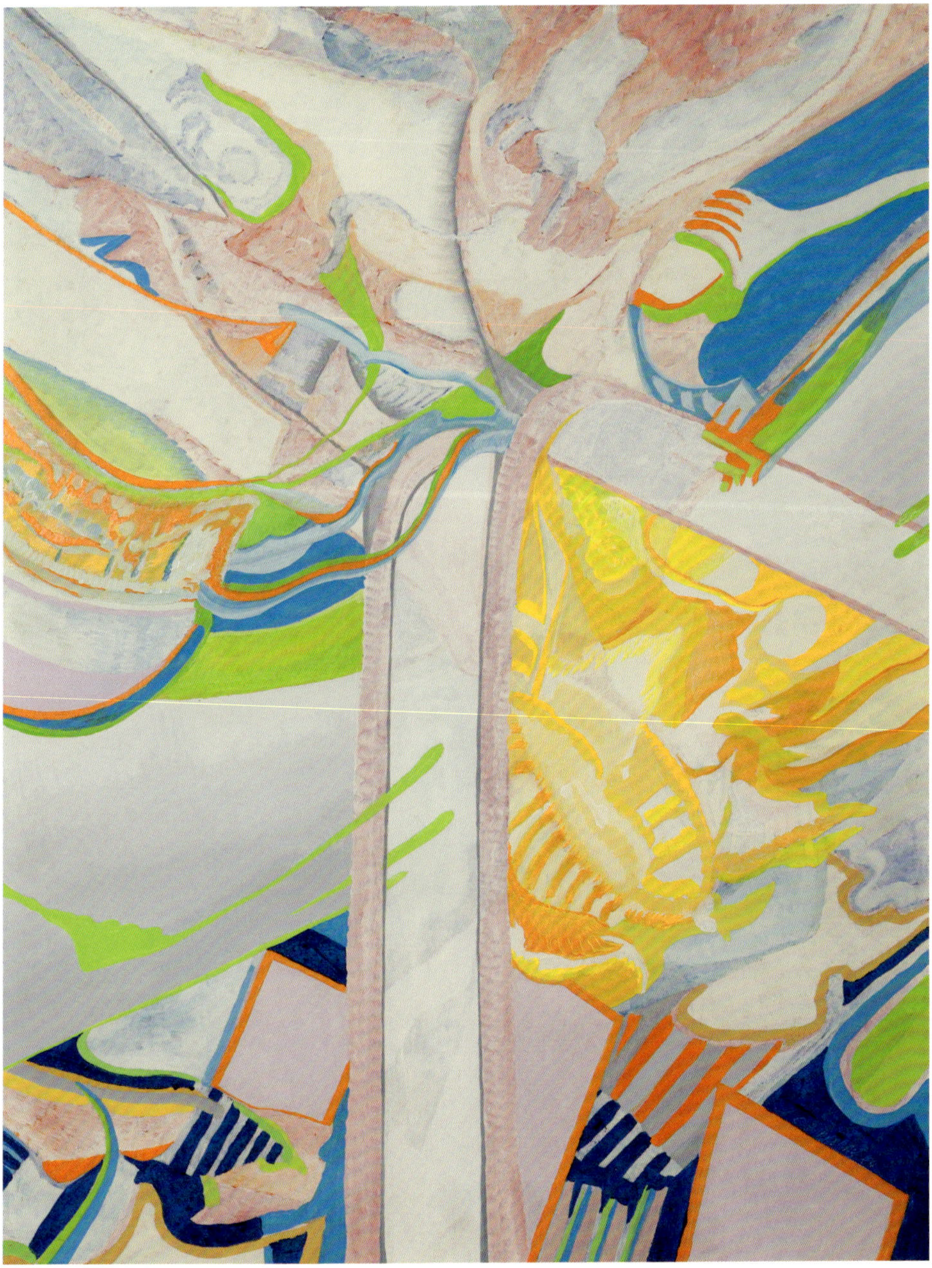

74
Das einzige legitime Barockbild des 20. Jahrhunderts, 1984
Öl-Tempera auf Holzfaserplatte, 85 x 65 cm
The Only Legitimate Baroque Painting of the Twentieth Century, 1984
oil tempera on fiberboard, 85 x 65 cm

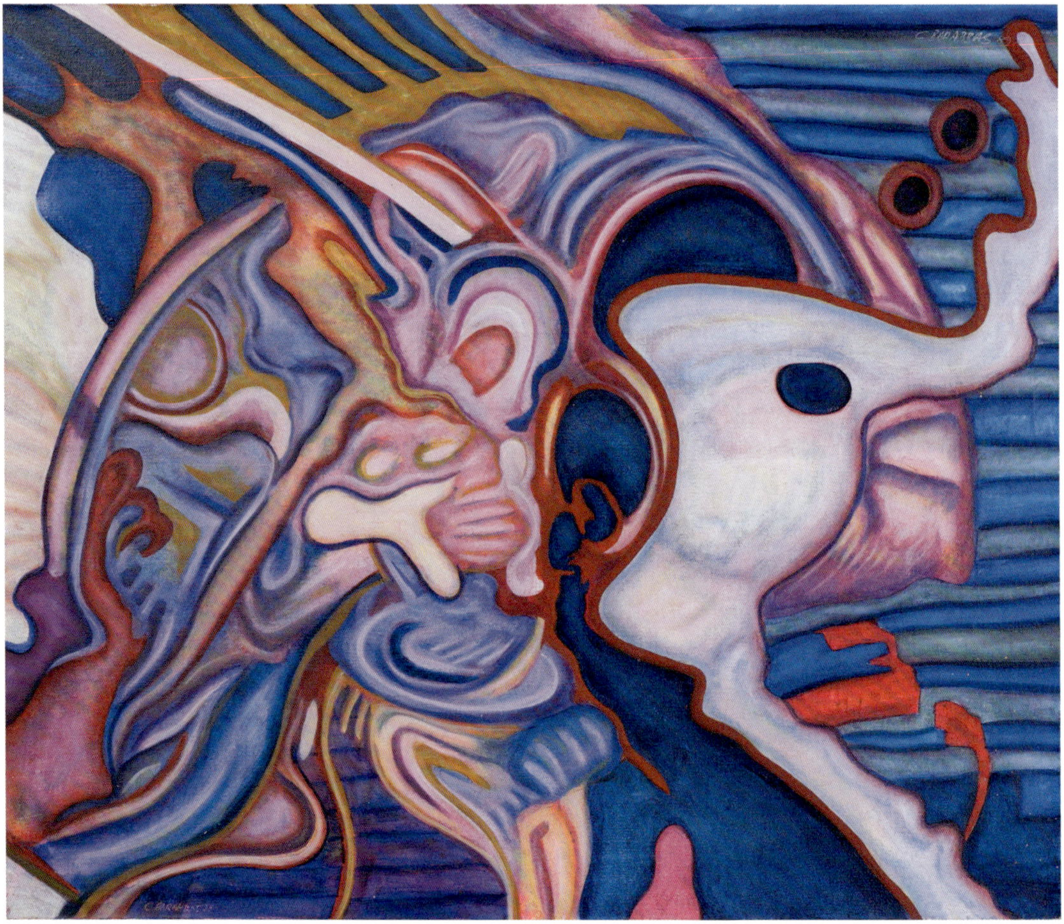

75
The Birth (Bahá'u'lláhs Geburtstag), 12.11.1988
Öl auf Leinwand, 46 x 56 cm
The Birth (Bahá'u'lláhs Birthday), November 12, 1988
oil on canvas, 46 x 56 cm

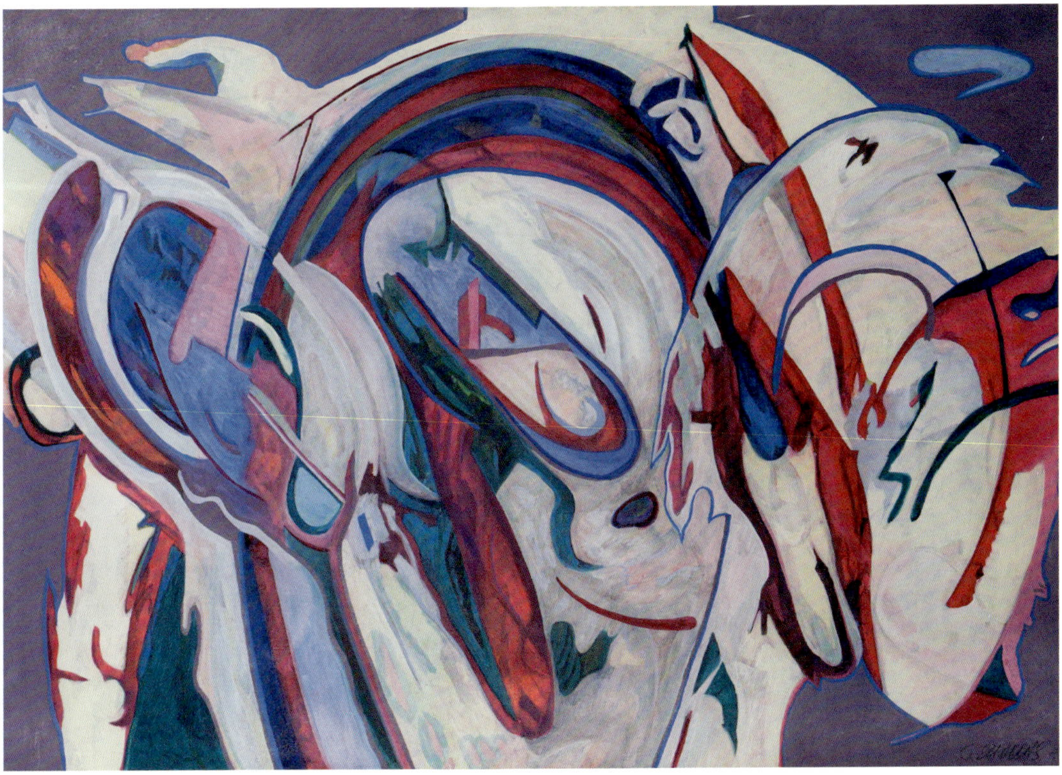

76
Quantum Detector, 1987
Öl auf Leinwand, 51 x 66 cm
Quantum Detector, 1987
oil on canvas, 51 x 66 cm

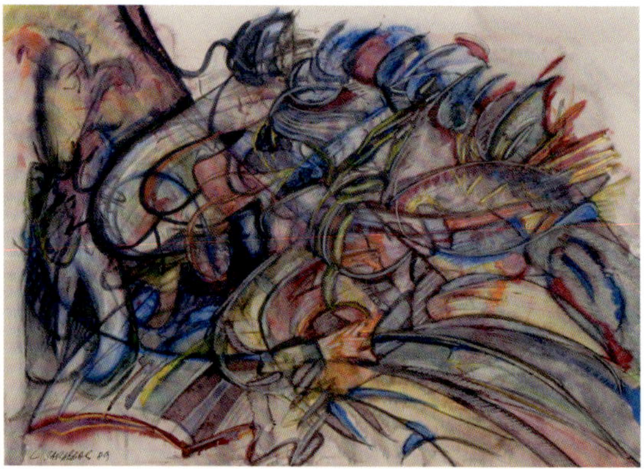

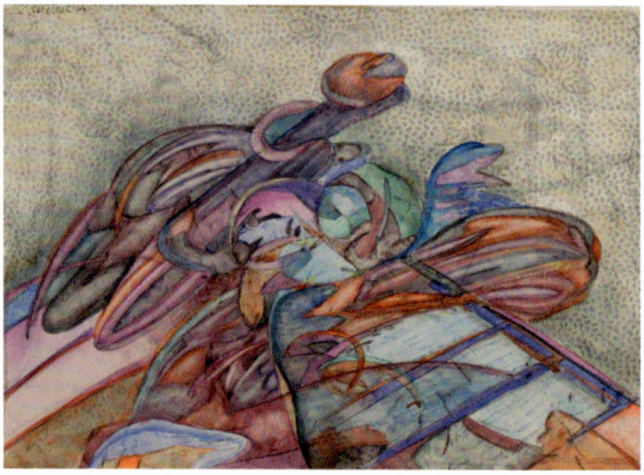

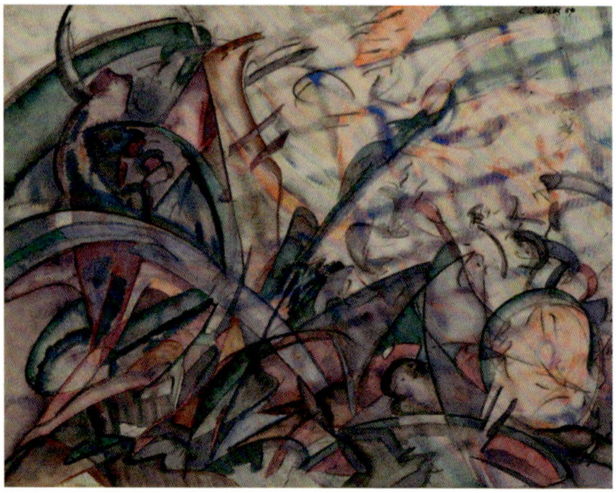

77
O.T., 1989
Aquarell auf Papier, 35 x 48,5 cm
Untitled, 1989
watercolor on paper, 35 x 48,5 cm

78
O.T., 1989
Aquarell auf Papier, 43 x 61 cm
Untitled, 1989
watercolor on paper, 43 x 61 cm

79
O.T., 1989
Aquarell auf Papier, 49 x 63 cm
Untitled, 1989
watercolor on paper, 49 x 63 cm

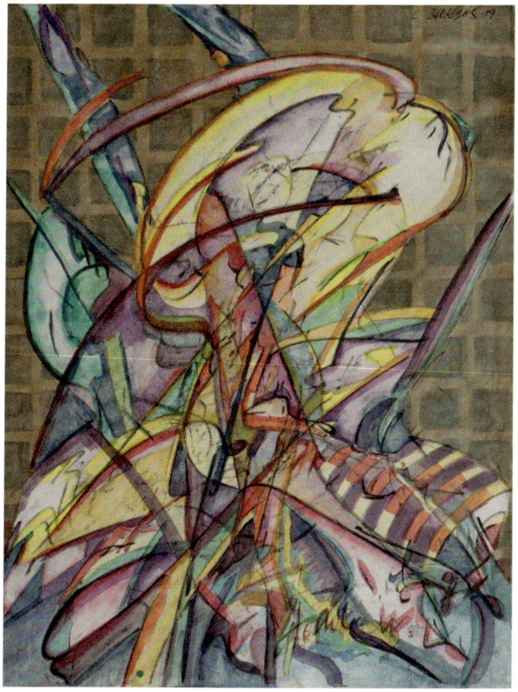

80
O.T. 1989
Aquarell auf Papier, 49 x 62 cm
Untitled, 1989
watercolor on paper, 49 x 62 cm

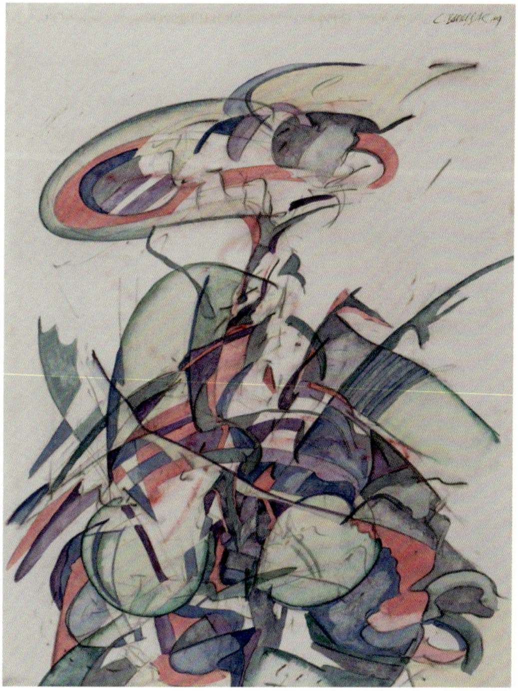

81
O.T., 1989
Aquarell auf Papier, 64 x 50 cm
Untitled, 1989
watercolor on paper, 64 x 50 cm

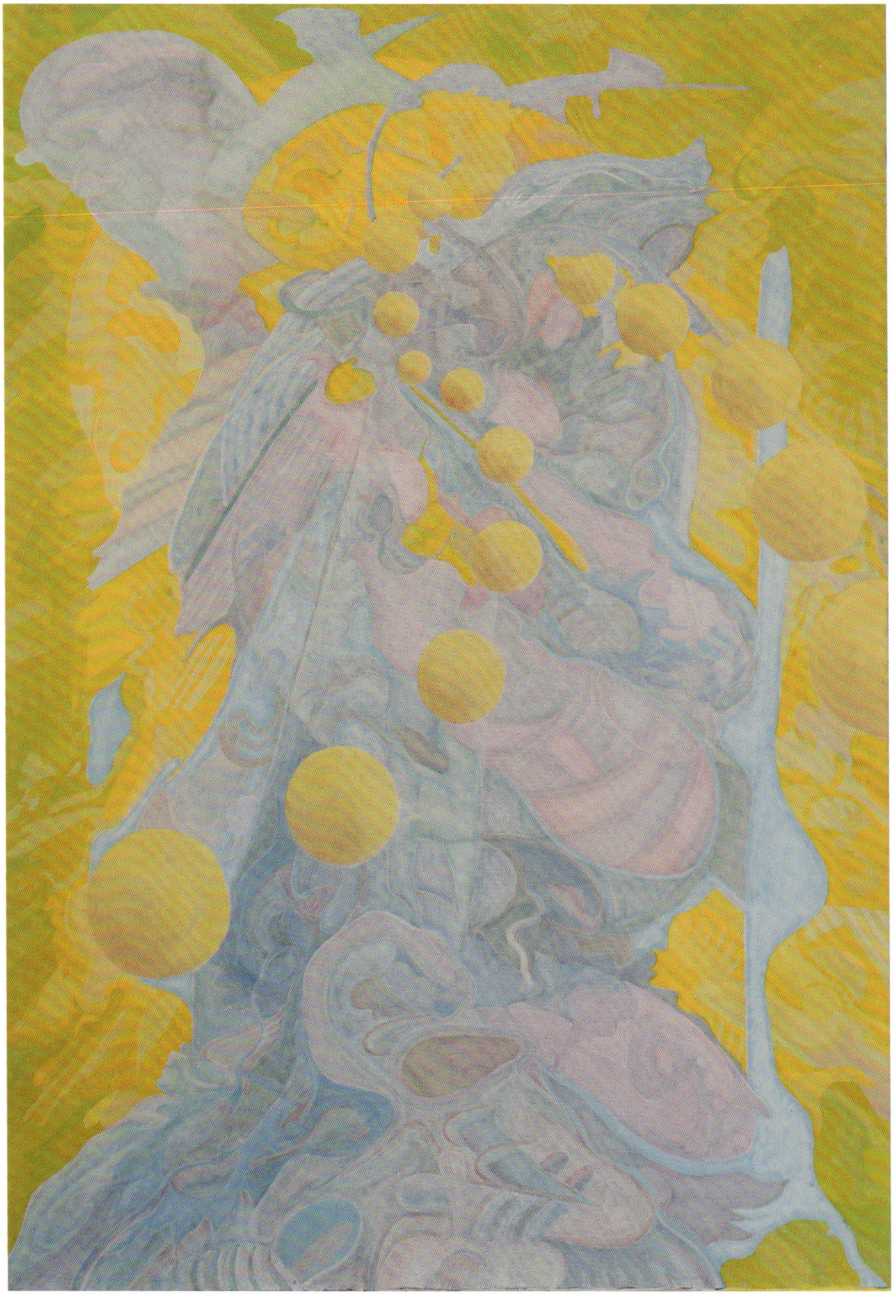

82
The Dawn-Breakers, 1988, Bali
Öl auf Leinwand, 140 x 100 cm
The Dawn-Breakers, 1988, Bali
oil on canvas, 140 x 100 cm

83
O.T., 3.10.1988, Bali
Öl auf Leinwand, 129 x 90 cm
Untitled, October 3, 1988, Bali
oil on canvas, 129 x 90 cm

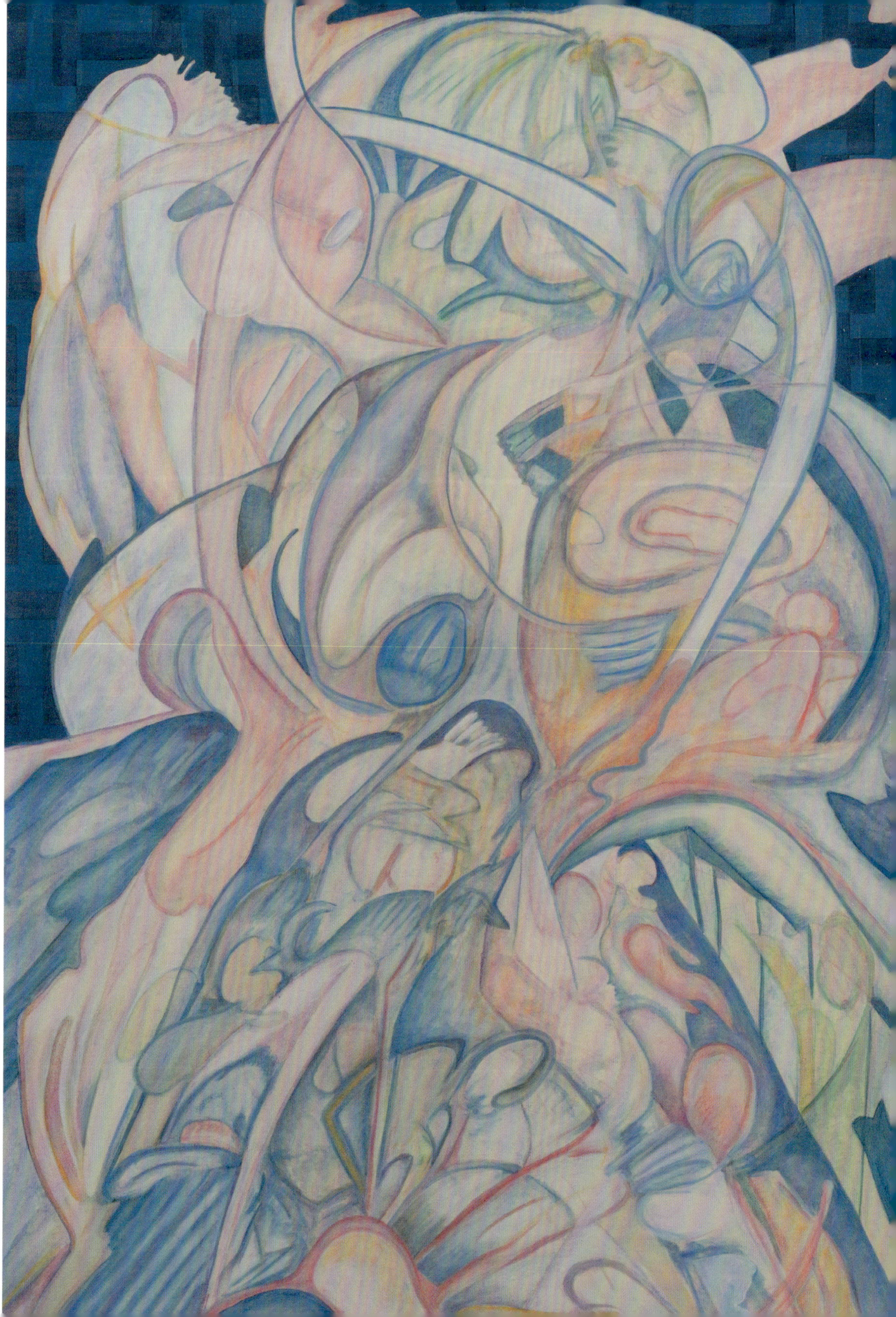

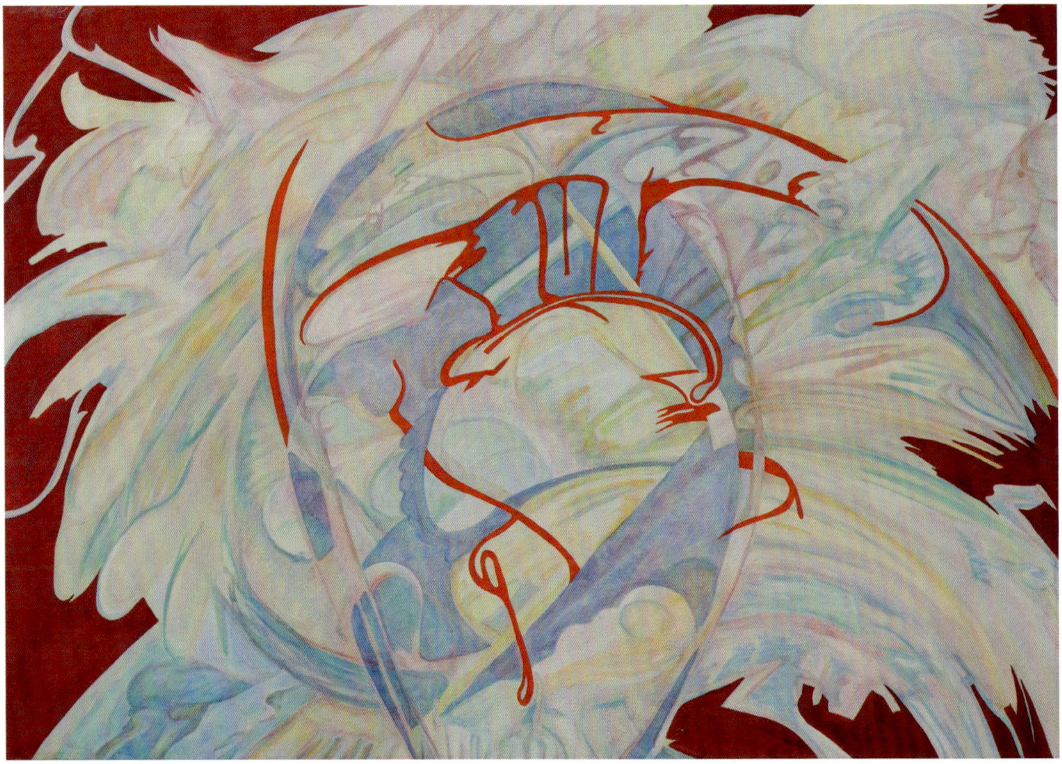

84
Bunga, 31.8.1988, Bali
Öl auf Leinwand, 70 x 100 cm
Bunga, August 31, 1988, Bali
oil on canvas, 70 x 100 cm

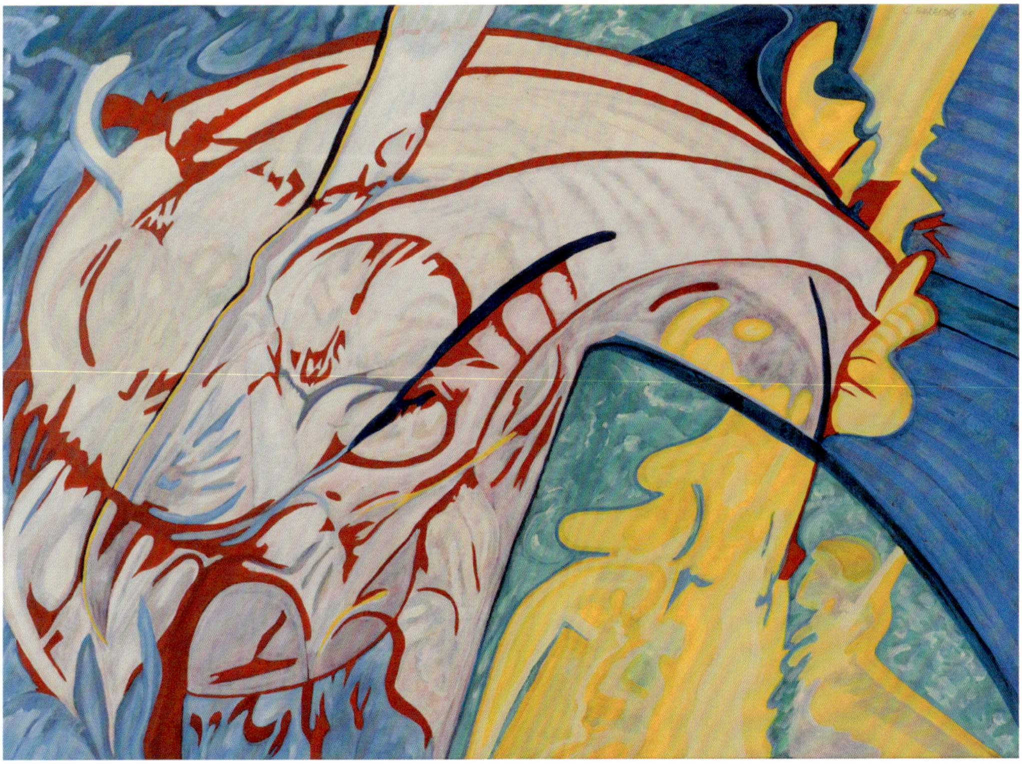

85
O.T., 1988, Bali
Öl auf Leinwand, 67 x 93 cm
Untitled, 1988, Bali
oil on canvas, 67 x 93 cm

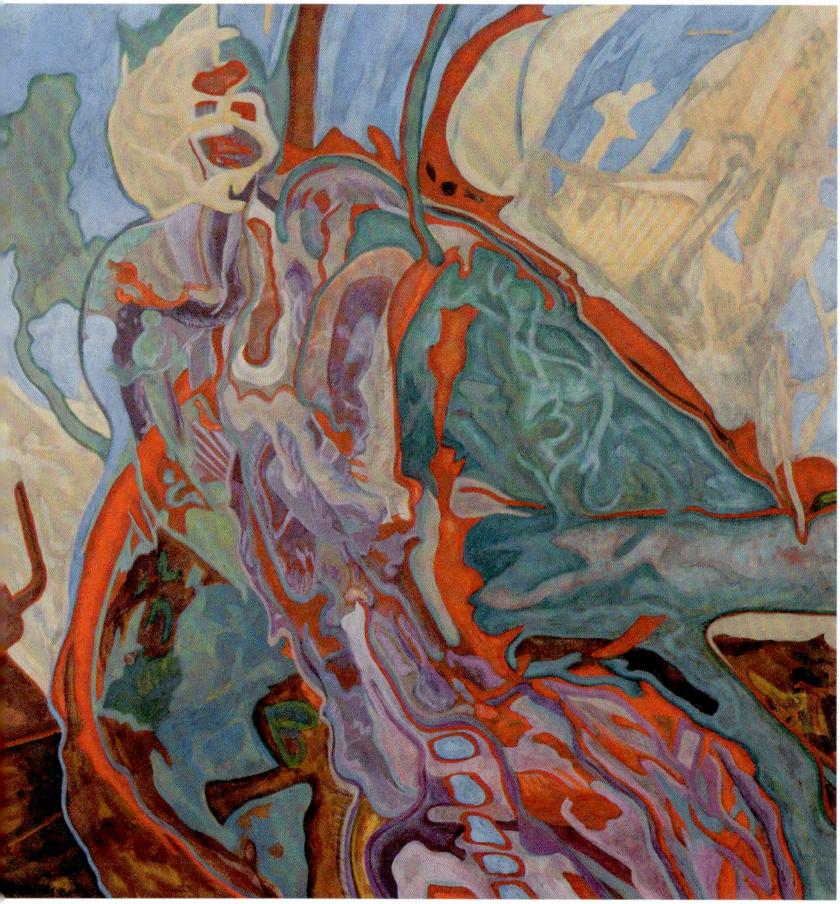

86
Warnumbungles, 1990, Australien
Öl auf Leinwand, 70 x 70 cm
Warnumbungles, 1990, Australia
oil on canvas, 70 x 70 cm

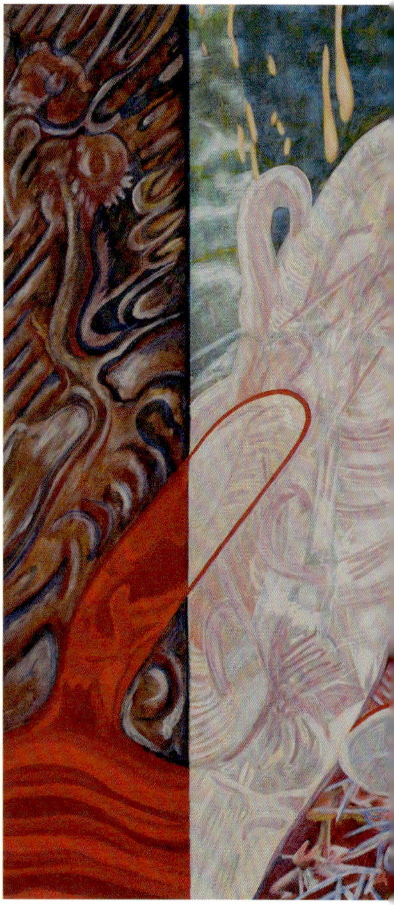

87
View, 1990, Australien
Öl auf Leinwand, 70 x 70 cm
View, 1990, Australia
oil on canvas, 70 x 70 cm

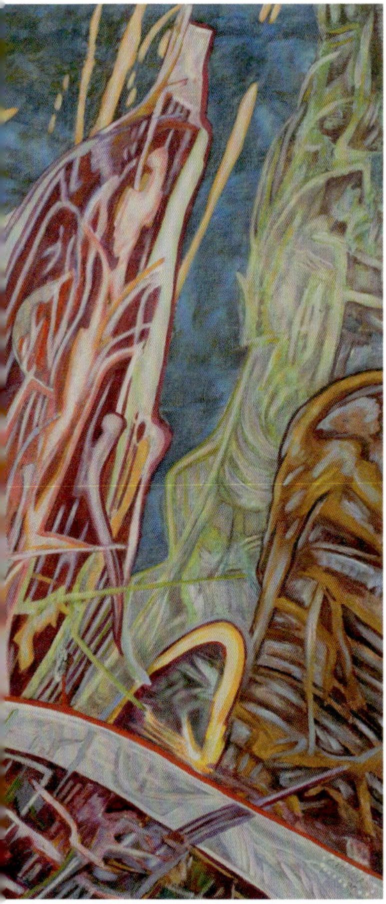

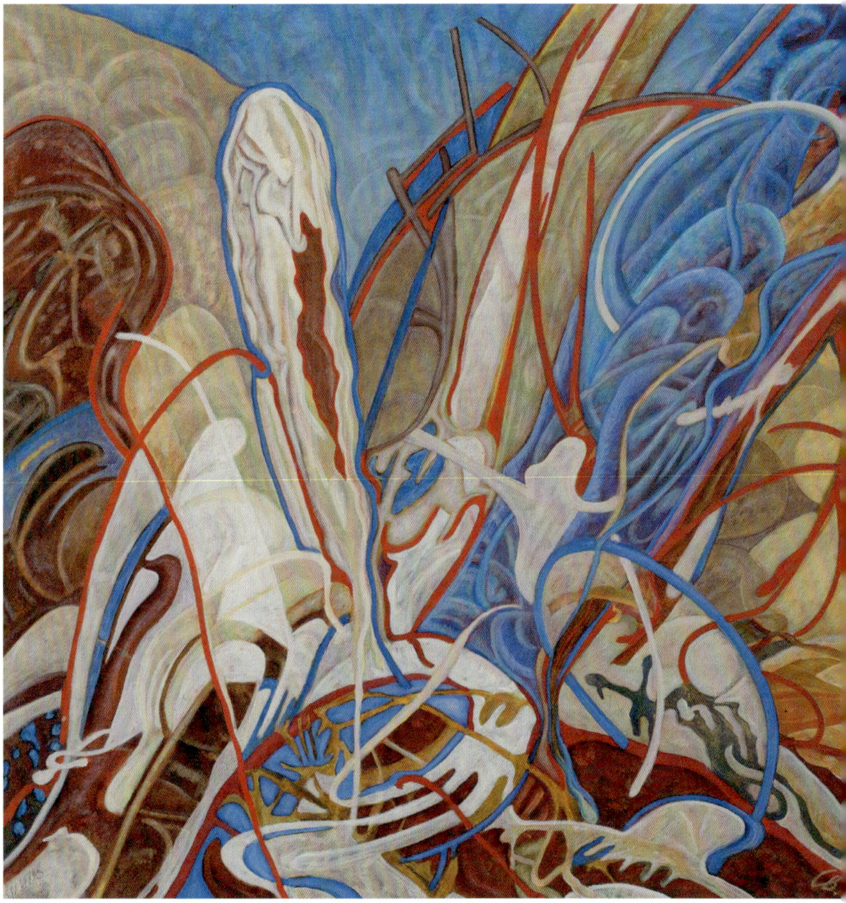

88
The Spirit of Coonawarra (Wüstenwind), 1990, Australien
Öl auf Leinwand, 70 x 70 cm
The Spirit of Coonawarra (Desert Wind), 1990, Australia
oil on canvas, 70 x 70 cm

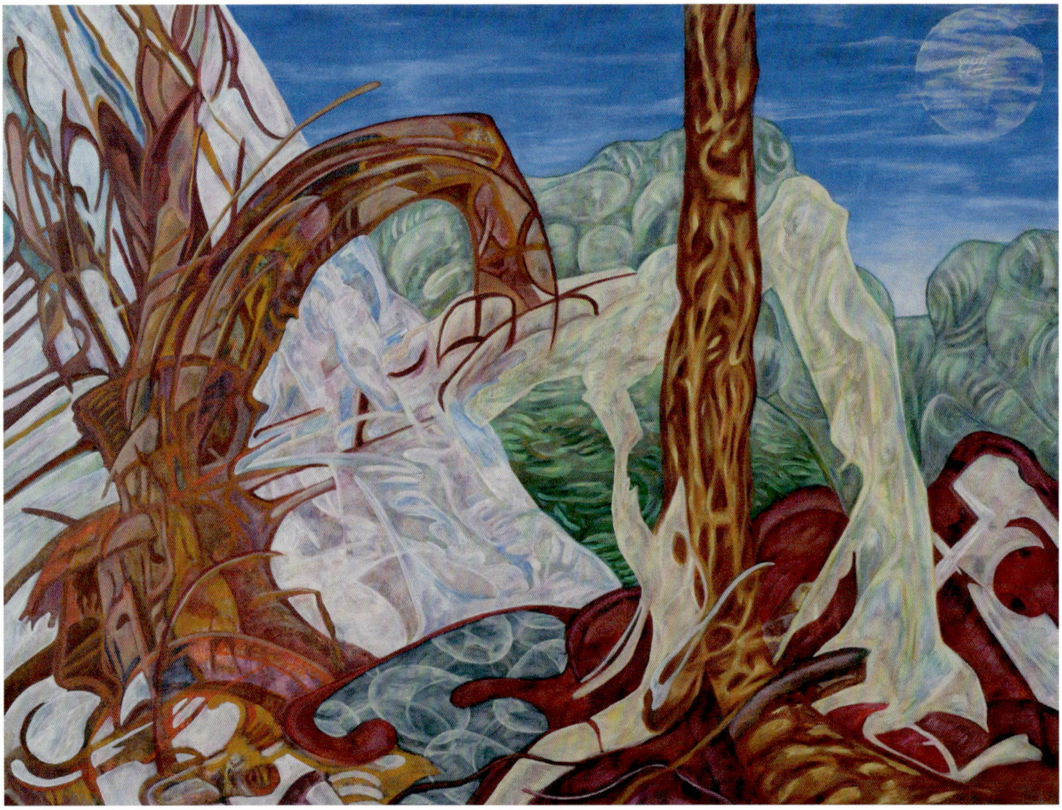

89
Time Cycle, 1990, Australien
Öl auf Leinwand, 75 x 101 cm
Time Cycle, 1990, Australia
oil on canvas, 75 x 101 cm

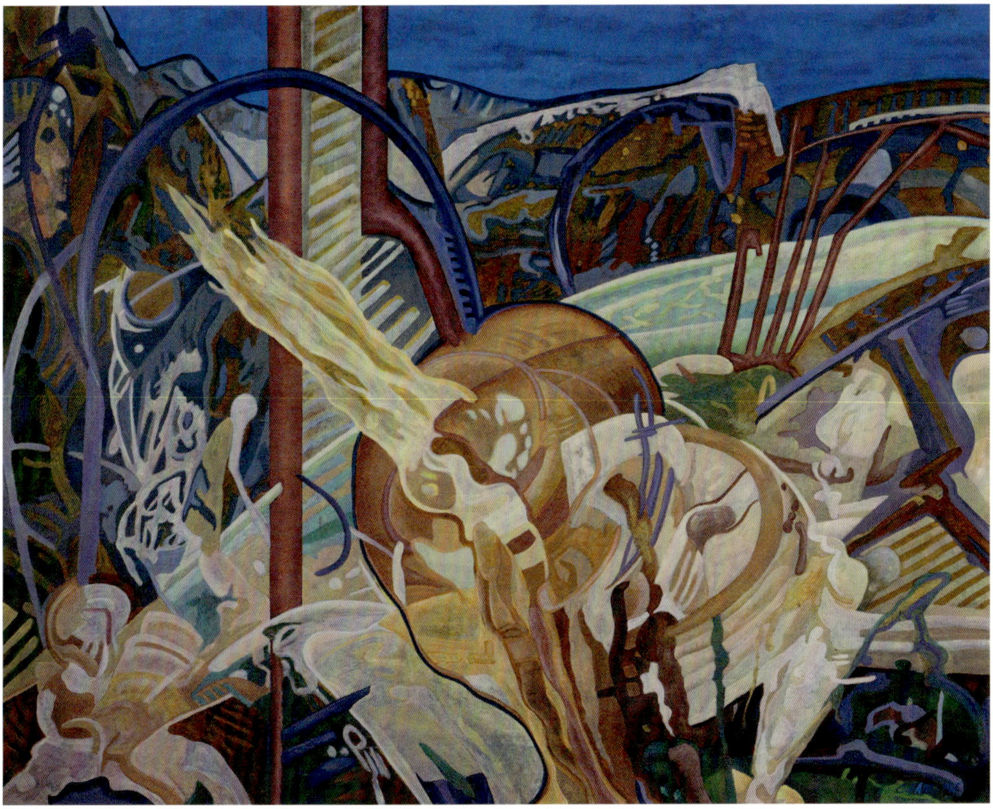

90
Transfiction, November 1990
Öl auf Leinwand, 83,5 x 106,5 cm
Transfiction, November 1990
oil on canvas, 83,5 x 106,5 cm

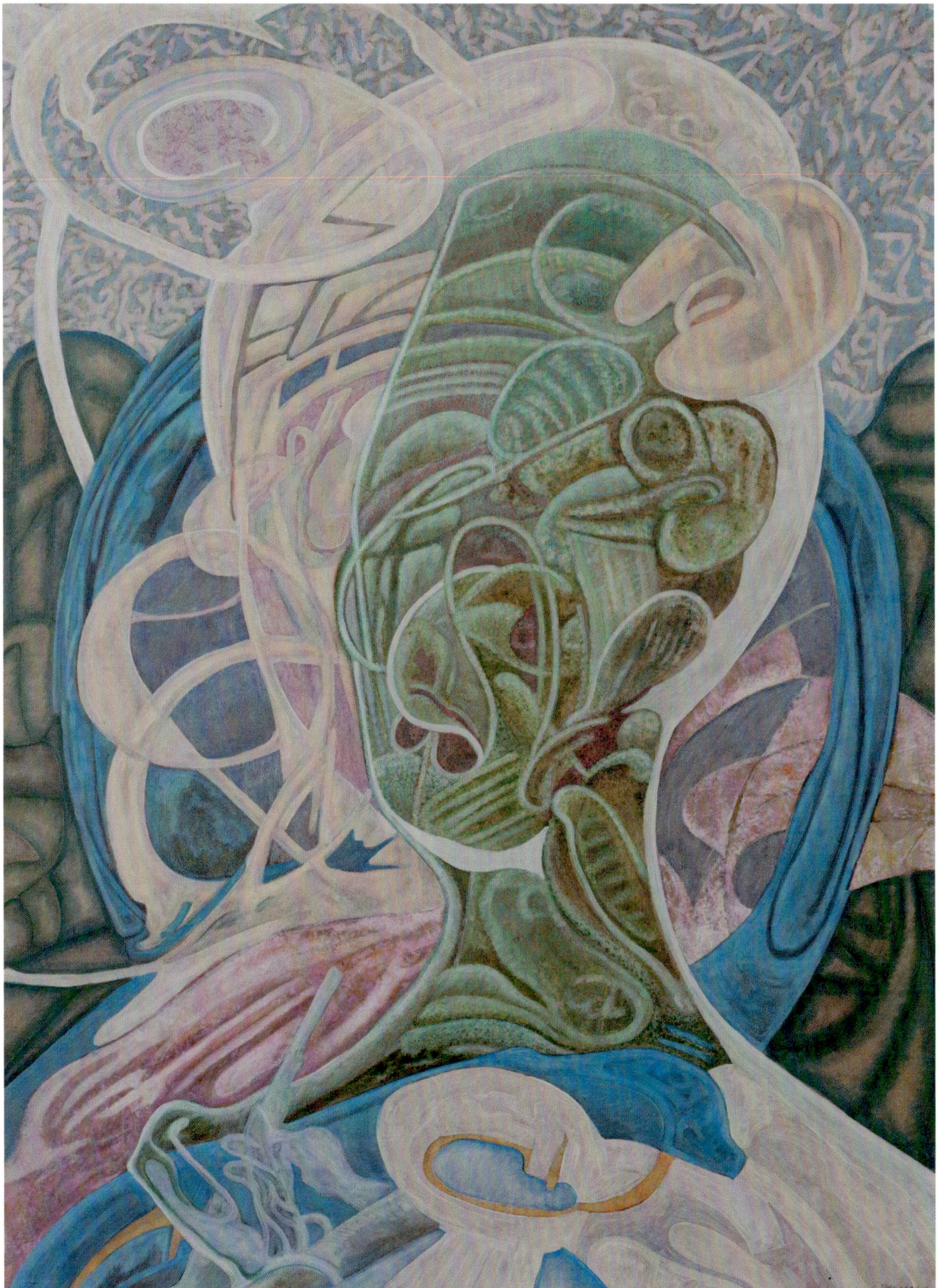

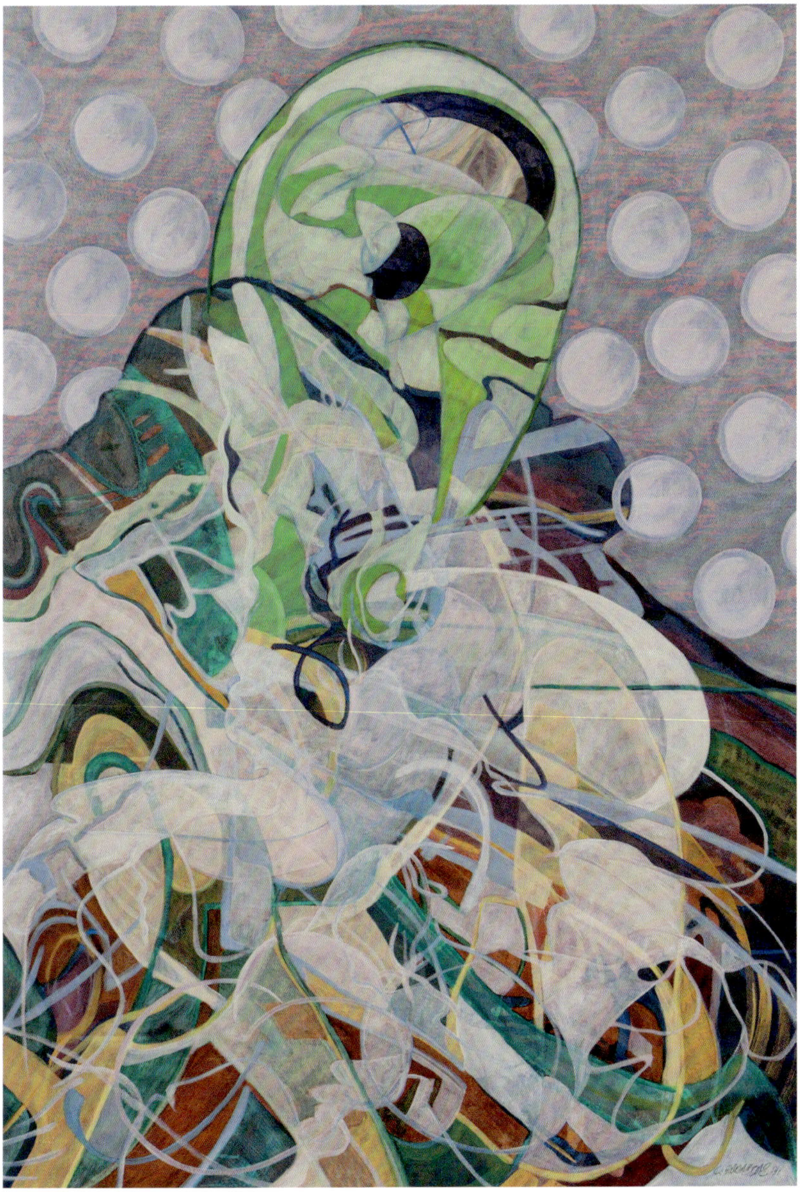

91
Milky Head, 1991, Australien
Öl auf Leinwand, 101 x 75,5 cm
Milky Head, 1991, Australia
oil on canvas, 101 x 75,5 cm

92
Travel through the 4th Dimension, 1991, Australien
Öl auf Leinwand, 101 x 71 cm
Travel through the 4th Dimension, 1991, Australia
oil on canvas, 101 x 71 cm

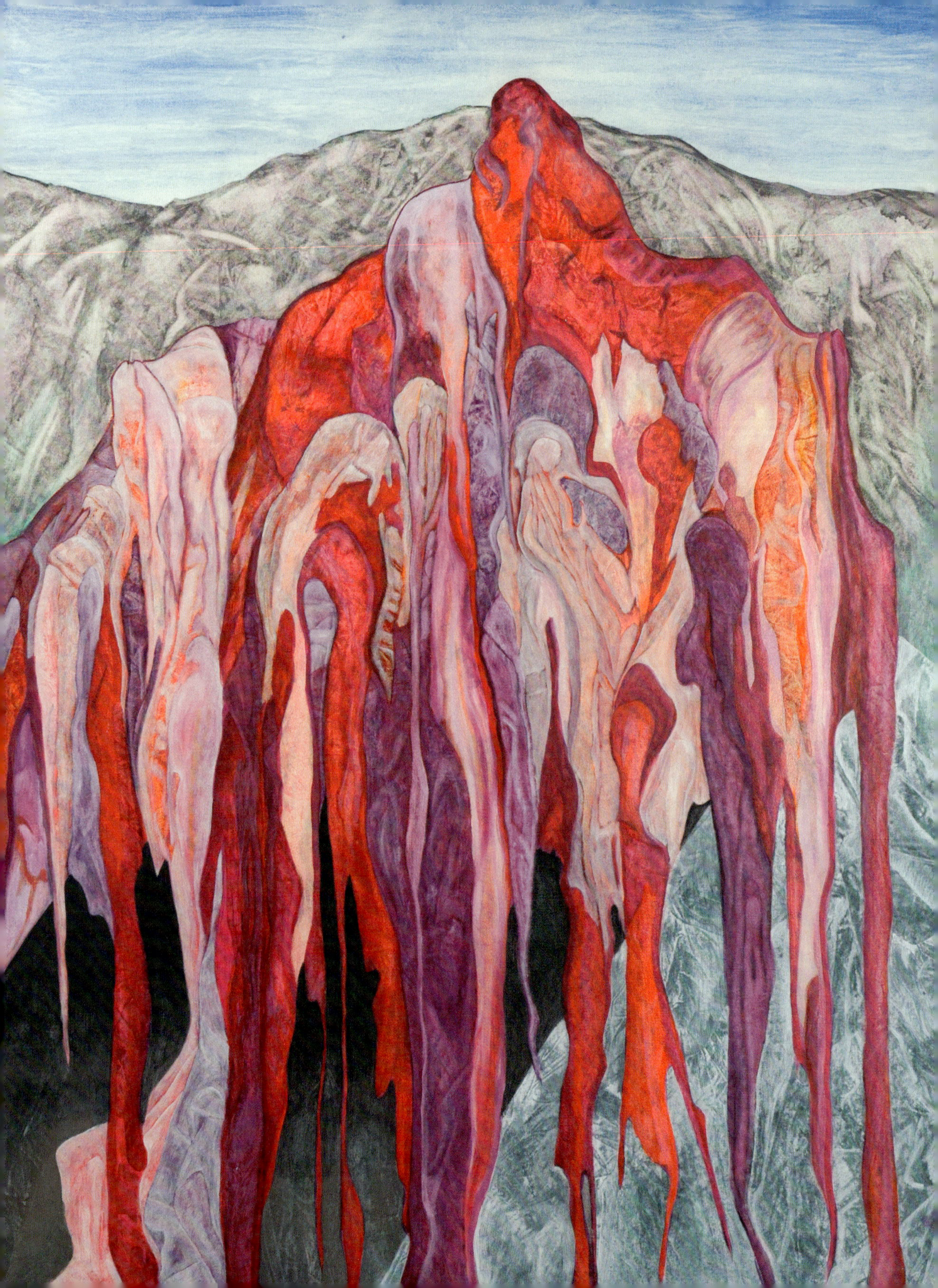

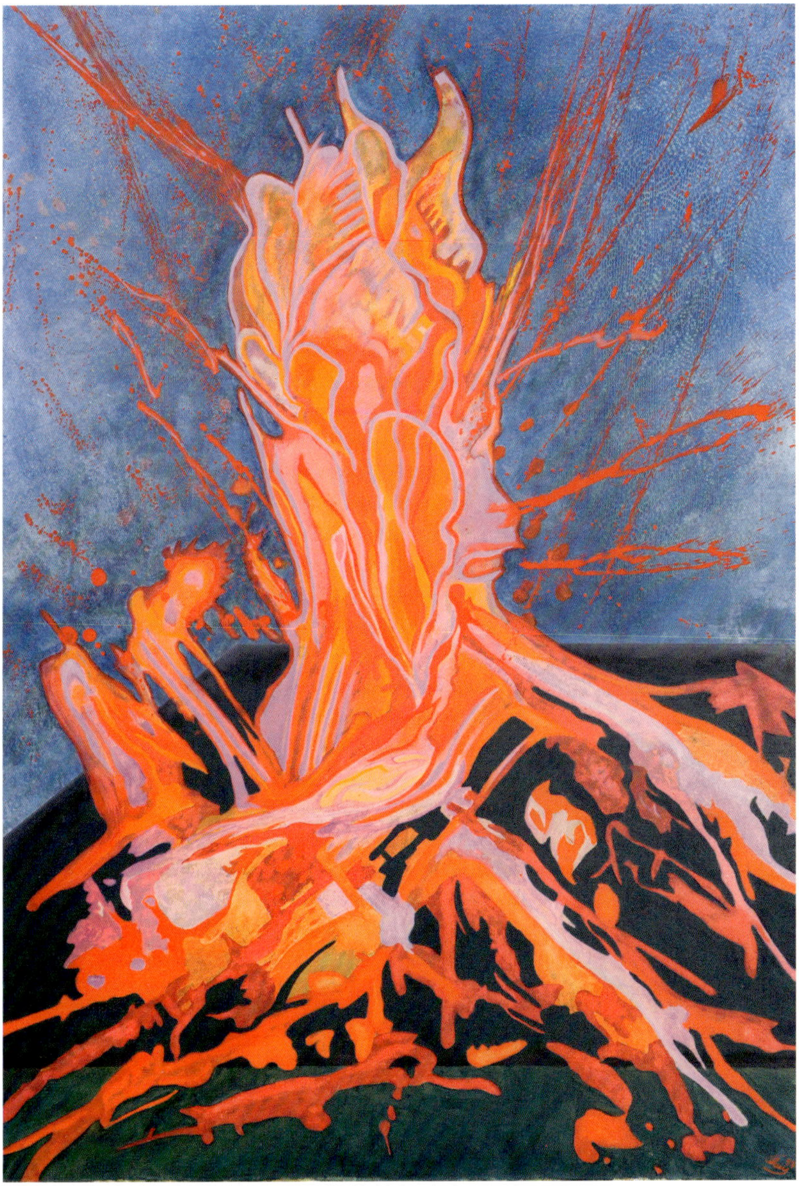

93
Krvavela gora, 1999
Öl auf Leinwand, 97 x 80 cm
Krvavela gora, 1999
oil on canvas, 97 x 80 cm

94
Tintish, 1996
Öl auf Leinwand, 101 x 71 cm
Tintish, 1996
oil on canvas, 101 x 71 cm

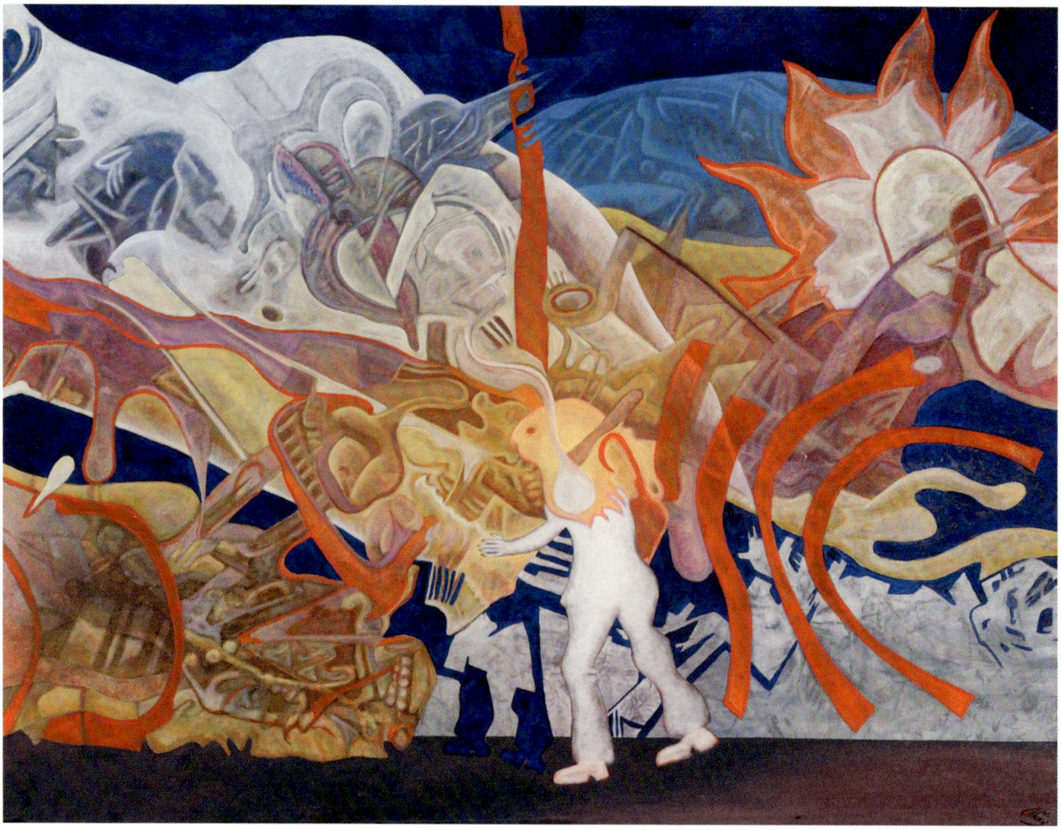

95
E = mc², 1996
Öl auf Leinwand, 84 x 110 cm
E = mc², 1996
oil on canvas, 84 x 110 cm

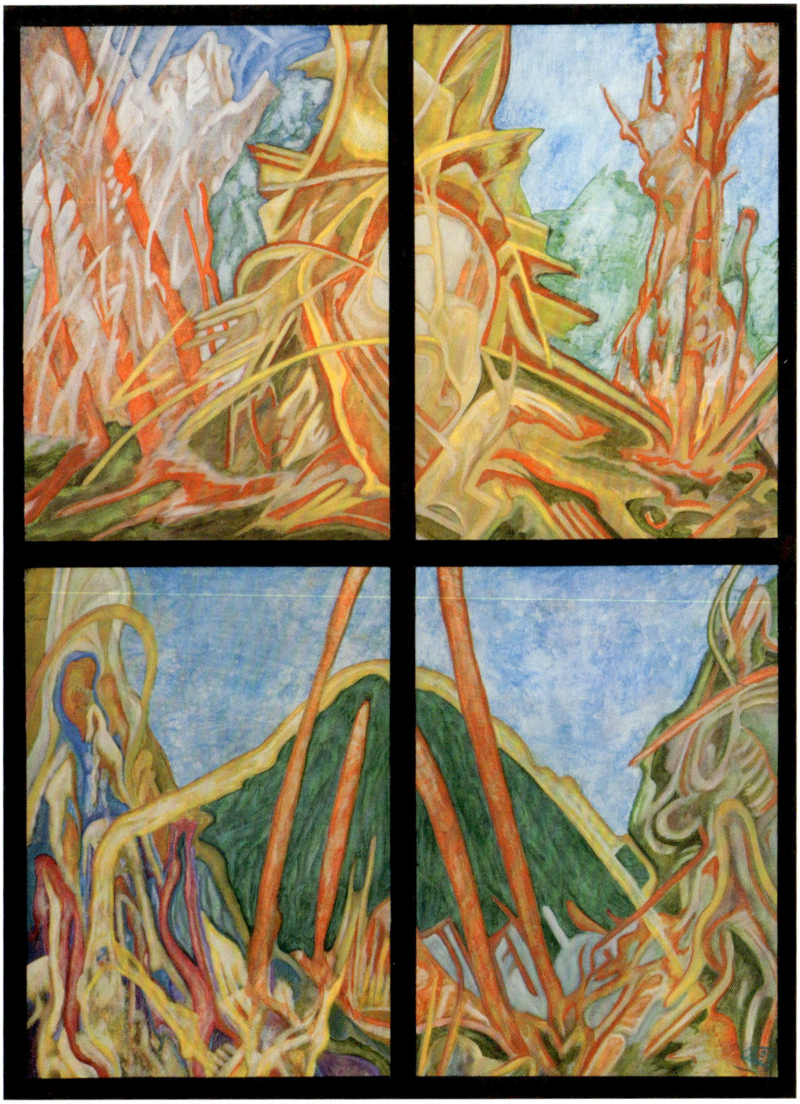

96
From possibility to reality, 1999
Öl auf Leinwand, 101 x 96 cm
From possibility to reality, 1999
oil on canvas, 101 x 96 cm

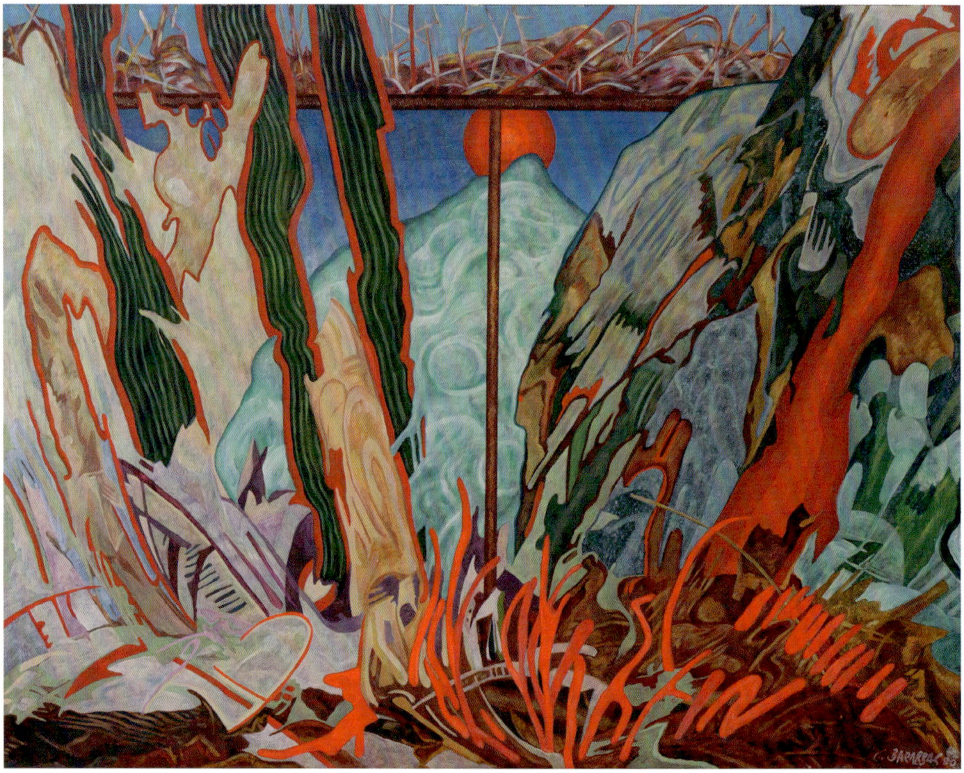

97
Aftermath (Nach der Flut), 1990
Öl auf Leinwand, 88,5 x 115 cm
Aftermath (Nach der Flut), 1990
oil on canvas, 88,5 x 115 cm

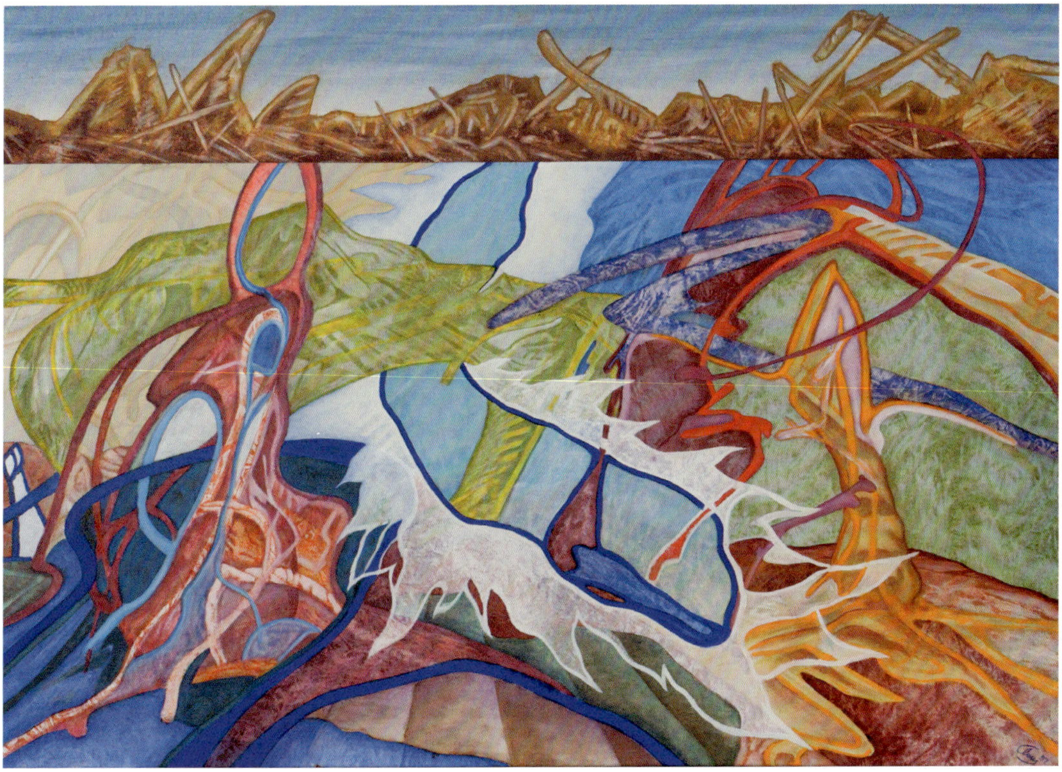

98
Serenity (Heiterkeit – Ruhe), 1997, Australien
Öl auf Leinwand, 71 x 100 cm
Serenity (Heiterkeit – Ruhe), 1997, Australia
oil on canvas, 71 x 100 cm

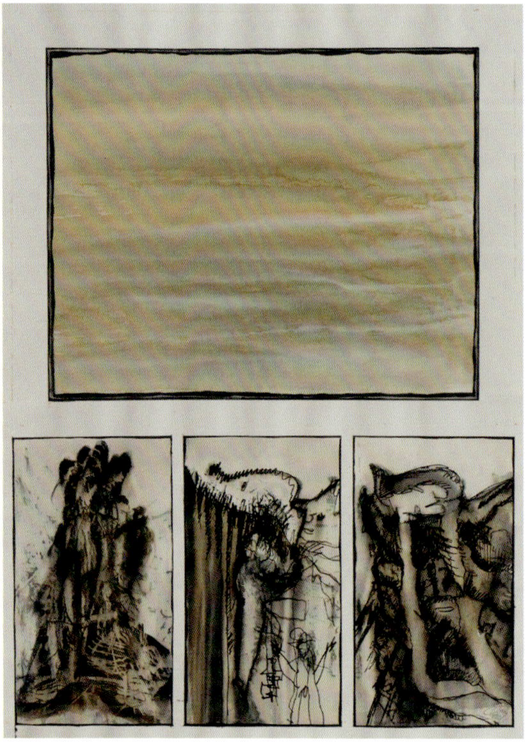

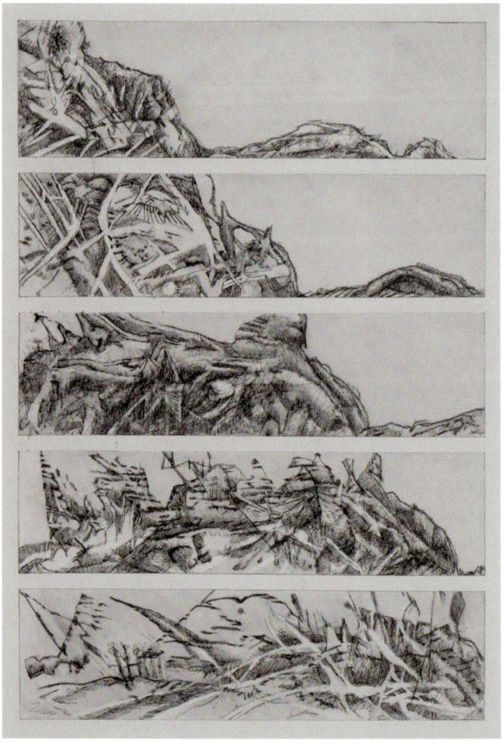

99
Four Possibilities to Reality
Examples of Trans-Realistic Visions in the Gibson Desert, 1999
Tusche auf Papier, 76 x 56 cm
Four Possibilities to Reality
Examples of Trans-Realistic Visions in the Gibson Desert, 1999
drawing ink on paper, 76 x 56 cm

100
Transrealistic Variations on a Landscape, 1999
Tusche auf Papier, 59 x 42 cm
Transrealistic Variations on a Landscape, 1999
drawing ink on paper, 59 x 42 cm

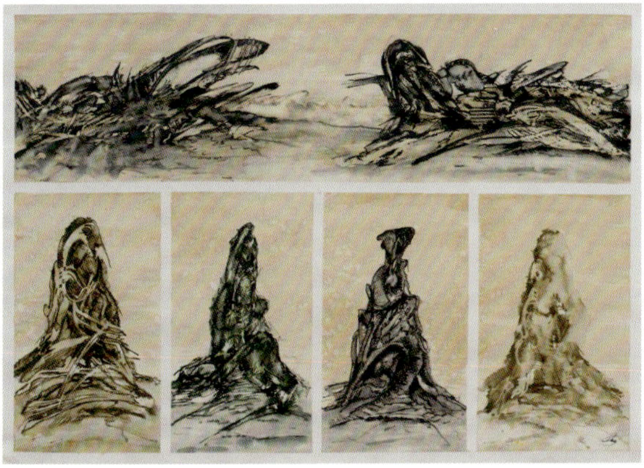

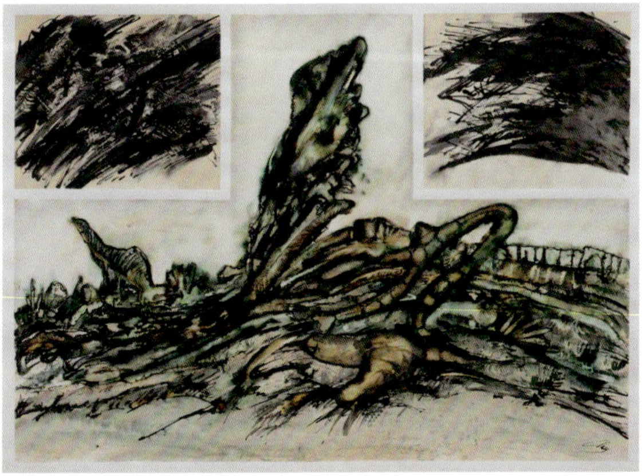

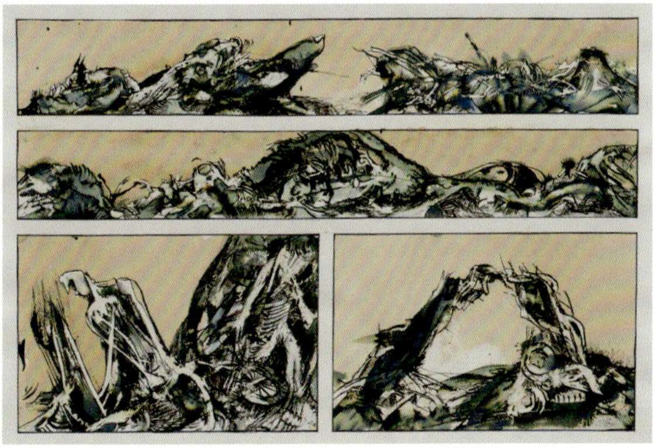

101
Models of Ideal Perfection, 1998
Tinte, Wachs, Kaffee, 56 x 78 cm
Models of Ideal Perfection, 1998
ink, wax, coffee, 56 x 78 cm

102
Aftermath Nr. 3, 1998
Tusche auf Papier, 56 x 76 cm
Aftermath No. 3, 1998
drawing ink on paper, 56 x 76 cm

103
„Friedensreich" may you be in peace, 2000
Mischtechnik, 38 x 56 cm
"Friedensreich" may you be in peace, 2000
mixed technique, 38 x 56 cm

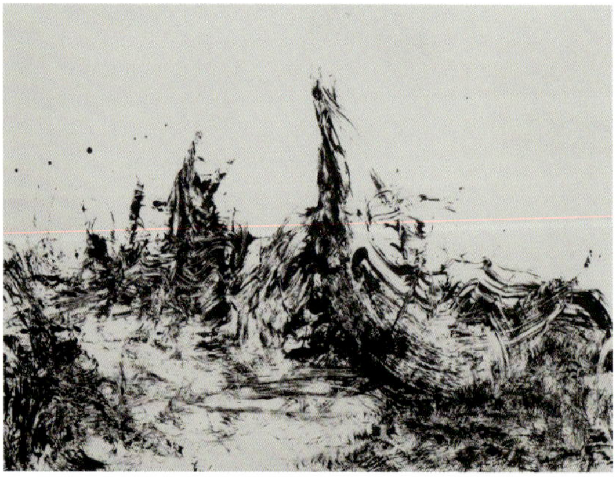

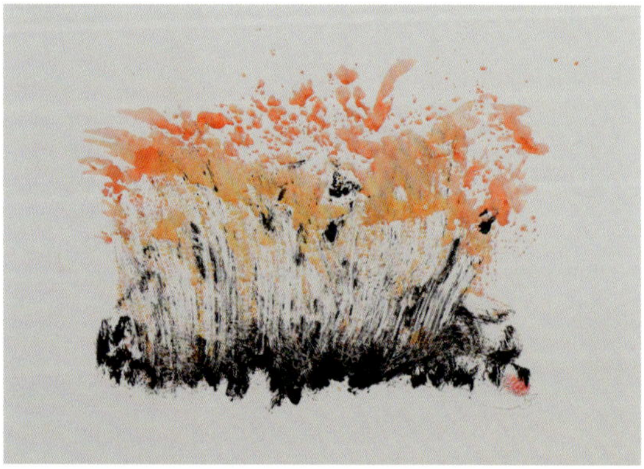

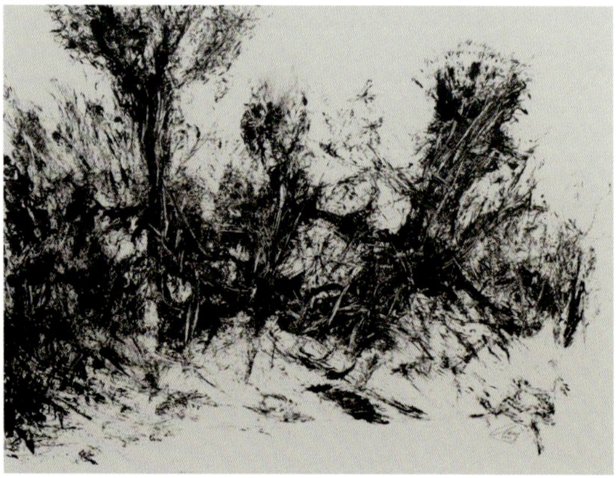

104
O.T., 2001
Enamel auf Papier, 42 x 58 cm
Untitled, 2001
Enamel on paper, 42 x 58 cm

105
O.T., 2001
Enamel auf Papier, 42 x 58 cm
Untitled, 2001
Enamel on paper, 42 x 58 cm

106
O.T., 2001
Enamel auf Papier, 42 x 58 cm
Untitled, 2001
Enamel on paper, 42 x 58 cm

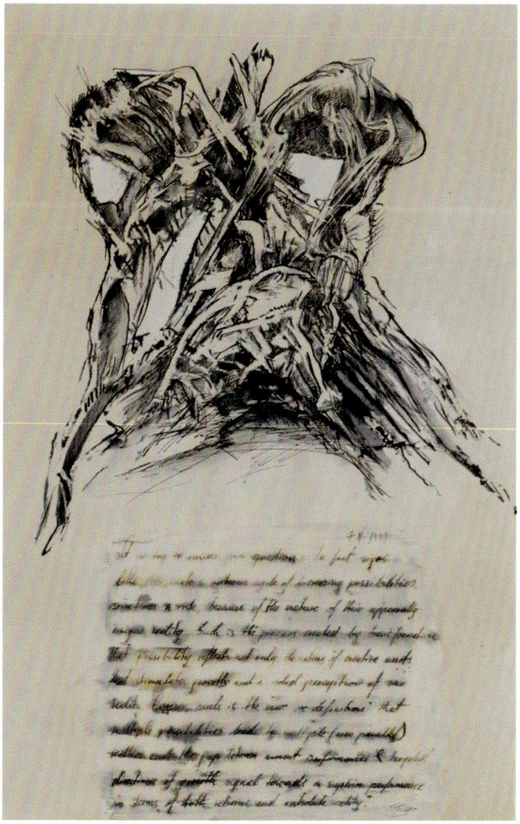

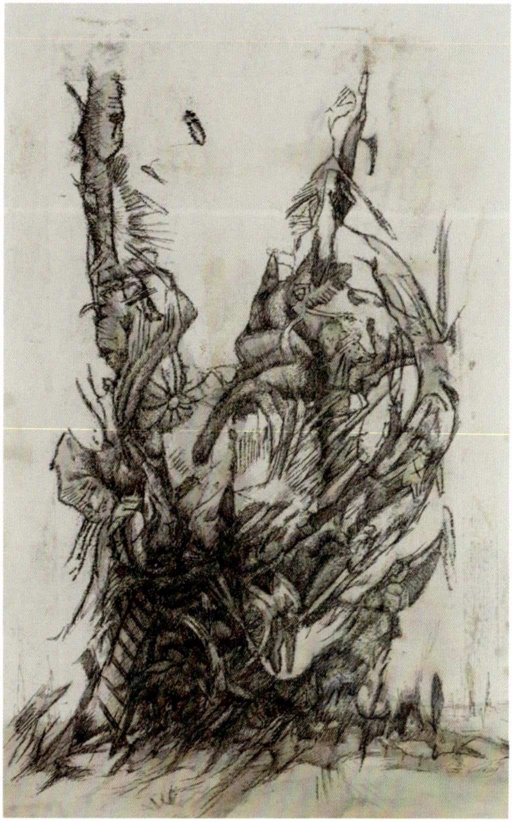

107
Sign, 1999
Mischtechnik auf Papier, 64 x 45 cm
Sign, 1999
mixed technique on paper, 64 x 45 cm

108
Desert Sculpture, 1999
Mischtechnik auf Papier, 56 x 38 cm
Desert Sculpture, 1999
mixed technique on paper, 56 x 38 cm

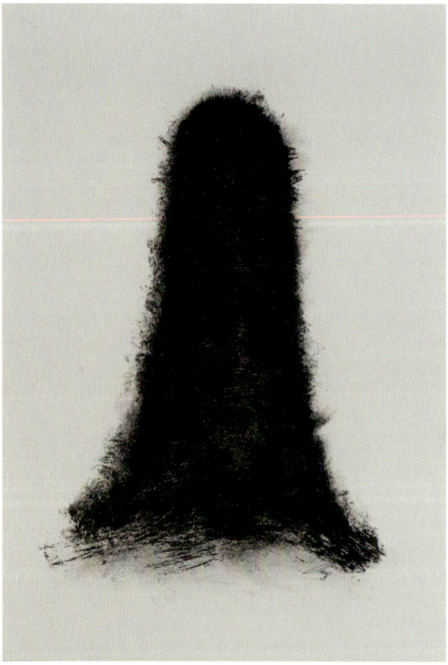

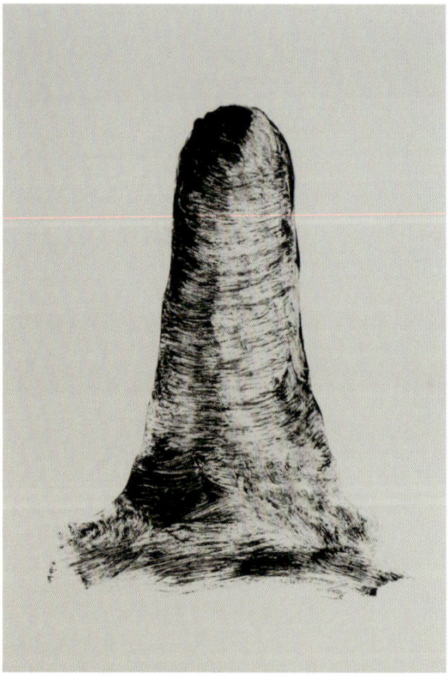

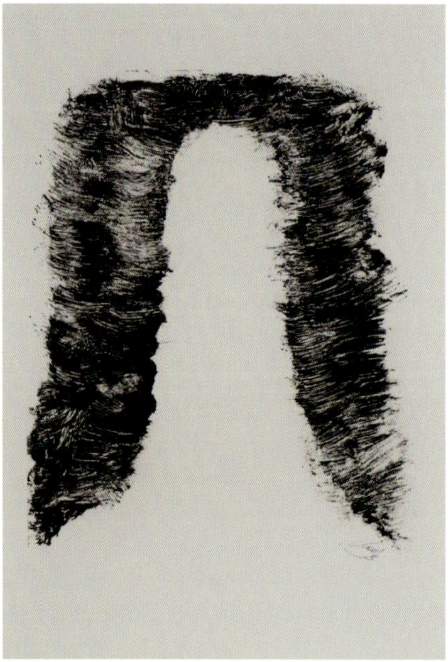

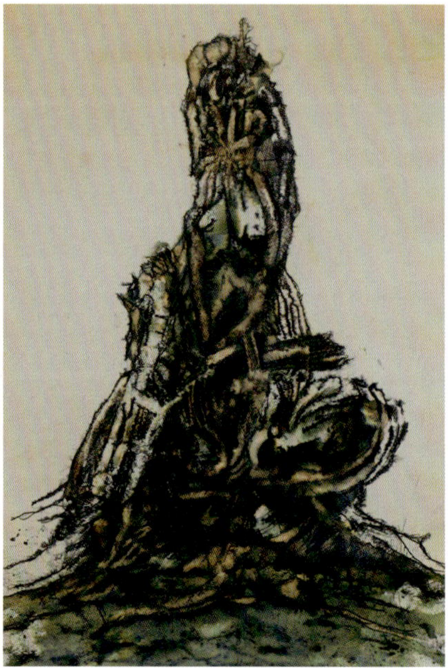

109
Tower
Enamel auf Papier, 59 x 42 cm
Tower
Enamel on paper, 59 x 42 cm

110
O.T.
Enamel auf Papier, 59 x 42 cm
Untitled
Enamel on paper, 59 x 42 cm

111
O.T.
Enamel auf Papier, 59 x 42 cm
Untitled
Enamel on paper, 59 x 42 cm

112
Effective Presentation of a Monument, 1999
Mischtechnik auf Papier, 57 x 38 cm
Effective Presentation of a Monument, 1999
mixed technique on paper, 57 x 38 cm

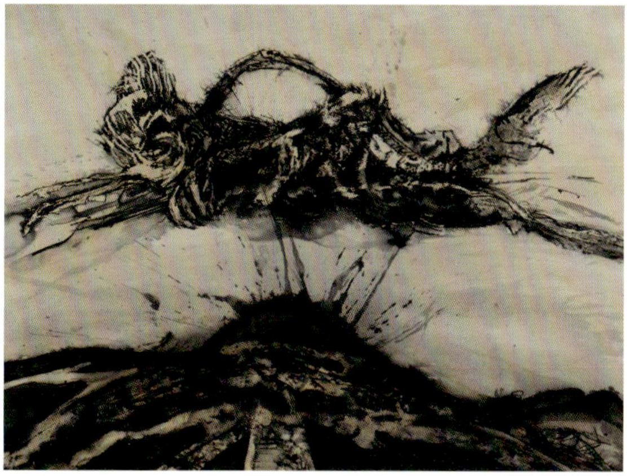

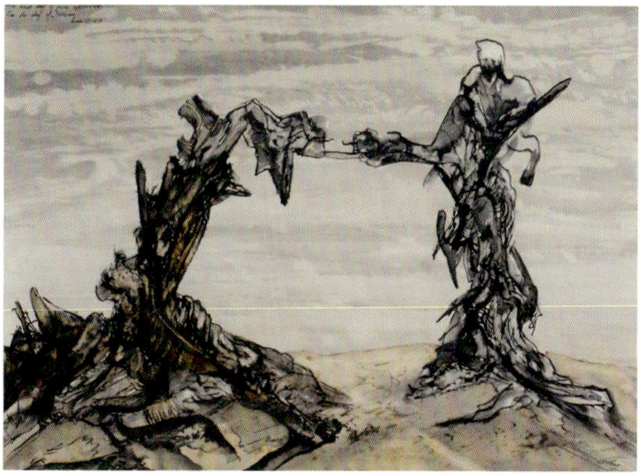

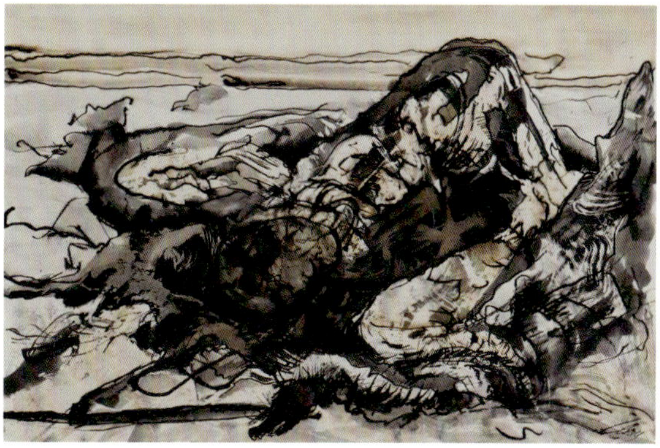

113
Conquest of the Sky, 2001
Mischtechnik auf Papier, 57 x 76 cm
Conquest of the Sky, 2001
mixed technique on paper, 57 x 76 cm

114
For What a Day?, 1999
Mischtechnik auf Papier, 56 x 76 cm
For What a Day?, 1999
mixed technique on paper, 56 x 76 cm

115
Wüstenformation, 2000
Mischtechnik auf Papier, 38 x 56 cm
Desert Formation, 2000
mixed technique on paper, 38 x 56 cm

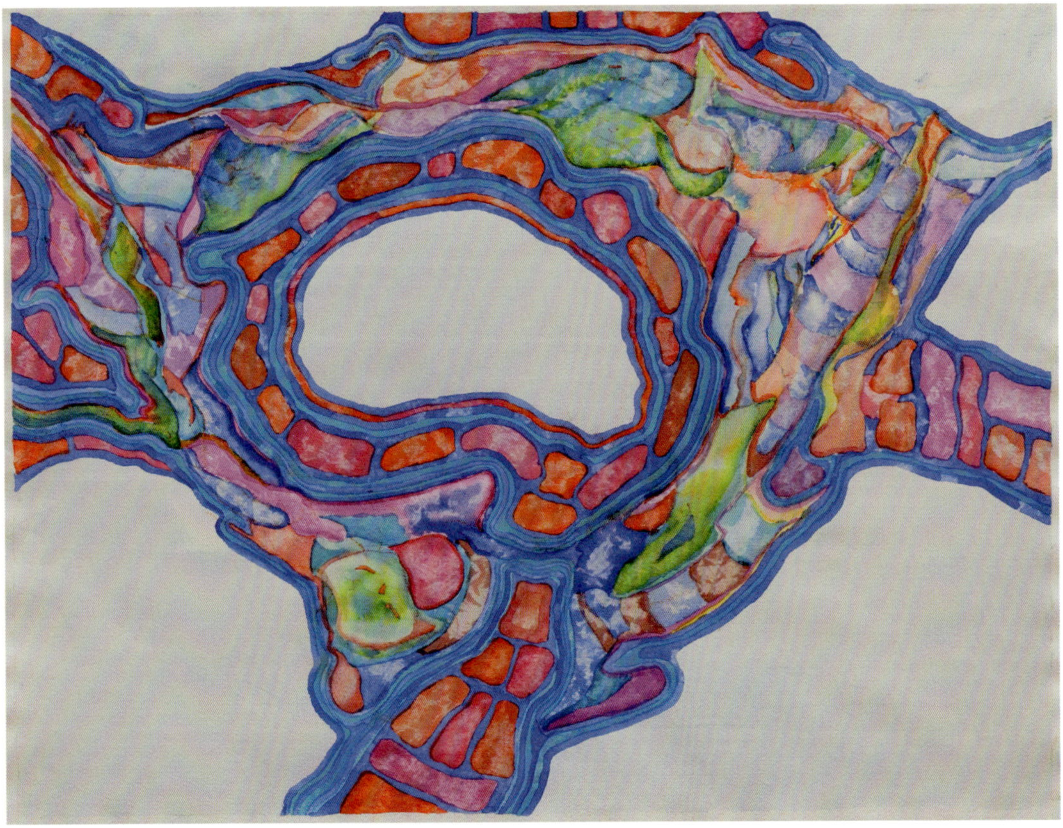

116
Die Mitte, 2007
Aquarell auf Papier, 50 x 65 cm
The Center, 2007
watercolor on paper, 50 x 65 cm

117
Odysseus, 2002
Öl auf Leinwand, 102 x 75 cm
Odysseus, 2002
oil on canvas, 102 x 75 cm

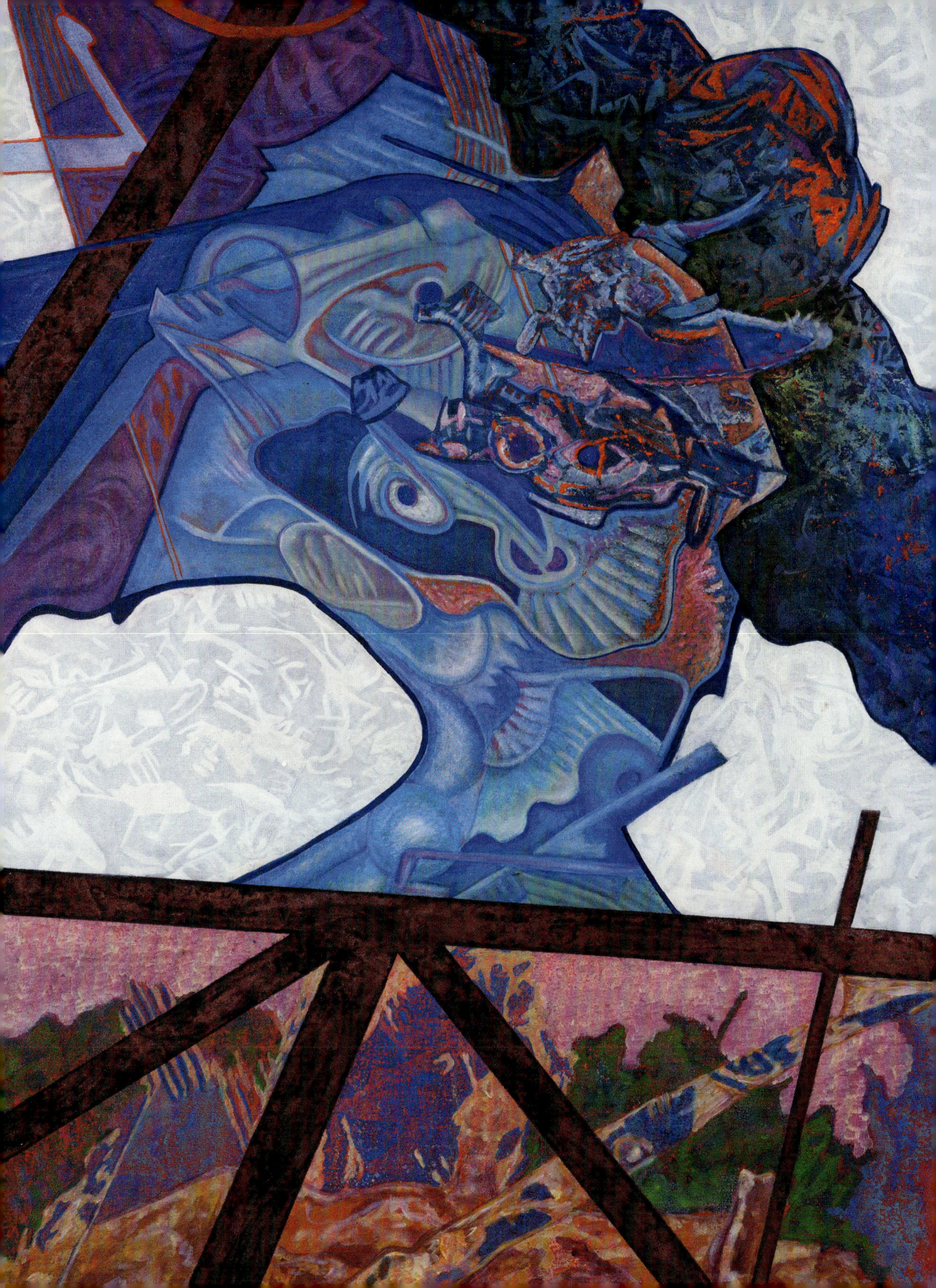

# Saxophonic Brushstrokes

**Claus Mayrhofer Barabbas the Musician**

*Andreas Felber*

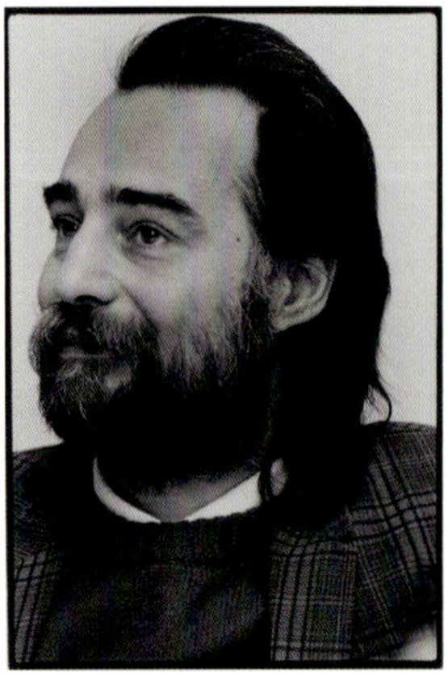

Claus Mayrhofer Barabbas
Claus Mayrhofer Barabbas

What went down on December 13, 1969, in the grand auditorium of the Konzerthaus in Vienna had all the makings of a scandal. The "Masters of Unorthodox Jazz" took the stage, a quintet of musicians wearing long beards, and some went by rather exotic-sounding names: Alaeddin Adlernest (or Eagle's Nest), Harun Ghulam Barabbas, Richard Ahmad Pechoc, Anton Michlmayr, and Walter Muhammad Malli. But what irritated the audience and the critics – who were looking forward to the evening's main act, the pianist Thelonious Monk – most were the unwonted sounds these five men produced.

Over the next few days, the *Kurier* wrote of a "chamber of tonal horrors";[1] the *Volksblatt* called it "jazz to turn you off jazz for life" and a "musical dark ride," and the same review called for the establishment of an "association dedicated to the protection of musical instruments."[2] The daily *Express* reported: "Roughly equal parts of the audience applauded and booed, but the number of people pleading to musicians to 'Stop!' kept growing. The Masters packed up their instruments and left the stage, elated that the listeners had failed to understand them."[3]

Although we should note the apologetic tinge of the reviews that appeared in *Die Presse* and in the *Salzburger Nachrichten,*[4] reactions like these are unthinkable now, forty-three years later. So who were the musicians who provoked such vociferous responses as late as 1969?

First things first: the "Masters" were in fact Austrian born and bred; more specifically, the musicians hailed from Vienna and Graz.[5] Their experience with hostile reactions from the public reached back years, to 1958. That was when Walter Muhammad Malli and Richard Ahmad Pechoc, then 18 and 19, respectively – one came from Graz, the other was born in Vienna – and both students of Albert Paris Gütersloh's at the Academy of Fine Arts Vienna, first took their hobby before an audience at Adebar, a famous artists' pub on Annagasse in downtown

# Saxofonistische Pinselstriche

## Claus Mayrhofer Barabbas als Musiker

*Andreas Felber*

Es roch nach Skandal, was sich am 13. Dezember 1969 im Großen Saal des Wiener Konzerthauses abspielte. Ein Quintett mit dem Namen „Masters of Unorthodox Jazz" stand auf der Bühne, bestehend aus Musikern mit langen Bärten und teilweise exotisch klingenden Namen: Alaeddin Adlernest, Harun Ghulam Barabbas, Richard Ahmad Pechoc, Anton Michlmayr und Walter Muhammad Malli. Vor allem aber waren es die ungewohnten Klänge, die diese fünf Männer von sich gaben, die Publikum und Kritiker – in Erwartung des Hauptprogrammpunkts des Abends, des Pianisten Thelonious Monk – heftig irritierten.

Von einem „tönende[n] Gruselkabinett" war in den darauffolgenden Tagen im „Kurier" zu lesen,[1] im „Volksblatt" von „Jazz zum Abgewöhnen" und einer „musikalische[n] Geisterbahn", wobei im selben Artikel auch der Ruf nach Gründung eines „Instrumentenschutzvereines" laut wurde.[2] Und die Tageszeitung „Express" berichtete: „Das Publikum klatschte und buhte zu etwa gleichen Teilen, plädierte aber schließlich immer öfter für ‚Aufhören!' Die Masters packten ihre Instrumente ein und verließen die Bühne mit dem Hochgefühl, unverstanden geblieben zu sein."[3]

Auch wenn nicht verschwiegen sei, dass in der „Presse" und den „Salzburger Nachrichten" apologetisch gefärbte Rezensionen erschienen,[4] so sind Reaktionen wie diese 43 Jahre später nicht mehr denkbar. Wer also waren diese Musiker, die noch im Jahr 1969 derartig lautes Echo provozierten?

Gleich vorweg: Hinter den „Masters" steckten durchwegs waschechte Österreicher, konkret: Wiener und Grazer Musiker.[5] Ihre Erfahrungen mit unfreundlichen Publikumsreaktionen reichten bereits Jahre zurück, bis 1958, in das berühmte Künstlerlokal Adebar in der Annagasse in der Wiener Innenstadt. Damals hatten Walter Muhammad Malli und Richard Ahmad Pechoc, der eine 18 Jahre jung und aus Graz stammend, der andere 19 und gebürtiger Wiener, beide Studenten bei Albert Paris Gütersloh an der Akademie der bildenden Künste, in der Adebar erstmals öffentlich ihrem Hobby gefrönt. Immer dann, wenn die Hausband pausierte, begannen sie am Flügel abwechselnd spontan zu improvisieren – obwohl beide

Vienna. Whenever the joint's hired band went on a break, they took turns on the grand, launching into spontaneous improvisation. Both were autodidacts on the piano, and a popular and oft-repeated story has it that the waiter, hardly delighted by their efforts, threatened to give them a slap in the face if they didn't leave the instrument alone. The Adebar was also where a trained bassist by the name of Toni Michlmayr joined the two teenagers and raised their experiments above the domain of freewheeling dilettantism.

Over the years that followed, as they toured the city's jazz venues with growing frequency, Malli, Pechoc & Co.'s nocturnal musical experiments continued to unsettle potential audiences. Their performances were always short and came to abrupt ends: on one occasion – or so the story goes – a bar owner even removed the keys from his piano to stop Richard Ahmad Pechoc from playing. Walter Malli, who died in 2012, recalled: "The mere possibility of playing that sort of thing was utopian at the time [...] Our demeanor alone shocked people."[6] In another interview, he remembered that "when I walked into a music joint with Barabbas, some old-established jazzmen blanched! The very sight of us was obviously terrifying; they were scared that we might join in on the ongoing session."[7]

## Galerie zum roten Apfel as an experimental laboratory

If they were a "terrifying" sight, their unusual appearance was a major part of it: Malli and Pechoc dressed in fezzes and harem pants; like the Arabic names Muhammad and Ahmad, this choice of garb grew out of the two friends and fellow students' conversion to Islam in 1958 and, later on, to the Baha'i faith. Claus Mayrhofer Barabbas, then called Harum Ghulam Barabbas – he, too, had become a Muslim and subsequently a Baha'i – stood out most in terms of appearance: he wore robes in luminous colors and kept his hair long, which was still unusual back then (later on, he would cut it to a Mohawk). He had first gotten to know his colleagues in 1960, at Galerie zum roten Apfel at 74 Landstraßer Hauptstraße. Setting up at Richard Pechoc's parents' apartment, the two friends had established not only a venue for presentations of their visual art, but also a sort of sheltered workshop for their musical adventures, a space where they were free to indulge their musical preferences without restraint or hindrance; sympathetic art-opening audiences provided encouragement and positive feedback.

Galerie zum roten Apfel, which has recently been the subject of a growing body of literature,[8] opened on July 11, 1959, and existed until 1965. During those years, the venue quickly grew into a fixture of the Vienna gallery scene. Jürgen Leskowa,

pianistische Autodidakten waren. Oft und gerne erzählt wird die Geschichte des darob wenig begeisterten Ober, der die beiden unter Androhung von Ohrfeigen vom Klavier zu vertreiben suchte. Allerdings gesellte sich in der Adebar auch ein ausgebildeter Bassist namens Toni Michlmayr zu den beiden Teenagern und enthob damit deren Experimente der Sphäre unbekümmerten Dilettierens.

In den folgenden Jahren mehrten sich die nächtlichen Jazzlokaltouren, im Zuge derer Malli, Pechoc und Kollegen mit ihren musikalischen Experimenten potenzielle Auditorien verunsicherten. Es waren dies stets kurze, unsanft beendete Auftritte: Einmal – so wird erzählt – habe ein Lokalbesitzer sogar die Klaviatur aus seinem Flügel entfernt, um Richard Ahmad Pechoc am Spielen zu hindern. Der 2012 verstorbene Walter Malli erzählte: „Damals war ja überhaupt die Möglichkeit, das zu spielen, eine Utopie. [...] Allein unser Auftreten hat die Leute schon schockiert."[6] Und an anderer Stelle: „Wenn ich zusammen mit Barabbas in ein Musiklokal eingetreten bin, wurde so mancher alteingesessene Jazzer bleich im Gesicht! Bereits unser Anblick war offenbar furchterregend; die hatten Angst, dass wir in die laufende Session einsteigen könnten."[7]

## Die Galerie zum roten Apfel als Experimentierlabor

Der „furchterregende" Anblick hatte mit dem unüblichen Äußeren zu tun: Malli und Pechoc kleideten sich mit Fez und Pluderhosen, was – wie auch die arabischen Namen Muhammad und Ahmad – daher rührte, dass die beiden Freunde und Studienkollegen 1958 zum Islam und später zur Baha'i-Religion konvertiert waren. Claus Mayrhofer Barabbas, der damalige Harun Ghulam Barabbas – auch er war Muslim und später Baha'i geworden –, war der optisch Hervorstechendste: Er trug farbenprächtige, leuchtend bunte Gewänder, zudem – damals noch ungewöhnlich – lange Haare, später eine Irokesen-Frisur. Seine Kollegen hatte er im Jahr 1960 in der Galerie zum roten Apfel in der Landstraßer Hauptstraße 74 kennen gelernt. Hier, in der Wohnung der Eltern von Richard Pechoc, hatten sich die beiden Freunde nicht nur eine eigene Präsentationsmöglichkeit für ihre bildnerischen Werke, sondern auch eine Art geschützte Werkstätte für ihre musikalischen Umtriebe geschaffen, einen Freiraum, in dem sie ohne alle Hemm- und Hindernisse ihrer Musik frönen konnten und von Seiten eines wohlwollenden Vernissagen-Publikums Zuspruch und Bestätigung erfuhren.

Diese in den letzten Jahren publizistisch in den Blickpunkt gerückte Galerie zum roten Apfel[8] wurde am 11. Juli 1959 eröffnet und bestand bis 1965. In dieser Zeit entwickelte sie sich rasch zu einem Fixpunkt in Wiens Galerien-Szene. Jürgen Leskowa, Martha Jungwirth und einmal auch Hermann Nitsch stellten hier

Martha Jungwirth, and, on one occasion, Hermann Nitsch showed their pictures there; Alfred Schmeller, who would later lead the Museum des 20. Jahrhunderts, as well as Walter Koschatzky, who became director of the Graphic Arts Collection of the Albertina in 1962, regularly graced the gallery's openings with their presence. Malli and Pechoc made acquaintance not only with fellow artists, but also with people who shared their musical interests such as Karl Anton Fleck, who first showed his art at Galerie zum roten Apfel on March 27, 1961; a trained jazz drummer (he had attended Walter Heidrich's jazz school in Vienna in the late 1940s[9]), he was quickly integrated into the band's sessions as well: on May 28, 1961, the "Ahmad Pechoc Trio," with Fleck as percussionist, Walter Malli on the drums, and Richard Pechoc at the piano, gave Austria's first free jazz concert at Forum Stadtpark, a venue in Graz that had recently opened its doors.[10] And then there was the abovementioned Claus Mayrhofer Barabbas, who first exhibited pictures at Galerie zum roten Apfel in 1960, when he was only seventeen years old, and started performing on the saxophone in 1962.

## From Claus Mayrhofer to Harun Ghulam Barabbas

Who was this Barabbas? He was born Claus Mayrhofer in Vienna on May 2, 1943. His earliest musical socialization came in the form of piano lessons he began to receive as a child. His piano teacher, a devotee of Arnold Schoenberg's music, familiarized him with the works of the Second Viennese School early on. And there were other sounds that thrilled the teenager: *"I lived on Glanzinggasse in the 19th district, in the American-occupied zone. So friendships offered opportunities for me to listen to jazz [...] Although the names didn't mean anything to me at the time, I was able to reconstruct in retrospect that I'd listened to bebop or swing. There were Lionel Hampton and Dizzy Gillespie, and of course there was Charlie Parker as well."*[11]

One important influence on the young Mayrhofer Barabbas was an acquaintance of his sister's: Padhi Frieberger, a scenester, painter and object artist, pigeon breeder, and, in the 1950s, Dixieland drummer. Mayrhofer Barabbas's senior by twelve years, Frieberger first took the teenager along to Galerie nächst St. Stephan, where he introduced him to artists like Andreas Urteil, Josef Mikl, and Arnulf Rainer. Mayrhofer Barabbas recalled: *"Disregarding the practical jokes and snide remarks you would expect people to treat a fifteen-year-old to, I had the feeling that I was being accepted. So I discovered I was an artist, and that's what I articulated."*[12]

As an outward expression of this realization of his artistic calling, Claus Mayrhofer Barabbas left school at the age of fifteen and replaced his last name

Bilder aus, Alfred Schmeller, später Direktor des Museums des 20. Jahrhunderts, und auch Walter Koschatzky, der 1962 das Direktorat der Graphischen Sammlung Albertina übernahm, waren gern gesehene Vernissagengäste. Hier schlossen Malli und Pechoc nicht nur mit Künstlerkollegen Bekanntschaft, sondern auch mit musikalisch Gleichgesinnten, etwa mit Karl Anton Fleck, der am 27. März 1961 erstmals in der Galerie zum roten Apfel ausstellte und der als gelernter Jazzschlagzeuger (er hatte Ende der 1940er Jahre Walter Heidrichs Institut für Jazzmusik in Wien besucht)[9] rasch auch in die Sessions integriert wurde: Am 28. Mai 1961 bestritt er als Perkussionist gemeinsam mit Walter Malli (Schlagzeug) und Richard Pechoc (Klavier) im „Ahmad Pechoc Trio" im kurz zuvor eröffneten Forum Stadtpark in Graz das erste Free-Jazz-Konzert Österreichs.[10] Und da war der bereits erwähnte Claus Mayrhofer Barabbas, der 1960 als 17-Jähriger erstmals in der Galerie zum roten Apfel Bilder ausstellte und ab 1962 als Saxofonist auch musizierend in Erscheinung trat.

## Von Claus Mayrhofer zu Harun Ghulam Barabbas

Wer war dieser Barabbas? Geboren worden war er am 2. Mai 1943 als Claus Mayrhofer in Wien. Seine früheste musikalische Sozialisation vollzog sich in Gestalt von Klavierunterricht, den er ab dem Kindesalter erhielt. Durch seine Klavierlehrerin, eine Liebhaberin der Musik Arnold Schönbergs, wurde er schon früh mit der Musik der Zweiten Wiener Schule vertraut gemacht. Und da waren auch andere Klänge, die den Jugendlichen elektrisierten: *„Ich wohnte in der Glanzinggasse im XIX. Bezirk, in der amerikanischen Besatzungszone. So hatte ich durch Freundschaften die Möglichkeit, Jazz zu hören. [...] Obwohl mir Namen damals nichts sagten, konnte ich später rekonstruieren, dass diese Musik Bebop oder Swing war. Da war Lionel Hampton, Dizzy Gillespie und natürlich auch Charlie Parker."*[11]

Ein wichtiger früher Einfluss für Mayrhofer Barabbas bedeutete ein Bekannter seiner Schwester: Padhi Frieberger, Szenefigur, Maler und Objektkünstler, Taubenzüchter, in den 1950er Jahren zudem als Dixieland-Schlagzeuger aktiv. Frieberger, zwölf Jahre älter als Mayrhofer Barabbas, nahm den Jugendlichen in die Galerie nächst St. Stephan mit und stellte ihn Künstlern wie Andreas Urteil, Josef Mikl und Arnulf Rainer vor. Mayrhofer Barabbas: *„Bis auf das, dass man halt einen 15-Jährigen rollt und [über ihn] Schmäh führt, hatte ich das Gefühl, akzeptiert zu sein. So entdeckte ich, dass ich Künstler bin, und artikulierte es."*[12]

Um der Erkenntnis seiner künstlerischen Berufung auch nach außen hin Ausdruck zu verleihen, verließ Claus Mayrhofer Barabbas 15-jährig das Gymnasium und ersetzte seinen Familiennamen durch das biblische „Barabbas", den Namen

with the biblical "Barabbas," the name of the insurrectionist whom Pontius Pilate, at the crowd's request, pardoned at Passover instead of Jesus of Nazareth. *"Because I'd always been a rebel,"* he remembered, he had often been called that name at home; now he adopted "Barabbas" as his *nom de guerre*.[13]

The young man's demeanor, too, was sometimes rebellious. The bassist Anton Michlmayr, later one of his fellow "Masters of Unorthodox Jazz," recalled the first encounter at Adebar in 1958: "He walked in, very bizarre, a total freak by the standards of the time, his hair very long, barefoot, wearing a T-shirt with a giant cross, a crucifix, painted on the back – so he came into Adebar, walked from table to table, saying, 'I'm a Christian!' Then he sat down and ordered a glass of water. Of course, the waiter viewed him with hostility right away."[14]

In early 1962, after Mayrhofer Barabbas had spent several months travelling through France and Germany, paying his way by playing the piano in a rhythm & blues style influenced by Little Richard and Ray Charles, he merged his musical energies with Pechoc's and Malli's. Switching from the piano – the instrument was already in Pechoc's hands – to the saxophone came easy to him. Pechoc remembers that the notes "gushed forth" from Mayrhofer Barabbas's new instrument at once "like water from a fountain."[15] According to Walter Malli, he was a "natural" and "played from the very first minute the way he then did over the years that followed."[16]

Without the assistance of a saxophone teacher or even fingering charts – he would have rejected them anyway – Mayrhofer Barabbas set out to explore the possibilities of his new instruments (he started on the alto and tenor saxes around the same time): an autodidact who followed only his own ear, he tested unconventional fingering combinations and developed special breathing techniques. He, too, was guided and inspired by the tradition of modern jazz: his absolute favorite was Thelonious Monk, and he regarded Monk's album "Brilliant Corners," recorded for Riverside in late 1956, as an especially important milestone, the more so since it also featured the saxophonists Ernie Henry and Sonny Rollins, whose aggressive edge and melodic inventiveness impressed him deeply. As Mayrhofer Barabbas himself said, he consciously avoided any stylistic imitation of his lodestars,[17] deliberately seeking to build an expressive idiom of his own. His approach to music, like Malli's and Pechoc's, was profoundly informed by his work as a visual artist. In retrospect, Mayrhofer Barabbas described their musical practice during those years as follows: *"The three of us were all painters, and in our painting we were in the middle of abstract expressionism or tachism at the time [Malli and Pechoc had already left that period behind, A.F.], so we wanted to do something similar in music. It was important to us to respond directly and cou-*

jenes Aufständischen, den Pontius Pilatus anlässlich des Passah-Festes anstelle von Jesus von Nazareth auf Wunsch des Volkes begnadigte. *„Da ich immer ein Rebell war"*, hatte man ihn zu Hause oft so genannt; nun nahm er „Barabbas" als seinen „nom de guerre" an.[13]

Rebellisch war mitunter auch das Auftreten des Jugendlichen. Bassist Anton Michlmayr, sein späterer Partner im Kontext der „Masters of Unorthodox Jazz", erinnert sich an die erste Begegnung in der Adebar anno 1958: „Der ist gekommen, ganz skurril, ganz ausgeflippt für damals, ganz lange Haare, barfuß, mit einem T-Shirt, hinten war ein riesiges Kreuz, ein Kruzifix, draufgemalt; da ist er reingekommen in die Adebar und ist von Tisch zu Tisch gegangen und hat gesagt: ‚I bin a Christ!' Dann hat er sich niedergesetzt und ein Glas Wasser bestellt. Der Kellner war ihm natürlich sofort feindlich gesinnt."[14]

Anfang 1962, nachdem Mayrhofer Barabbas mehrere Monate lang durch Frankreich und Deutschland gereist war und sich dabei mit an Little Richard und Ray Charles orientiertem Rhythm & Blues-Pianospiel verdingt hatte, vereinigten sich seine musikalischen Energien mit jenen Pechocs und Mallis. Der Umstieg vom Piano – das bereits durch Pechoc besetzt war – zum Saxofon fiel nicht schwer. Pechoc erinnert sich, die Töne seien aus Mayrhofer Barabbas' neuem Instrument sogleich „gesprudelt wie aus einer Quelle".[15] Laut Walter Malli hat das „Naturtalent [...] von der ersten Minute [an] schon so gespielt, wie er es dann auch in den folgenden Jahren praktiziert hat."[16]

Ohne auf Saxofonschulen oder Grifftabellen zurückgreifen zu können und zu wollen, ging Mayrhofer Barabbas daran, autodidaktisch und nur nach dem Gehör die Möglichkeiten seiner neuen Instrumente – er begann etwa gleichzeitig mit Alt- und Tenorsaxofon – mittels unkonventioneller Griffkombinationen und spezieller Atemtechniken auszuloten. Auch für ihn fungierte dabei die Tradition des modernen Jazz als Leitbild und Inspiration: Sein absoluter Favorit hieß Thelonious Monk; im Besonderen das Ende 1956 für Riverside eingespielte Monk-Album „Brilliant Corners" galt ihm als Markstein, zumal daran auch die Saxofonisten Ernie Henry und Sonny Rollins, dessen aggressiver Biss und melodischer Einfallsreichtum ihn beeindruckten, beteiligt waren. Bewusst vermied Mayrhofer Barabbas nach eigener Aussage eine stilistische Annäherung an seine Leitsterne[17] und versuchte stattdessen gezielt, sich eine eigene Ausdrucksweise anzueignen. Sein Zugang zur Musik war wie auch jener Mallis und Pechocs nachhaltig von der Tätigkeit als bildender Künstler geprägt. Rückblickend beschrieb Mayrhofer Barabbas die musikalische Praxis dieser frühen Jahre wie folgt: *„Da wir alle drei Maler waren und [uns] in unserer Malerei damals inmitten des abstrakten Expressionismus oder des Tachismus befanden [diese Zeit war für Malli und Pechoc bereits vo-*

*rageously to the given material, while also exerting a strong influence on the progression of the musical piece [...] Initially, as we understood the musical process, it was as though we were all painting on one and the same picture and responding to each other. Of course, that was very different from the developments and philosophies in music in the United States. Given the free use I made of my saxophone, my exploration of its various acoustic possibilities, the instrument naturally sometimes started to produce very unconventional sounds, groaning, smoking, crashing, singing, whistling [...] that was hardly surprising, of course [...] since the idea of expanding the saxophone was in the air [...] The importance and necessity of extending music into space – and I experienced it as spatial as well, as a gesture, like, for example, a sweeping motion, a vigorous brushstroke."*[18]

## Impulses: founding the "Masters" and the début LP "Overground"

Mayrhofer Barabbas not only quickly became an enthusiastic partner in the sessions his two older fellow artists staged, he soon also began to contribute his own ideas: he was the driving force behind the meeting of four musicians for a joint performance at a recording studio in Vienna on August 4, 1964. Besides himself, these were Walter Muhammad Malli (drums), Richard Ahmad Pechoc (piano), and the bassoonist Horst Brückl a.k.a. Alaeddin Adlernest, a friend from Malli's teenage years in Graz and now a member of the Graz Philharmonics. The improvisations recorded that day were never published, but the event marks a turning point: the desire to capture the results of their work on their music, to document their sonic practice, was also an expression of the musicians' awareness of its relevance. It was probably also on occasion of these recordings that they first used the provocative moniker "Masters of Unorthodox Jazz" – August 1964, that is to say, may be regarded as the ensemble's founding date.[19]

Over the next few years, Mayrhofer Barabbas remained a source of important impulses. Three years after the "Masters" – with the lineup Barabbas/Malli/Pechoc – delivered their official début concert performance at the Internationales Kulturzentrum on Vienna's Annagasse on June 22, 1966, he once more pushed to ensure that the music of the ensemble, now a quintet that had also performed at the Museum des 20. Jahrhunderts and the grand auditorium of the Konzerthaus, would not be lost to history. On May 16, 1969, the "Masters of Unorthodox Jazz" recorded four pieces at the Austrophon studio, located inside the Konzerthaus building, that were then pressed in vinyl and published as an LP by the bankroller's own label Barabbas Records. "Overground" was the title of Austria's first free jazz record.[20] It really was Mayrhofer Barabbas's brainchild: he rented the studio and organized the pressing and distribution; so this record may also

*rüber; Anm. A.F.], wollten wir Ähnliches in der Musik machen. Es war uns wichtig, auf das gegebene Material direkt und mutig zu reagieren, aber auch gleichzeitig starken Einfluss auf den Fortschritt des Musikstücks zu nehmen. [...] Wir verstanden im Anfang den Spielprozess [so], als wie wenn wir alle an einem gleichen Bild gemalt hätten und aufeinander reagiert hätten. Das natürlich unterschied sich ziemlich stark von den musikalischen Entwicklungen und Philosophien in den Vereinigten Staaten. Dass natürlich mein Saxophon durch die freie Verwendung, durch das Erforschen der verschiedenen klanglichen Möglichkeiten, anfing, manchmal sehr unkonventionell zu klingen, stöhnend, rauchend, krachend, singend, pfeifend, [...] war natürlich auch klar, [...] da es ja in der Luft lag, das Saxophon zu erweitern [...]. [Es war] die Bedeutung und Notwendigkeit, die Musik räumlich auszudehnen – und ich erlebte sie auch räumlich, als Geste, wie zum Beispiel ein Schwung, ein starker Pinselstrich."*[18]

## Impulse: Gründung der „Masters" und LP-Debüt „Overground"

Mayrhofer Barabbas mutierte nicht nur rasch zum begeisterten Session-Partner seiner beiden älteren Künstler-Kollegen, er begann alsbald selbst Akzente zu setzen: Er war es, der am 4. August 1964 vier Musiker dazu veranlasste, sich in ein Wiener Tonstudio zu begeben und dort Aufnahmen zu machen. Neben ihm selbst waren dies Walter Muhammad Malli (Schlagzeug), Richard Ahmad Pechoc (Klavier) und der Fagottist Horst Brückl alias Alaeddin Adlernest, ein Grazer Jugendfreund Mallis, nunmehr im Orchester der Grazer Philharmoniker beschäftigt. Die an diesem Tag konservierten Improvisationen blieben unveröffentlicht, bedeuteten aber doch eine Zäsur: Das Bestreben, die musikalischen Resultate festhalten, dokumentieren zu wollen, war auch ein Ausdruck des Bewusstseins um die Relevanz der klingenden Aktivitäten. Anlässlich dieser Aufnahmen fand vermutlich auch der provokante Name „Masters of Unorthodox Jazz" erstmals Verwendung. Der August 1964 kann also als Gründungsdatum gelten.[19]

Von Mayrhofer Barabbas gingen auch in den folgenden Jahren wichtige Impulse aus. Nachdem die „Masters" – in der Besetzung Barabbas/Malli/Pechoc – am 22. Juni 1966 im Internationalen Kulturzentrum in der Wiener Annagasse ihr offizielles Konzertdebüt gegeben hatten, sorgte er drei Jahre später erneut dafür, dass die Musik des nunmehr als Quintett auftretenden Ensembles, zu diesem Zeitpunkt bereits im Museum des 20. Jahrhunderts und im Großen Konzerthaussaal zu hören, nicht undokumentiert blieb. Am 16. Mai 1969 nahmen die „Masters of Unorthodox Jazz" im Austrophon-Studio in den Räumen des Wiener Konzerthauses vier Stücke auf, die anschließend auf Vinyl gepresst und auf des Financiers eigenem Label Barabbas Records als Schallplatte veröffentlicht wurden. „Overground" war der Titel von Österreichs erster Free-Jazz-LP.[20] Sie war tatsäch-

be Austria's first jazz LP produced and distributed by the musicians themselves. Mayrhofer Barabbas's friends objected to his plan to put a painting by himself on the cover; at Malli's initiative, Arnulf Rainer gave them a partly overpainted drawing they used as a template.

What hides behind cryptic track titles like "Magnetic Girl," "Space Girl," "Pissing Girl" – in which Mayrhofer paid homage to his three girls – and "Everyone a Master"? In the last piece, the musicians introduce themselves, one after the other, with brief solos; on the other tracks, by contrast, the vigorous energy collective predominates. The musicians improvise a dense and colorful fabric of sounds and lines that nonetheless remains transparent thanks to the distinctive individuality of the voices. Walter Malli at the drums produces a dynamic and yet delicate structure of percussive sounds; many passages seem composed of interlocking asynchronously retarded series of accents. Michlmayr at the upright bass often reaches for the bow to lay out a stimulating and expressive texture between tremolos, pizzicato interjections, and scrunched sonic fragments. Meanwhile, Pechoc at the piano generates clusters of notes that sparkle with pointillistic luster. The winds could hardly be more different: there is Horst Brückl's lean bassoon nimbly alternating between staccato passages and melodic lines integrating wide interval jumps. And there is Mayrhofer Barabbas's alto sax brimming with elemental force, a performance that frequently recalls Albert Ayler: with its penchant for quotations of melodic fragments, for example, but also in the way it systematically sounds out the instrument's acoustic possibilities down into the realm of noise. Listening to the extraordinary chromatic wealth of this music, which seems alive with the forces of nature itself, is an unadulterated pleasure. Even to today's ears, "Overground" remains an impressive and multifaceted record.

## Complex characters

*"In artists' circles, our music was regarded as an 'action'; in jazz circles, it was perceived as a threat,"* Mayrhofer Barabbas summed up how the music of the "Masters" was received, especially in the 1960s.[21] The concert in the grand auditorium of the Konzerthaus mentioned at the beginning of these notes, where the "Masters" performed as an opening act for the pianist Thelonious Monk, took place in the fall of 1969, only months after the LP "Overground" came out. In retrospect, it is surprising that the reviewers in the audience that night were so aghast; some of the musicians had staged similar performances for almost a decade – but had apparently flown beneath the music journalists' radar. The Museum des 20. Jahrhunderts had hosted a first concert in November 1968, and in 1970, it started to

lich Mayrhofer Barabbas' Produkt: Er mietete das Studio, er kümmerte sich um Pressung und Vertrieb; möglicherweise handelte es sich bei diesem Tonträger also auch um die erste von Musikern selbst produzierte und verlegte Jazz-LP Österreichs. Mayrhofer Barabbas' Plan, auf dem Cover ein eigenes Bild zu platzieren, scheiterte am Widerstand seiner Freunde; auf Initiative Mallis stellte dafür stattdessen Arnulf Rainer eine teilübermalte Grafik als Vorlage zur Verfügung.

Was verbirgt sich hinter den kryptischen Stücktiteln „Magnetic Girl", „Space Girl", „Pissing Girl" – in denen Mayrhofer Barabbas seinen drei Töchtern Reverenz erwies – und „Everyone a Master"? Während sich im Zuge letzteren Stücks die Musiker einzeln mit kurzen Solodarbietungen vorstellen, regiert in den anderen Piecen das kraftvolle Kollektiv. Es ist ein dichtes, farbenreiches und ob der distinkten Individualität der einzelnen Stimmen zugleich transparentes Gewebe an Klängen und Linien, das hier improvisiert wird. Walter Malli erzeugt am Schlagzeug ein energiereiches und doch filigranes perkussionistisches Soundgefüge, in dem sich oft asynchron retardierte Akzentreihen ineinander zu verzahnen scheinen. Michlmayr erarbeitet am Kontrabass unter oftmaligem Griff zum Bogen eine stimulierende, expressive Textur zwischen Tremoli, Pizzicato-Einwürfen und knirschenden Klangsplittern, während Pianist Pechoc pointillistisch schillernde Tontrauben hervorbringt. Die Bläser könnten gegensätzlicher kaum sein: Da ist Horst Brückls schlankes, virtuos zwischen Staccato-Passagen und melodischen Linien mit großen Intervallsprüngen changierendes Fagott. Und da ist Mayrhofer Barabbas' urwüchsiges, kraftstrotzendes Altsaxofon, das immer wieder Assoziationen an Albert Ayler aufkommen lässt: etwa durch die Neigung zur Zitierung von Melodiefragmenten, aber auch durch das konsequente Ausloten der klanglichen Möglichkeiten des Instruments bis hin in den Geräuschbereich. Es ist das pure Vergnügen, diesen extrem farbenreichen, naturereignishaften Klängen zu lauschen. „Overground" ist bis heute ein beeindruckendes, vielschichtiges Stück Musik geblieben.

## Komplexe Charaktere

*„In Künstlerkreisen sah man unsere Musik als ‚Aktion', in Jazzkreisen als Bedrohung"*, resümierte Mayrhofer Barabbas die Rezeption der Musik der „Masters" – insbesondere im Hinblick auf die 1960er Jahre.[21] Nur wenige Monate nach Erscheinen der LP „Overground" im Herbst 1969 fand das eingangs erwähnte Konzert im Großen Konzerthaussaal im Vorprogramm zu Pianist Thelonious Monk statt. Die entgeisterten medialen Reaktionen überraschen retrospektiv auch deshalb, weil die Musiker zu diesem Zeitpunkt teilweise schon fast ein Jahrzehnt einschlägig aktiv waren – offenbar aber nicht auf dem Radar der Musikjournalisten aufgeschienen

serve as a home of sorts for city's free jazz avant-garde, which is to say, primarily for the "Masters" and the "Reform Art Unit" Fritz Novotny founded in 1965, an ensemble that still exists. In the venue in Vienna's Schweizergarten park, the "Masters" had found not only a prominent setting for their concerts that matched their self-image as artists, but also a framework that helped publicize the group to audiences that took an interest in such things. Public figures from the art world one might run into during the "Masters" concerts at the so-called 20er-Haus included Friedrich Achleitner, Arnulf Rainer, and Hermann Nitsch, as well as the composers Gerhard Lampersberg, Otto M. Zykan, and Kurt Schwertsik. The latter two at some point even floated the idea of a joint project, Mayrhofer Barabbas recalled:

*"Kurt Schwertsik [...] and Otto Zykan heard me perform during a concert and were very impressed. The two were working on a collaborative music project at the time. Be that as it may, I was approached (by Kurt) with the question: would I be interested in doing a concert with them? The concept was roughly this: parts were notated, also in graphical systems, etc., but then I was also supposed to play freely. I explained that I wasn't terribly good at reading scores, had no experience performing with an orchestra, and had never played under a conductor, etc., but if they'd be patient with me I would be interested indeed, no problem! (I mean, a saxophone in concert with an orchestra – I was thrilled!) But the other Masters weren't. They pestered me with the usual phrases until I finally gave in and cancelled on Schwertsik/Zykan.*[22]

Mayrhofer Barabbas as a soloist with the ensemble "MOB art & tone Art" Schwertsik, Zykan, and HK Gruber had founded in 1968: that would no doubt have been an exciting combination. The gig never happened; still, the episode offers a glimpse of how it wasn't always easy to find a common denominator among the five musicians' diverse interests: the history of the "Masters of Unorthodox Jazz" is the history of a fascinating ensemble bucking up against the conservative restraints of the era with uncompromising verve, but it is also the history of five individualistic and complex characters. That is one of the reasons why, after producing a second record titled "Vienna Jazz Avantgarde" (a joint double LP with the "Reform Art Unit") in 1972 and another performance that drew a great deal of attention as part of the music program of the steirischer herbst festival in Graz in 1974, the musicians parted ways in the mid-1970s, though they never officially dissolved the band. The last concerts in a representative framework took place in August 1975 at the Künstlerhaus, Vienna, where the major retrospective "Barabbas 1958–1975" also featured the first public exhibition of the frieze "Big Bang," a work in acrylic measuring 165 by almost 12 feet whose themes were inspired by the Baha'i philosophy. Mayrhofer Barabbas

waren. Tatsächlich mutierte nach dem ersten Konzert im Museum des 20. Jahrhunderts im November 1968 das Gebäude im Wiener Schweizergarten ab 1970 zu einer Art Heimstätte für die Wiener Free-Jazz-Avantgarde, also im Wesentlichen für die „Masters" und Fritz Novotnys 1965 gegründete, bis heute existente „Reform Art Unit". Womit die „Masters" nicht nur einen prominenten konzertanten Rahmen gefunden hatten, der ihrem künstlerischen Selbstverständnis entsprach, sondern auch einen Ort, der die Gruppe einem einschlägig interessierten Publikum bekannt machte. Unter den Persönlichkeiten des kulturellen Lebens, die sich bei den „Masters"-Konzerten im sogenannten 20er-Haus begegneten, waren unter anderem Friedrich Achleitner, Arnulf Rainer und Hermann Nitsch sowie die Komponisten Gerhard Lampersberg, Otto M. Zykan und Kurt Schwertsik. Letztere Herren äußerten dabei einmal die Idee eines gemeinsamen Projekts, so Mayrhofer Barabbas:

*„Kurt Schwertsik [...] und Otto Zykan hörten mich in einem Konzert und waren von meiner Spielweise sehr beeindruckt. Beide kollaborierten damals miteinander in einem musikalischen Projekt. Wie auch immer, man trat an mich heran (Kurt), mit der Anfrage, ob ich daran interessiert sei, ein Konzert mit ihnen zu spielen. Das Konzept war ungefähr so: Teile waren notiert, auch graphisch usw., und ich soll aber auch frei spielen. Ich erklärte, dass ich nicht einer der besten Notenleser sei, und auch keine Orchestererfahrung habe und noch nie mit einem Dirigenten gespielt habe etc., doch wenn man mit mir Geduld hätte, dann wäre ich schon interessiert, no problem! (No, na, ein Saxophonkonzert mit Orchester – ich war begeistert!) Aber die anderen Masters waren es nicht. Man bearbeitete mich, mit den üblichen Phrasen, so lange, bis ich nachgab und Schwertsik/Zykan absagte."*[22]

Mayrhofer Barabbas als Solist des 1968 von Schwertsik, Zykan und HK Gruber gegründeten Ensembles „MOB art & tone Art", das wäre zweifellos eine reizvolle Kombination gewesen. Es kam nicht dazu; die Begebenheit eröffnet auch einen Blick auf die nicht immer einfach auf einen Nenner zu bringenden Interessen der fünf Musiker: Die Geschichte der „Masters of Unorthodox Jazz" ist die Geschichte eines spannenden, den konservativen Hemmnissen der Zeit mit kompromisslosem Nachdruck trotzenden Ensembles, es ist jedoch auch die Geschichte von fünf individualistischen, komplexen Persönlichkeiten. Diesem Umstand ist es unter anderem zuzuschreiben, dass die Musiker Mitte der 1970er Jahre, nachdem 1972 die zweite Platte „Vienna Jazz Avantgarde" (Doppel-LP, gemeinsam mit der „Reform Art Unit") erschienen war und das Ensemble 1974 noch einen viel beachteten Auftritt im Rahmen des Musikprotokolls im steirischen herbst in Graz absolvierte, auseinandergingen, ohne dass die Formation jemals offiziell aufgelöst worden wäre. Die letzten Konzerte im repräsentativen Rahmen fan-

continued to pursue his interest in improvisation until the mid-1980s, in ensembles like "Athanor" (with Malli and a succession of other fellow musicians), "Rhythm & Breath" (with Markus Pillhofer, Sepp Mitterbauer, and Fritz Kotrba), and "Starlight" (with Pillhofer and Susanna Surabaia).

Individualism, impulsiveness, precision: these three terms may serve to sum up the musician Claus Mayrhofer Barabbas. He was a rebellious character who always charted his own paths and confidently flaunted his independent mind and his idiosyncrasies, an autodidact at his instruments whose performances often had the force of a natural phenomenon and contained a spark of self-transcending ecstasy. Mayrhofer Barabbas created physically intense music of fervid expressivity, like a sweeping gesture bursting with energy and a wealth of acoustic color. And yet with all his will to intensity, Mayrhofer Barabbas was also a strategic thinker and capable of taking the initiative: if it had not been for him, the music of the "Masters of Unorthodox Jazz" might never have come out on a record. The history of this legendary Austrian free jazz ensemble would no doubt have been different without him. An uncompromising individualist, an impulsive man who lived for the moment, a thinker and planner, Claus Mayrhofer Barabbas has left his mark on the history of music in Austria – a mark that will not fade.

den im August 1975 im Wiener Künstlerhaus statt, wo im Zuge der großen Retrospektive „Barabbas 1958–1975" auch der 50 Meter lange und knapp vier Meter breite, thematisch von der Baha'i-Philosophie inspirierte Acryl-Fries „Big Bang" erstmals gezeigt wurde. Mayrhofer Barabbas verfolgte seine improvisatorischen Interessen bis Mitte der 1980er Jahre in Ensembles wie „Athanor" (mit Malli und wechselnden weiteren Kollegen), „Rhythm & Breath" (mit Markus Pillhofer, Sepp Mitterbauer und Fritz Kotrba) und „Starlight" (mit Pillhofer und Susanna Surabaia) weiter.

Individualismus, Impulsivität, Genauigkeit: Auf diese drei Begriffe lässt sich der Musiker Claus Mayrhofer Barabbas bringen. Er war ein rebellischer Charakter, der stets eigene, selbstbestimmte Wege ging. Der seine Unabhängigkeit, sein Anderssein selbstbewusst zur Schau trug. Dessen autodidaktisch angeeigneter Instrumentalismus oft von naturereignisnaher Kraft war, ein Moment der selbstentäußernden Ekstase in sich trug. Mayrhofer Barabbas schuf körperhafte Musik von hitziger Expressivität, einer klangfarbenreichen Energiespur gleich. Wobei Mayrhofer Barabbas bei allem Willen zur Intensität auch strategisch dachte und Fähigkeit zur Initiative zeigte: Ohne ihn wäre die Musik der „Masters of Unorthodox Jazz" möglicherweise niemals auf LP erschienen. Die Geschichte des legendären österreichischen Free-Jazz-Ensembles wäre ohne ihn zweifellos anders verlaufen. Der kompromisslose Individualist, der impulsive Mann des Moments, der Denker und Planer Claus Mayrhofer Barabbas hat Spuren hinterlassen in Österreichs Musikgeschichte. Spuren, die bleiben werden.

1 Igo Sicka, "Graue Eminenz zum Gruseln," Kurier, December 15, 1969, 9.
2 P[eter] H[irsch], "Jazz zum Abgewöhnen," Volksblatt, December 17, 1969.
3 t. o., "Unter keinem guten Stern," Express, December 15, 1969.
4 See Claus Pack, "Monk und Masters," Die Presse, December 16, 1969, 4; Ruediger Engerth, "Erinnerungen an Minton's Playhouse," Salzburger Nachrichten, December 17, 1969.
5 For extensive information on the "Masters of Unorthodox Jazz," see Andreas Felber, Die Wiener Free-Jazz-Avantgarde: Revolution im Hinterzimmer (Vienna: Böhlau, 2005).
6 Walter Malli in conversation with the author, April 22, 1995.
7 Walter Malli, "art is shit – entertainment is great," interview with Klaus Peham, Jazzlive, no. 58 (November 1988), 10.
8 See Semirah Heilingsetzer, ed., Die Galerie "zum Roten Apfel" 1959–1965: Künstlerpositionen der 60er Jahre in Wien (Frankfurt am Main: Peter Lang, 2003); and see also Felber, Die Wiener Free-Jazz-Avantgarde, 63–71.
9 See Andreas Felber, "Randfigur mit Potenzial: Karl Anton Fleck, der Jazzmusiker," in Karl Anton Fleck: Anthropologische Maschine, ed. Romana Schuler, exh. cat., Leopold Museum, Vienna (Weitra: Publication PNo 1, 2005), 125–34.
10 See Felber, Die Wiener Free-Jazz-Avantgarde, S. 71–80.
11 Claus Mayrhofer Barabbas in conversation with the author, August 10, 1995.
12 Ibid.
13 Claus Mayrhofer Barabbas, email to the author, March 13, 2001.
14 Anton Michlmayr in conversation with the author, August 7, 1995.
15 Richard Pechoc in conversation with the author, May 18, 1995.
16 Walter Malli, "art is shit – entertainment is great," 10.
17 Claus Mayrhofer Barabbas in conversation with the author, August 10, 1995.
18 Ibid.
19 See Felber, Die Wiener Free-Jazz-Avantgarde, 94–96.
20 Ibid., 118–24.
21 Claus Mayrhofer Barabbas, email to the author, August 5, 2002.
22 Claus Mayrhofer Barabbas, email to the author, March 13, 2001. I have been unable to determine which piece this was going to be. In a phone conversation on November 29, 2000, Kurt Schwertsik confirmed that he knew the "Masters" and had heard them perform, but he knew nothing about a plan to engage Mayrhofer Barabbas. He did recall, however, that someone had proposed to ask the "Masters" to contribute to a friend's filmic portrait of Schwertsik. That plan came to nothing because the "Masters" declined, fearing – according to Schwertsik – that they would be disparaged in the film.

1 Igo Sicka, Graue Eminenz zum Gruseln, in: Kurier, 15.12.1969, S. 9.
2 P[eter] H[irsch], Jazz zum Abgewöhnen, in: Volksblatt, 17.12.1969.
3 t. o., Unter keinem guten Stern, in: Express, 15.12.1969.
4 Vgl. Claus Pack: Monk und Masters, in: Die Presse, 16.12.1969, S. 4. Ruediger Engerth: Erinnerungen an Minton's Playhouse, in: Salzburger Nachrichten, 17.12.1969.
5 Für ausführlichere Informationen zu den „Masters of Unorthodox Jazz" siehe Andreas Felber, Die Wiener Free-Jazz-Avantgarde. Revolution im Hinterzimmer, Wien 2005.
6 Walter Malli, Gespräch mit dem Autor, 22.4.1995.
7 Walter Malli, art is shit – entertainment is great [Interview von Klaus Peham], in: Jazzlive Nr. 58 (November 1988), S. 10.
8 Vgl. Semirah Heilingsetzer (Hg.), Die Galerie „zum Roten Apfel" 1959–1965. Künstlerpositionen der 60er Jahre in Wien, Frankfurt am Main 2003. Siehe auch Felber, Die Wiener Free-Jazz-Avantgarde, S. 63–71.
9 Vgl. Andreas Felber, Randfigur mit Potenzial. Karl Anton Fleck, der Jazzmusiker, in: Romana Schuler (Hg.), Karl Anton Fleck – Anthropologische Maschine. Katalog zur Ausstellung im Leopold Museum, Wien/Weitra 2005, S. 125–134.
10 Vgl. Felber, Die Wiener Free-Jazz-Avantgarde, S. 71ff.
11 Claus Mayrhofer Barabbas, Gespräch mit dem Autor, 10.8.1995.
12 Ebd.
13 Claus Mayrhofer Barabbas, E-Mail an den Autor, 13.3.2001.
14 Anton Michlmayr, Gespräch mit dem Autor, 7.8.1995.
15 Richard Pechoc, Gespräch mit dem Autor, 18.5.1995.
16 Walter Malli, art is shit – entertainment is great, S. 10.
17 Claus Mayrhofer Barabbas, Gespräch mit dem Autor, 10.8.1995.
18 Ebd.
19 Siehe dazu Felber, Die Wiener Free-Jazz-Avantgarde, S. 94–96.
20 Ebd., S. 118ff.
21 Claus Mayrhofer Barabbas, E-Mail an den Autor, 5.8.2002.
22 Claus Mayrhofer Barabbas, E-Mail an den Autor, 13.3.2001. Um welches Stück es sich dabei handelte, konnte nicht eruiert werden. Kurt Schwertsik bestätigte in einem Telefonat am 29.11.2000, dass er die „Masters" gekannt und auch in Konzerten gehört hätte, vom Plan, Mayrhofer Barabbas zu engagieren, wusste er nichts; er erinnerte sich aber daran, dass für ein Schwertsik-Filmporträt eines Freundes die Idee im Raum stand, die „Masters" zu engagieren. Der Plan scheiterte, weil diese absagten, da sie – so Schwertsik – befürchteten, dabei verunglimpft zu werden.

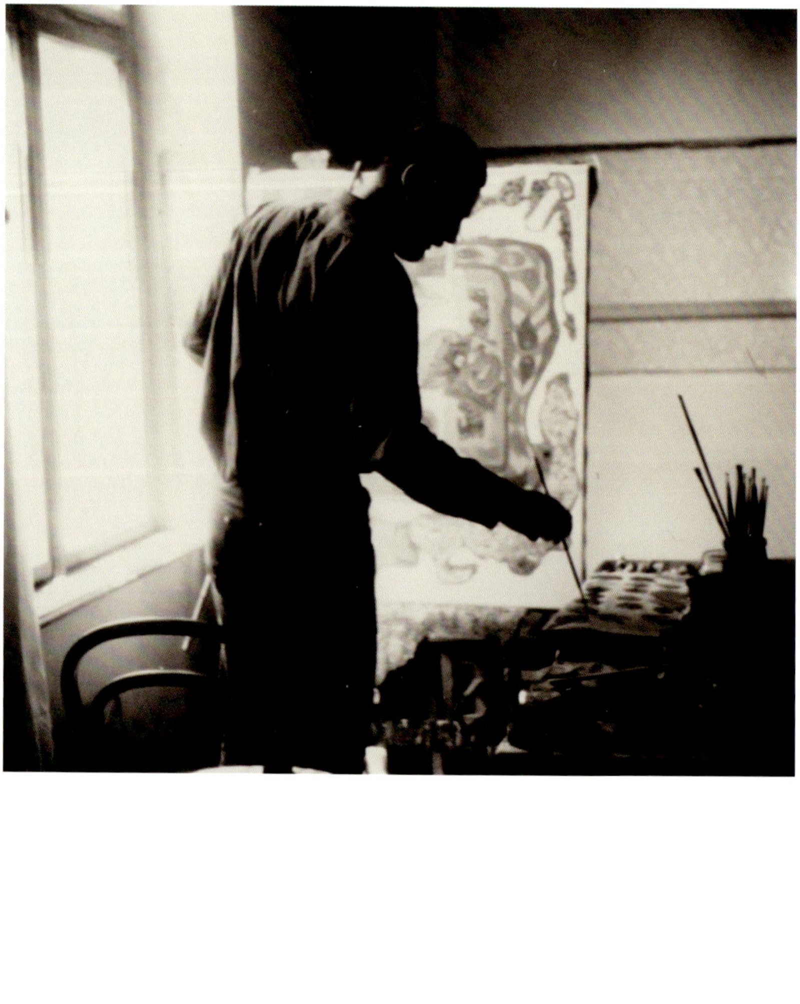

Barabbas bei der Arbeit, Reichenau 1966
Barabbas at work, Reichenau, 1966

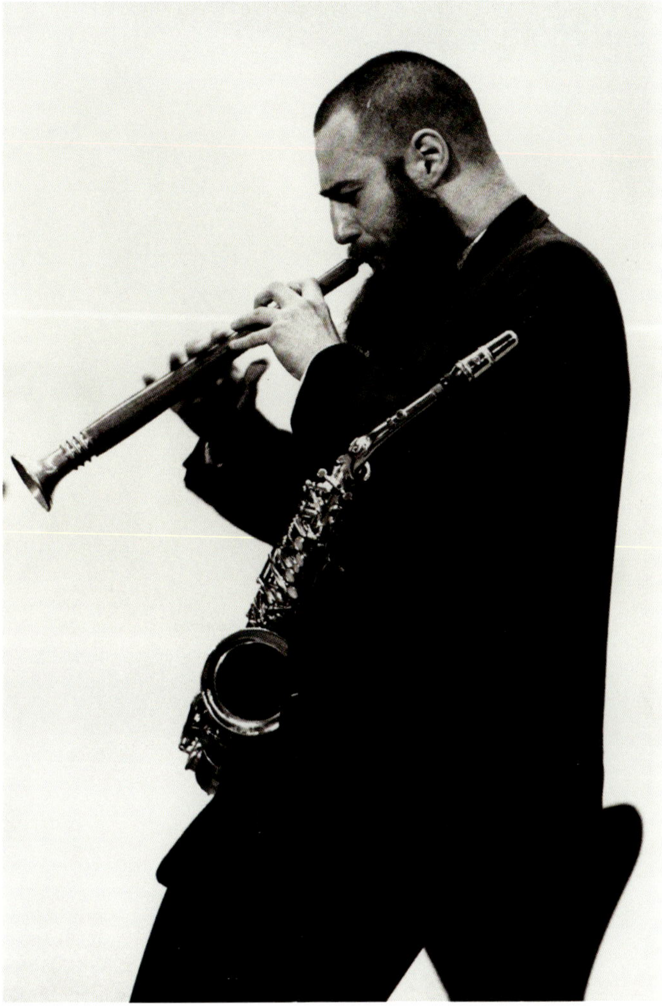

Konzert im Museum des 20. Jahrhunderts, Wien, 23.1.1970.
Barabbas spielt auf der Shenai, einem indischen Doppelrohrblattinstrument
Concert at the Museum des 20. Jahrhunderts, Vienna, January 23, 1970.
Barabbas is playing the shenai, an Indian double-reed wind instrument

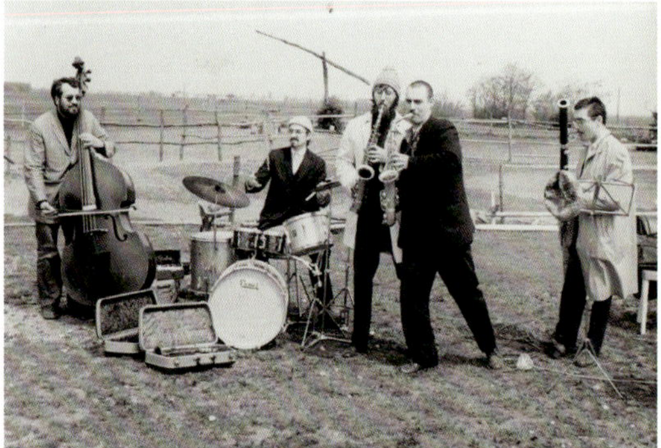

1

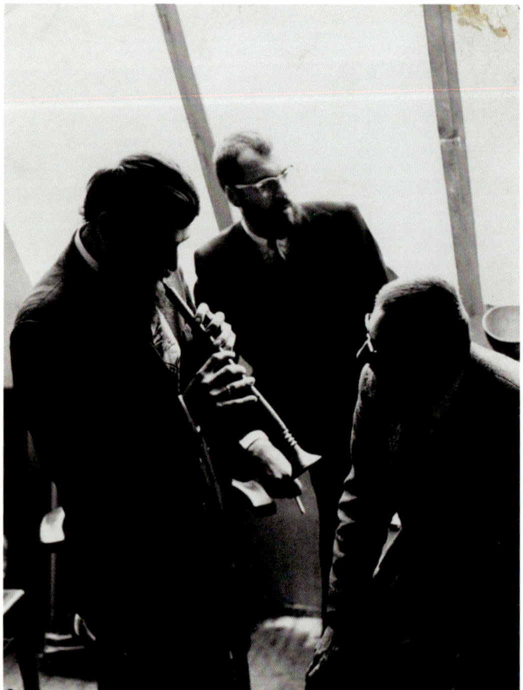

2

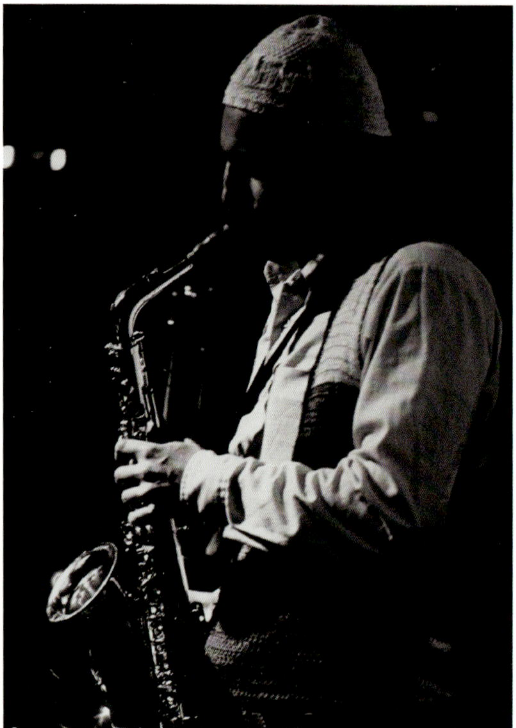

3

1
„Masters of Unorthodox Jazz": Walter Malli (Schlagzeug), Richard Pechoc (Altsaxofon), Anton Michlmayr (Bass), Horst Brückl (Fagott), Claus Mayrhofer Barabbas (Altsaxofon), Frauenkirchen, Seewinkel/Burgenland. Foto: Gerhard Trumler
"Masters of Unorthodox Jazz": Walter Malli (drums), Richard Pechoc (alto saxophone), Anton Michlmayr (bass), Horst Brückl (bassoon), Claus Mayrhofer Barabbas (alto saxophone), Frauenkirchen, Seewinkel/Burgenland. Photograph: Gerhard Trumler

2
Claus Mayrhofer Barabbas (Shenai), Anton Michlmayr, Richard Pechoc
Claus Mayrhofer Barabbas (Shenai), Anton Michlmayr, Richard Pechoc

3
Claus Mayrhofer Barabbas (Altsaxofon). Foto: Manfred Winter
Claus Mayrhofer Barabbas (alto saxophone). Photograph: Manfred Winter

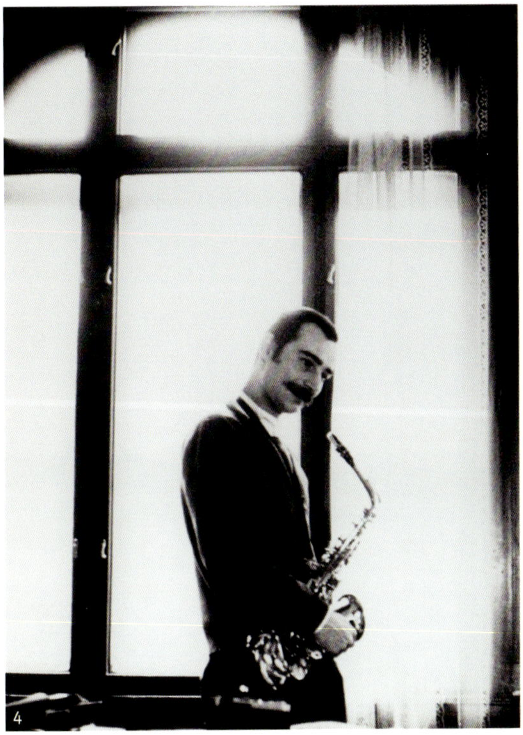

4

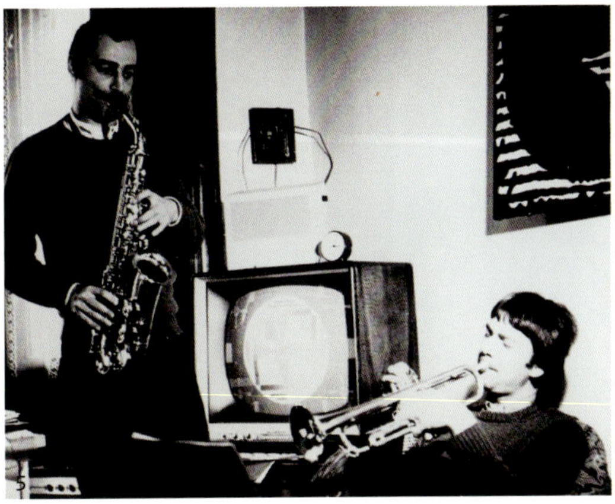

5

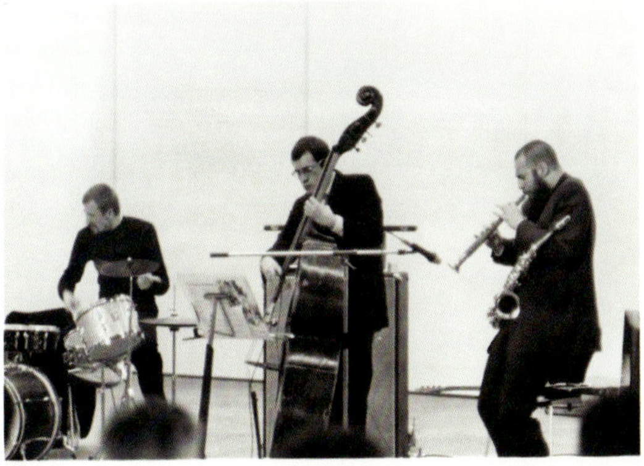

6

4
Claus Mayrhofer Barabbas (Altsaxofon). Foto: Manfred Winter
Claus Mayrhofer Barabbas (alto saxophone).
Photograph: Manfred Winter

5
Claus Mayrhofer Barabbas (Altsaxofon),
Franz Koglmann (Trompete)
Claus Mayrhofer Barabbas (alto saxophone),
Franz Koglmann (trumpet)

6
Konzert im Museum des 20. Jahrhunderts, 23.1.1970.
Von links nach rechts: Malli (Schlagzeug), Michlmayr (Bass) und Barabbas (Shenai und Saxofon)
Concert at the Museum des 20. Jahrhunderts, January 23, 1970.
Left to right: Malli (percussions), Michlmayr (bass), and Barabbas (shenai and saxophone)

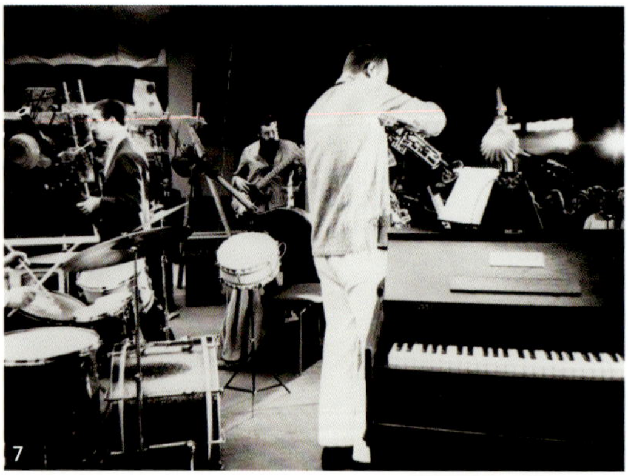

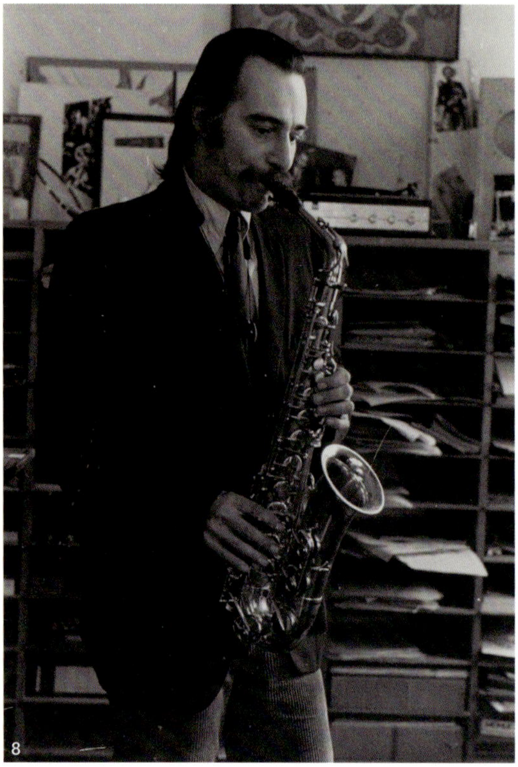

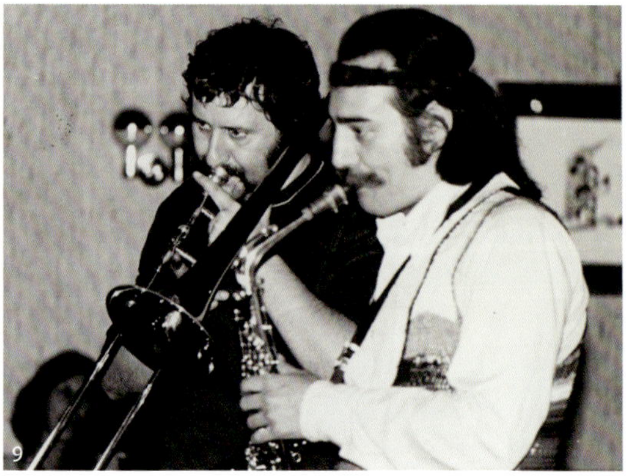

7
„Masters of Unorthodox Jazz": Horst Brückl (Fagott),
Anton Michlmayr (E-Bass), Claus Mayrhofer Barabbas (Trompete),
Konzert in der Z-Zentrale, Wien, November 1973
"Masters of Unorthodox Jazz": Horst Brückl (bassoon),
Anton Michlmayr (electric bass), Claus Mayrhofer Barabbas
(trumpet), concert at the Z-Zentrale, Vienna, November 1973

8
Claus Mayrhofer Barabbas (Altsaxofon)
Claus Mayrhofer Barabbas (alto saxophone)

9
Josef Traindl (Posaune), Claus Mayrhofer Barabbas (Altsaxofon),
Nickelsdorf 1978
Josef Traindl (trombone), Claus Mayrhofer Barabbas
(alto saxophone), Nickelsdorf 1978

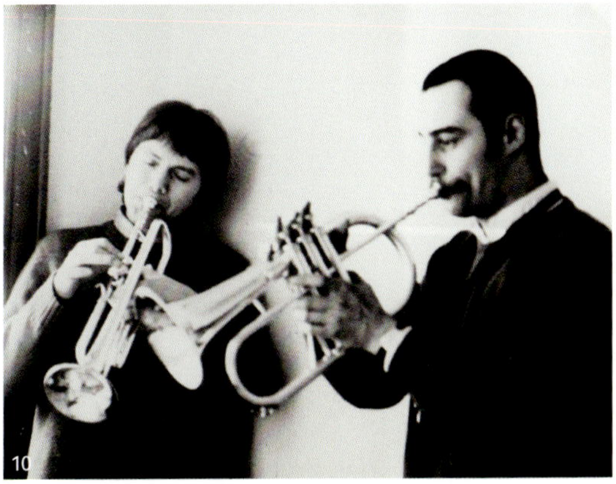

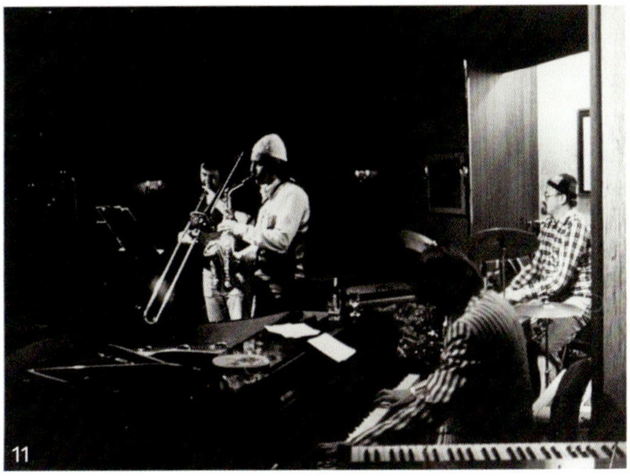

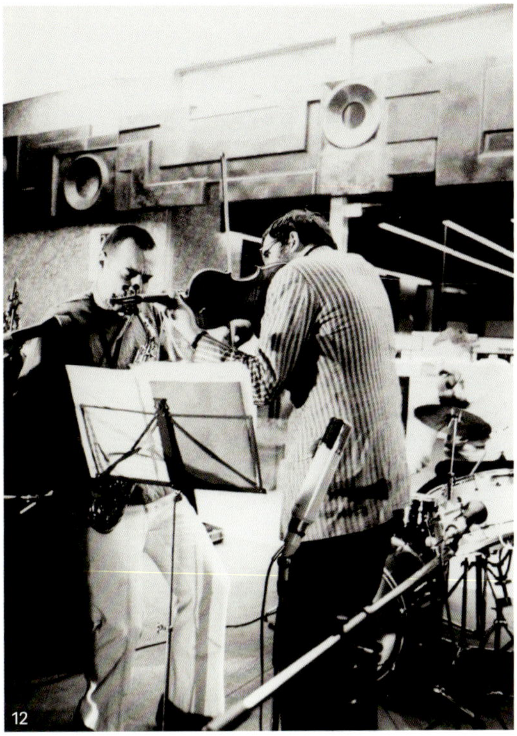

10
Franz Koglmann (Trompete), Claus Mayrhofer Barabbas (Flügelhorn)
Franz Koglmann (trumpet), Claus Mayrhofer Barabbas (flugelhorn)

11
Claus Mayrhofer Barabbas (Altsaxofon), Josef Traindl (Posaune), Richard Pechoc (Klavier), Walter Malli (Schlagzeug), Nickelsdorf 1978
Claus Mayrhofer Barabbas (alto saxophone), Josef Traindl (trombone), Richard Pechoc (piano), Walter Malli (percussion), Nickelsdorf 1978

12
„Masters of Unorthodox Jazz" im 20er-Haus: Claus Mayrhofer Barabbas (Altsaxofon), Anton Michlmayr (Violine), Walter Malli (Schlagzeug)
"Masters of Unorthodox Jazz" at the 20er-Haus: Claus Mayrhofer Barabbas (alto saxophone), Anton Michlmayr (violin), Walter Malli (percussion)

# Biographical sketch Claus Mayrhofer Barabbas

**(during the 1960s and 1970s: Harun Ghulam Barabbas)**

Born in Vienna on May 2, 1943.
Spends his childhood with his parents and his sister Ilse in the Döbling district of Vienna; attends the Schottengymnasium, Vienna, with his future fellow painter Heinz Stangl.

1958 drops out of school. Friendship with Padhi Frieberger, who introduces him to the Viennese arts scene (Galerie nächst St. Stephan). Adopts the alias Barabbas.

1960 visits Friedensreich Hundertwasser in Bellême, France.
Joins the group "Zum roten Apfel." Plays free jazz with Walter Malli, Richard Pechoc, and Karl Anton Fleck. The ensemble grows into the legendary "Masters of Unorthodox Jazz" (Barabbas, Brückl, Malli, Michlmayr, Pechoc).

1964–1969 lives in his parents' villa in Reichenau an der Rax. The artists' colony he hopes to establish lasts only a few years. Frequent visitors include Ernst Fuchs, Malli, Pechoc, Heinz Stangl, Othmar Zechyr, and the photographer Gerhard Trumler.

1969 Barabbas produces the album "Overground" featuring the "Masters of Unorthodox Jazz."

1970–1981 member of the artists' group "Der Kreis."

1975 grand retrospective at the Künstlerhaus, including the 1980-square-foot painting "Genesis" a.k.a. "Big Bang."

1974 stays in New York.

1976–1984 black period.

1986–1989 lives in Bali.

1989–2009 lives in Australia.
On January 10, 2009, Barabbas is found dead in his sister's home in Bendigo, Australia (near Melbourne).

# Kurzbiografie Claus Mayrhofer Barabbas

**(in den 1960er und 1970er Jahren: Harun Ghulam Barabbas)**

| | |
|---|---|
| | Geboren 2. Mai 1943 in Wien.<br>Kindheit mit Eltern und Schwester Ilse in Wien-Döbling, Besuch des Wiener Schottengymnasiums, gemeinsam mit dem späteren Malerkollegen Heinz Stangl. |
| 1958 | Abbruch der Schule. Freundet sich mit Padhi Frieberger an und wird von diesem mit der Wiener Kunstszene (Galerie nächst St. Stephan) bekannt gemacht. Er legt sich den Künstlernamen Barabbas zu. |
| 1960 | Besuch bei Friedensreich Hundertwasser in Bellême, Frankreich.<br>Mitglied der Gruppe „Zum roten Apfel". Spielt mit Walter Malli, Richard Pechoc und Karl Anton Fleck Freejazz. Daraus entwickeln sich die legendären „Masters of Unorthodox Jazz" (Barabbas, Brückl, Malli, Michlmayr, Pechoc). |
| 1964–1969 | lebt er in Reichenau an der Rax in der Villa seiner Eltern. Eine geplante Künstlerkolonie hat nur wenige Jahre Bestand. Häufige Gäste: Ernst Fuchs, Malli, Pechoc, Heinz Stangl, Othmar Zechyr und der Fotograf Gerhard Trumler. |
| 1969 | produziert Barabbas die Schallplatte „Overground" mit den „Masters of Unorthodox Jazz". |
| 1970–1981 | Mitglied der Künstlergruppe „Der Kreis". |
| 1975 | große Retrospektive im Künstlerhaus mit dem knapp 200 m² großen Gemälde „Genesis" oder „Big Bang". |
| 1974 | Aufenthalt in New York. |
| 1976–1984 | schwarze Phase. |
| 1986–1989 | Aufenthalt auf Bali. |
| 1989–2009 | lebt er in Australien.<br>Am 10. Januar 2009 wird er im Haus seiner Schwester in Bendigo, Australien (in der Nähe von Melbourne) tot aufgefunden. |

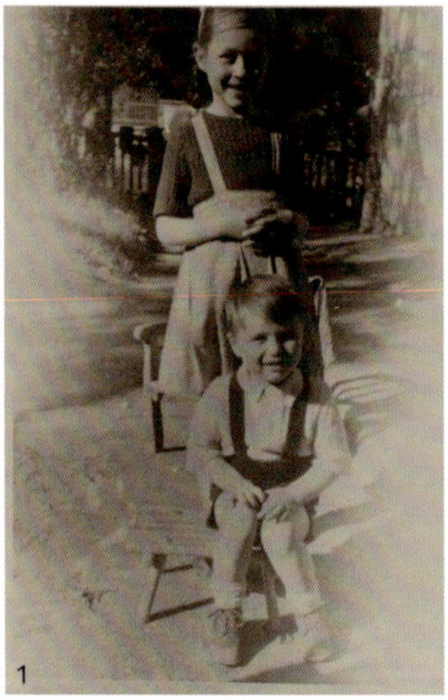

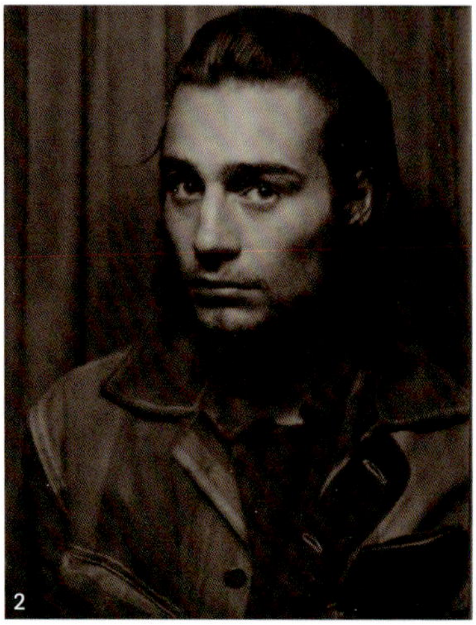

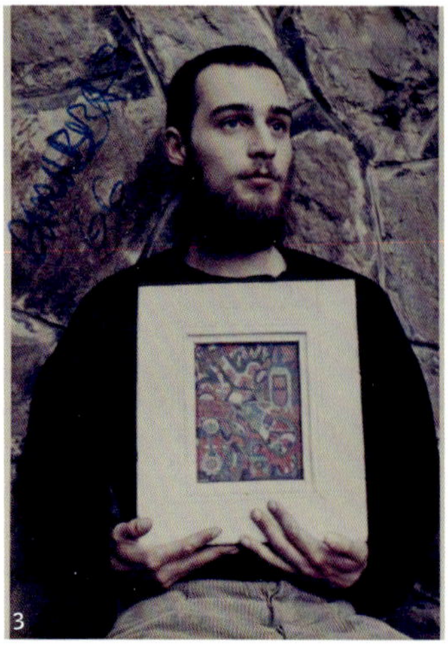

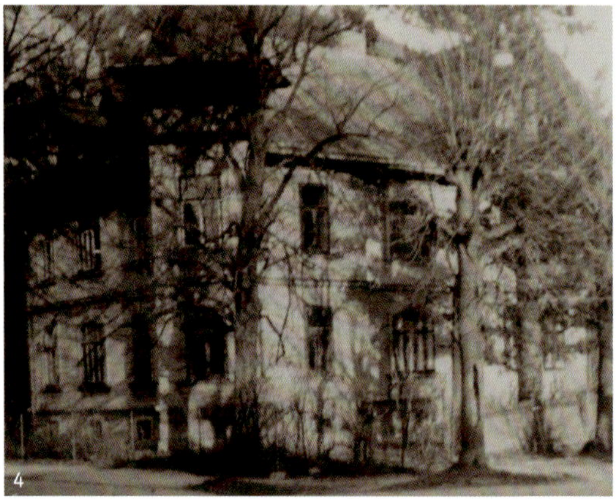

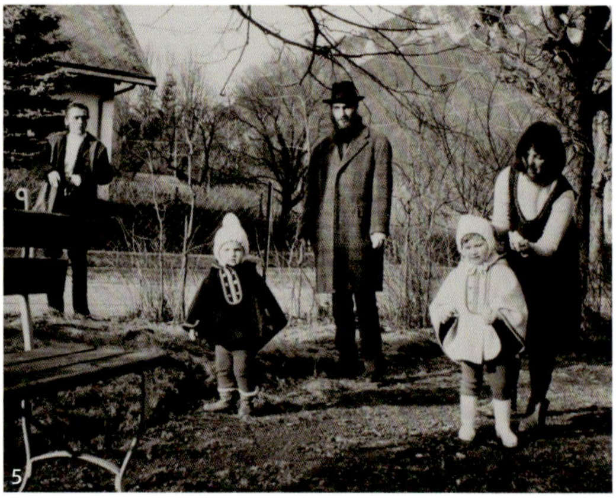

1
Der zweijährige Claus (Barabbas) mit seiner Schwester Ilse, 1945
Claus (Barabbas) at the age of two with his sister Ilse, 1945

2
Der neunzehnjährige Barabbas, 1962.
Er trug damals – sehr ungewöhnlich für die Zeit – langes Haar und Kleidung aus buntem Liegestuhlstoff.
Barabbas at the age of nineteen, 1962. He wore his hair long, which was very unusual at the time, and made his clothes out of colorful deck-chair fabrics.

3
Barabbas mit Selbstporträt, 1963
Barabbas with a self-portrait, 1963

4
Von 1965 bis 1969 lebte Barabbas mit seiner Familie in dieser Villa in Reichenau, einer Erbschaft seiner Mutter. Ab 1967 wohnte für eineinhalb Jahre auch Othmar Zechyr mit seiner Familie in dem Haus. Barabbas, Malli, Pechoc und Zechyr planten, dort eine Art Künstlerkolonie zu gründen.
Between 1965 and 1969, Barabbas and his family lived in this villa in Reichenau, which his mother had inherited. In 1967, Othmar Zechyr and his family also moved into the house; they would stay for a year and a half. Barabbas, Malli, Pechoc, and Zechyr planned to establish a sort of artists' colony on the property.

5
Barabbas mit seiner Familie im Garten der elterlichen Villa in Reichenau, 1967. Von links nach rechts: Othmar Zechyr, Tochter Esther (ein Jahr), Barabbas, Tochter Chadidja (zwei Jahre) und die mit Daphne schwangere Wardi (Rosemarie Sebek)
Barabbas with his family in the garden of his parents' villa in Reichenau, 1967. Left to right: Othmar Zechyr, the one-year-old daughter Esther, Barabbas, the two-year-old daughter Chadidja, and Wardi (Rosemarie Sebek), who is pregnant with Daphne

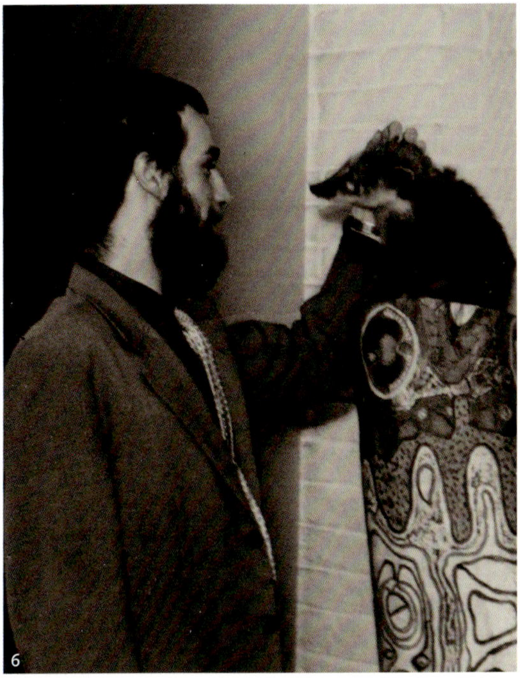

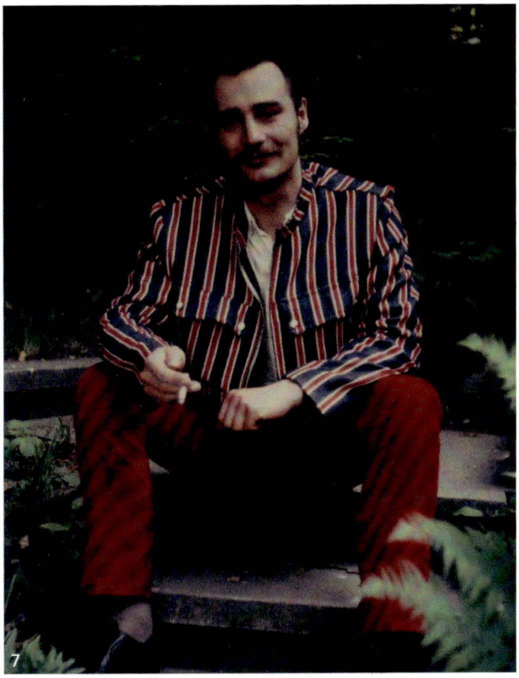

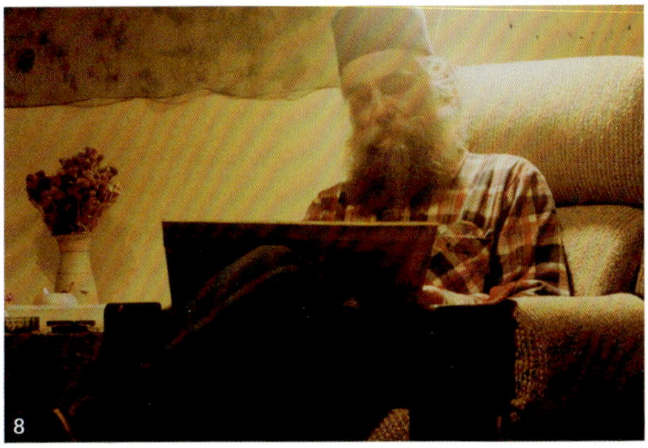

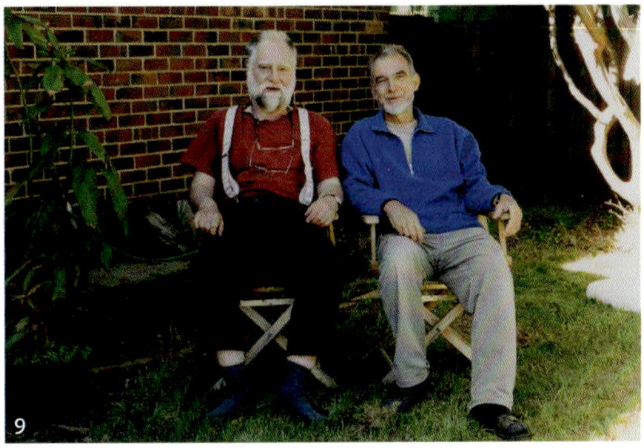

6
Barabbas mit einem Waschbären anlässlich der Gemeinschaftsausstellung „Zwei Genies" mit Othmar Zechyr in der Galerie Fuchs-Fischhof in der Millöckergasse, Wien 6, 1966. Für diese Ausstellung stellte der Tierfänger und Händler Josef Pieber Tiere zur Verfügung.
Barabbas with a raccoon on occasion of the group exhibition "Zwei Genies" ("Two Geniuses," with Othmar Zechyr) at Galerie Fuchs-Fischhof, Millöckergasse, Vienna, 6th district, 1966. The animal catcher and dealer Josef Pieber supplied animals for the show.

7
Barabbas auf den Stufen vor dem Wohnhaus seiner Eltern in Glanzing, Wien 19, 1972
Barabbas on the steps outside his parents' house in Glanzing, Vienna, 19th district, 1972

8
Barabbas malend in seinem Haus in Bendigo, Australien, 1995
Barabbas painting at his home in Bendigo, Australia, 1995

9
Barabbas und Dr. Friedrich Jelinek, der 2006 seinen Freund in Australien besuchte
Barabbas and Dr. Friedrich Jelinek, who visited his friend in Australia in 2006

# Exhibitions

| | |
|---|---|
| 1959 & 1963 | Galerie zum roten Apfel, Vienna, solo |
| 1960 | Bellême, Normandy, with Friedensreich Hundertwasser |
| 1963 | Galerie Fuchs, Vienna |
| 1964 | "Die Kultur bin ich," Galerie Tao, Vienna, solo |
| 1966 | "Zwei Genies," Galerie Fischhof, Vienna (with Othmar Zechyr) |
| 1967 | "Integrale Malerei," K.-O.-Braun-Museum, Ludwigshafen, Germany, solo |
| 1968 | Galerie Krokodil, Hamburg, solo |
| 1968 | Galerie Basilisk, Vienna, solo |
| 1969 | Galerie nächst St. Stephan, Vienna |
| 1969 | Galerie Matthias, Cologne, solo |
| 1969 | Galerie 10, Vienna |
| 1970 | "Roter Apfel in der Galerie Basilisk," Galerie Basilisk, Vienna |
| 1970 | "Der Kreis," Vienna (Barabbas will continue to participate in the shows held by the artists' group "Der Kreis" until its dissolution in 1981) |
| 1971 | "Heimat bist du großer Söhne," Galerie Nagl, Vienna, solo |
| 1971 | "Phantastische Kunst," Villa Angeli, Reichenau an der Rax |
| 1971 | Marcarios Gallery, New York |
| 1972 | Galerie Wolfrum, Vienna, solo |
| 1975 | "Das Riesenbild von Wien," retrospective of works from between 1958 and 1975, Künstlerhaus, Vienna, solo |
| 1975 | Cologne Art Fair |
| 1977 | International Art Fair, Basel |
| 1981 | Exhibition "Der Kreis" at the Historical Museum of the City of Vienna |
| 1984 | Galerie Upupa, Villach, Austria, solo |
| 1985 | Galerie Schwarz auf Weiß, Vienna, solo |
| 1991 | AFFA Gallery, Bendigo, Australia, solo |
| 1992 | Stuart Gerstman Gallery, Melbourne, Australia |
| 1993 | Tog's Gallery, Castlemaine, Australia |
| 1996 | Galerie Peithner-Lichtenfels, Vienna, solo |
| 1999 | Gabriel Gallery, Melbourne, Australia |
| 2000 | Penfold's Fine Art Gallery, Bendigo, Australia, solo |
| 2001 | Central Goldfields Gallery, Maryborough, Australia |
| 2002 | Castlemaine Art Gallery, Castlemaine, Australia, solo |
| 2002 | Gamma Space Gallery, Melbourne, Australia, solo |
| 2003 | "Roter Apfel," Galerie Chobot, Vienna |
| 2007 & 2008 | Galerie Gans, Vienna |

# Ausstellungen

| | |
|---|---|
| 1959 & 1963 | Galerie zum roten Apfel, Wien, Pers. |
| 1960 | Bellême, Normandie, mit Friedensreich Hundertwasser |
| 1963 | Galerie Fuchs, Wien |
| 1964 | „Die Kultur bin ich", Galerie Tao, Wien, Pers. |
| 1966 | „Zwei Genies", Galerie Fischhof, Wien (gemeinsam mit Othmar Zechyr) |
| 1967 | „Integrale Malerei", K.-O.-Braun-Museum, Ludwigshafen, Deutschland, Pers. |
| 1968 | Galerie Krokodil, Hamburg, Deutschland, Pers. |
| 1968 | Galerie Basilisk, Wien, Pers. |
| 1969 | Galerie nächst St. Stephan, Wien |
| 1969 | Galerie Matthias, Köln, Deutschland, Pers. |
| 1969 | Galerie 10, Wien |
| 1970 | „Roter Apfel in der Galerie Basilisk", Galerie Basilisk, Wien |
| 1970 | „Der Kreis", Wien (bis zur Auflösung 1981 Teilnahme an den Ausstellungen der Künstlergruppe „Der Kreis") |
| 1971 | „Heimat bist du großer Söhne", Galerie Nagl, Wien, Pers. |
| 1971 | „Phantastische Kunst", Villa Angeli, Reichenau an der Rax |
| 1971 | Marcarios Gallery, New York, USA |
| 1972 | Galerie Wolfrum, Wien, Pers. |
| 1975 | „Das Riesenbild von Wien", Retrospektive 1958–1975, Künstlerhaus, Wien, Pers. |
| 1975 | Kunstmesse Köln |
| 1977 | Internationale Kunstmesse, Basel |
| 1981 | Ausstellung „Der Kreis" im Historischen Museum der Stadt Wien |
| 1984 | Galerie Upupa, Villach, Pers. |
| 1985 | Galerie Schwarz auf Weiß, Wien, Pers, |
| 1991 | AFFA Gallery, Bendigo, Australien, Pers. |
| 1992 | Stuart Gerstman Gallery, Melbourne, Australien |
| 1993 | Tog's Gallery, Castlemaine, Australien |
| 1996 | Galerie Peithner-Lichtenfels, Wien, Pers. |
| 1999 | Gabriel Gallery, Melbourne, Australien |
| 2000 | Penfold's Fine Art Gallery, Bendigo, Australien, Pers. |
| 2001 | Central Goldfields Gallery, Maryborough, Australien |
| 2002 | Castlemaine Art Gallery, Castlemaine, Australien, Pers. |
| 2002 | Gamma Space Gallery, Melbourne, Australien, Pers. |
| 2003 | „Roter Apfel", Galerie Chobot, Wien |
| 2007 & 2008 | Galerie Gans, Wien |
| 2009 | „Landscapes. Ölbilder, Aquarelle, Mischtechnik auf Papier", |

| | |
|---|---|
| 2009 | "Landscapes: Ölbilder, Aquarelle, Mischtechnik auf Papier," Galerie Gans, Vienna, solo |
| 2010 | "Tradition and Avantgarde: Art in Austria, 1945–1980," Museum Liaunig, Neuhaus / Suha, Austria |
| 2010 | "Die Blöße," Galerie Lang, Vienna |
| 2010–2011 | "Landschaften und Akte," Galerie Gans, Vienna, solo |
| 2011 | "The 1960s: A Fantastic Modernism," MUSA, Vienna |
| 2011 | "Der Akt in der österreichischen Kunst 1900–2011," Galerie Lanserhaus, Eppan, Italy |

## Works in public collections

Department for Cultural Affairs of the City of Vienna – MUSA
Graphic Arts Collection, Albertina, Vienna
Wien Museum (Historical Museum of the City of Vienna)
State Museum of Lower Austria, St. Pölten, Austria
Museum Liaunig, Neuhaus / Suha, Austria
Sammlung Peter-Infeld-Privatstiftung, Vienna
Kleine Galerie, Linz, Austria
K.-O.-Braun-Museum, Ludwigshafen, Germany
Rudana Gallery, Peliatan, Indonesia
Bendigo Art Gallery, Bendigo, Australia
Castlemaine Art Gallery and Historical Museum, Castlemaine, Australia

Galerie Gans, Wien, Pers.

2010 „Tradition und Avantgarde. Kunst in Österreich 1945–1980", Museum Liaunig, Neuhaus / Suha, Kärnten

2010 „Die Blöße", Galerie Lang, Wien

2010–2011 „Landschaften und Akte", Galerie Gans, Wien, Pers.

2011 „Die sechziger Jahre. Eine phantastische Moderne", MUSA, Wien

2011 „Der Akt in der österreichischen Kunst 1900–2011", Galerie Lanserhaus, Eppan, Italien

## Werke in öffentlichen Sammlungen

Kulturabteilung der Stadt Wien – MUSA
Graphische Sammlung Albertina, Wien
Wien Museum (Historisches Museum der Stadt Wien)
Landesmuseum Niederösterreich, St. Pölten
Museum Liaunig, Neuhaus / Suha, Kärnten
Sammlung Peter-Infeld-Privatstiftung, Wien
Kleine Galerie, Linz
K.-O.-Braun-Museum, Ludwigshafen, Deutschland
Rudana Gallery, Peliatan, Indonesien
Bendigo Art Gallery, Bendigo, Australien
Castlemaine Art Gallery and Historical Museum, Castlemaine, Australien

## Literature

Peter Baum, Kunst in Österreich, in Tradition und Avantgarde: Kunst in Österreich 1945–1980, exh. cat., Neuhaus: Museum Liaunig, 2010.
Maria Buchsbaum, Barabbas: Das Ornamentale als Inhaltsträger, Vernissage 16, no. 8 (October 1996).
Berthold Ecker and Wolfgang Hilger, eds., The 1960s: A Fantastic Modernism, Collection of the Department for Cultural Affairs of the City of Vienna – MUSA, Vienna: Springer, 2011.
Rüdiger Engerth, "Overground," Protokolle: Wiener Jahresschrift für Literatur, bildende Kunst und Musik 72, no. 1 (1972).
Andreas Felber, Zur "europäischen" Identität der Wiener Free-Jazz-Avantgarde: Die Geschichte der Masters of Unorthodox Jazz und der Reform Art Unit, PhD diss., Vienna, 2001.
Andreas Felber, Die Wiener Free-Jazz-Avantgarde: Revolution im Hinterzimmer, Vienna, Cologne, and Weimar: Böhlau, 2005.
Heinrich Fuchs, Die österreichischen Maler des 20. Jahrhunderts, Vienna, 1985.
Gerhard Habarta, Lexikon der phantastischen Künstler, Norderstedt: Books on Demand, 2008.
Semirah Heilingsetzer, Die Galerie "Zum Roten Apfel" 1959–1965: Künstlerpositionen der 60er Jahre in Wien, Frankfurt am Main: Lang, 2003.
Renata Kassal-Mikula and Hans Bisanz, eds., Der Kreis: Dokumentation einer Wiener Künstlervereinigung, 1946–1980, exh. cat., Vienna: Historisches Museum der Stadt Wien, 1981.
Klaus Lingens and Robert , eds., Roter Apfel in der Galerie Basilisk, exh. cat., Vienna: Galerie Basilisk, 1970.
David Thomas and Allyn J. Fisher, eds., Claus Barabbas: Recent Paintings, exh. cat., Bendigo (Australia): Allyn Fisher Fine Arts, 1991.
Peter Weiermair, Eine Geschichte des Körpers: Der Akt in der österreichischen Kunst von 1900–2011, exh. cat., Eppan (South Tyrol): Galerie im Lanserhaus, 2011.

## Films

Das Zimmer der Sophie Baier, television film featuring the "Masters of Unorthodox Jazz," dir. Toni Michlmayr, 1974.
Film in conjunction with Barabbas's exhibition at Galerie Upupa, Villach, 1984, dir. Karl-Heinz Fessl, ca. 20 mins., 1984.

## Literatur


Peter Baum, Kunst in Österreich, in: Tradition und Avantgarde. Kunst in Österreich 1945–1980, Ausstellungskatalog Museum Liaunig, Neuhaus 2010.

Maria Buchsbaum, Barabbas. Das Ornamentale als Inhaltsträger, in: Vernissage, 16. Jg., Nr. 8, Oktober 1996.

Berthold Ecker/Wolfgang Hilger (Hg.), Die sechziger Jahre. Eine phantastische Moderne. Sammlung der Kulturabteilung der Stadt Wien – MUSA, Wien 2011.

Rüdiger Engerth, "Overground," Protokolle: Wiener Jahresschrift für Literatur, bildende Kunst und Musik 72, no. 1 (1972).

Andreas Felber, Zur „europäischen" Identität der Wiener Free-Jazz-Avantgarde. Die Geschichte der Masters of Unorthodox Jazz und der Reform Art Unit, Phil. Diss., Wien 2001.

Andreas Felber, Die Wiener Free-Jazz-Avantgarde. Revolution im Hinterzimmer, Wien, Köln und Weimar 2005.

Heinrich Fuchs, Die österreichischen Maler des 20. Jahrhunderts, Wien 1985.

Gerhard Habarta, Lexikon der phantastischen Künstler, Norderstedt, 2008.

Semirah Heilingsetzer, Die Galerie „Zum Roten Apfel" 1959–1965. Künstlerpositionen der 60er Jahre in Wien, Frankfurt am Main 2003.

Renata Kassal-Mikula/Hans Bisanz (Hg.), Der Kreis. Dokumentation einer Wiener Künstlervereinigung, 1946–1980, Ausstellungskatalog Historisches Museum der Stadt Wien, Wien 1981.

Klaus Lingens/Robert Kettner (Hg.), Roter Apfel in der Galerie Basilisk, Ausstellungskatalog Galerie Basilisk, Wien 1970.

David Thomas/Allyn J. Fisher (Hg.), Claus Barabbas – Recent Paintings, Ausstellungskatalog Allyn Fisher Fine Arts, Bendigo (Australien) 1991.

Peter Weiermair, Eine Geschichte des Körpers. Der Akt in der österreichischen Kunst von 1900–2011, Ausstellungskatalog Galerie im Lanserhaus, Eppan (Südtirol) 2011.


## Filme

Fernsehfilm „Das Zimmer der Sophie Baier" mit den „Masters of Unorthodox Jazz", von Toni Michlmayr, 1974.

Film zur Ausstellung von Barabbas in Galerie Upupa in Villach 1984, von Karl-Heinz Fessl (ca. 20 min.), 1984.

**Impressum | Imprint**

**Katalog | Catalogue**
**HerausgeberInnen für die Kulturabteilung der Stadt Wien (MA 7) |**
**Editors for the Department for Cultural Affairs of the City of Vienna (MA 7):**
Gunda Achleitner, Berthold Ecker, Elisabeth Voggeneder
**Redaktion | Editing:** Gunda Achleitner
**Texte | Texts:** Berthold Ecker, Andreas Felber, Manfred Lang, Elisabeth Voggeneder
**Lektorat | Proofreading:** Fanny Esterhazy
**Übersetzung | Translations:** Gerrit Jackson
**Grafik | Graphic design:** schultz+schultz-Mediengestaltung

AMBRA | V ist ein Unternehmen der Medecco Holding GmbH, Wien
Printed in Austria

**Umschlagbild | Cover photo:** Milchstraße mit weißem Loch, 1975, Mischtechnik auf Leinwand, 100 x 70 cm
Milky Way with White Hole, 1975, mixed technique on canvas, 100 x 70 cm, © Privatsammlung | private collection
**Druck | Printing:** Holzhausen Druck GmbH, A-1140 Wien | Vienna



Gedruckt auf säurefreiem, chlorfrei gebleichtem Papier | Printed on acid-free and chlorine-free bleached paper
Mit 141 farbigen Abbildungen | With 141 colored figures

Bibliografische Information der Deutschen Nationalbibliothek
Die Deutsche Nationalbibliothek verzeichnet diese Publikation in der Deutschen Nationalbibliografie; detaillierte bibliografische Daten sind im Internet über http://dnb.d-nb.de abrufbar.

ISBN 978-3-99043-556-4

**Ausstellung | Exhibition**
MUSA Museum Startgalerie Artothek
13.5. – 8.6.2013
Felderstraße 6-8, 1010 Wien | Vienna
www.musa.at

Ein Projekt der Kulturabteilung der Stadt Wien (MA 7) |
A Project of the Department for Cultural Affairs of the City of Vienna (MA 7)
Leiter der Kulturabteilung der Stadt Wien | Head of the Department for Cultural
Affairs of the City of Vienna: Bernhard Denscher
MUSA – Leiter| Director: Berthold Ecker
Kuratorin | Curator: Elisabeth Voggeneder
Projektleitung | Project management: Gunda Achleitner
Mitarbeit | Assistance: Roland Fink, Johannes Karel, Peter Schauer, Gabriele Strommer, Heimo Watzlik, Michael Wolschlager
Öffentlichkeitsarbeit | PR: Monika Anzelini

Ein besonderer Dank gilt der Familie des Künstlers, sowie Freunden und Sammlern für die Unterstützung des Projekts.
Special thanks for supporting the project go to the artists' family as well as friends and collectors.

MUSA WIEN KULTUR StaDt Wien